Mitchell
Beazley
Pocket
Guides

WINES OF SPAIN

FOREWORD BY HUGH JOHNSON

Jan Read

Wines of Spain
by Jan Read

First published in Great Britain in 1983 by Mitchell Beazley, an imprint of Octopus Publishing Group Limited, 2-4 Heron Quays, London E14 4JP.

This edition 2001.

Copyright © Octopus Publishing Group Limited 1983, 1988, 1992, 1997, 1998, 1999, 2001.
Text copyright © Jan Read 1983, 1988, 1992, 1997, 1998, 1999, 2001.

All rights reserved. No part of this work may be reproduced or utilised in any form by any means, electronic or mechanical, including photocopying, recording or by any information storage and retrieval system, without the prior written permission of the publishers.

A CIP catalogue record for this book is available from the British Library.

ISBN 1 840 00389 8

The author and publishers will be grateful for any information which will assist them in keeping future editions up to date. Although all reasonable care has been taken in the preparation of this book, neither the publishers nor the author can accept responsibility for any consequences arising from the use thereof or from the information contained therein.

Commissioning Editor/Editor: Adrian Tempany
Executive Art Editor: Philip Ormerod
Design: Colin Goody
Production: Nancy Roberts
Index: Ann Barrett

Typeset in Veljovic Book
Printed and bound in China

Contents

Key to Symbols	4
Foreword	5
Map of Spain	6
Introduction	8
How to Read an Entry	9
Anatomy of Spanish Wine	10
Laws and Labels	12
Glossary	14
A Spanish Selection for 2001-2	19
Aragón	20
Balearics and Canaries	26
Castilla-La Mancha	34
Castilla-León	44
Cataluña	59
Extremadura and the Southwest	84
Galicia	91
Montilla-Moriles and Málaga	103
Navarra and the Basque Country	114
Rioja	123
Sherry (Jerez) and Manzanilla	153
Valencia and Murcia	177
Sparkling Wines	187
Spirits, Aromatic Wines and Liqueurs	198
Index	209

Key to Symbols

r	red
p	rosé
w	white
am	amber
g	*generoso*
res	*reserva*
dr	dry
s/sw	semi-sweet
sw	sweet
sp	sparkling
pt	*pétillant*

Where any of the above codes appears in parentheses, it means that the product is a relatively unimportant part of the range. *See* page 9 for further information.

☆	everyday wine
☆ ☆	above average
☆ ☆ ☆	excellent quality, highly reputed
☆ ☆ ☆ ☆	grand, prestigious, expensive
★	if the star or stars appear black rather than in outline, then the wine is, in addition, usually good value in its class.
DO	*denominación de origen* – name and origin controlled (*see* pages 12–14)
DOP	*denominación de origen provisional* (*see* page 12)
VC	*vino comarcal* (*see* pages 12–14)
74, 75	recommended years which may be currently available
DYA	drink the youngest available
NV	vintage not normally shown on label
HARO	a name in small capitals indicates that the word appears as an entry in its own right within that chapter.

Foreword

Some wine historian of the future, reviewing the last quarter of the 20th century, will no doubt enjoy the question of which of the leading wine countries accelerated fastest from being a producer of wine at a fairly primitive, everyday level, to highly organised quality production on a grand scale. It will be surprising if the vote does not go to Spain.

In a quarter of a century, Spain has progressed from what was as dim a start as any winemaking land could have to being one of the world's most confident, most original and best-run producers.

Throughout this time, an English film writer and scholar with a passion for Spain has been more than just passively observing the revolution. He has been a much-valued commentator and critic at the heart of it.

Jan Read and his wife Maite (and their son Carlos, too) have been both interpreters and ambassadors for Spain, and at the same time creative inspirations at *bodega*-floor level.

To its maker, good wine is a very personal thing. It is not just anybody he takes into his confidence. Jan, above all, has been one of the people winemakers can trust to give them a frank opinion, technical advice, encouragement and friendship. He has also been the same to other writers studying Spanish wine. My own most rewarding journeys in this most rewarding of countries have been with Jan as a guide, philosopher and friend.

This book condenses more experience than any other writer can claim of one of the most exciting wine countries on earth. Can we ask for more?

Hugh Johnson

Map of Spain 7

Spain

The autonomous regions shown on this map are those used for the chapters of this guide. The definitive boundaries for individual wine-producing areas are shown on the regional maps at the start of each chapter.

Introduction

Since the time of Sir Francis Drake's 'rape of the barrels' in Cádiz (*see* page 153), Spain has been known first and foremost for a single wine: sherry. The sweet dessert Málagas achieved a certain vogue in England in Victorian times, but the better beverage wines have been slow to establish themselves in foreign markets. Until recently the image was of sturdy (though often drinkable) 'plonk'.

The reasons for this are to be found in the drinking habits of the Spanish themselves. What Richard Ford wrote in his *Gatherings from Spain* in 1846 long remained true: 'The Spaniard himself is neither curious in port, nor particular in Madeira; he much prefers quantity to quality and loves flavour less than he hates trouble...'

When I first began drinking Spanish wine some 40 years ago, the custom was to take an empty bottle to the wine shop and to fill it from a cask marked with the alcoholic degree and some such terse description as *tinto* (full-bodied red), *clarete* (light red), *blanco* (white), Moscatel or so on. It is true, of course, that better wines were available, sometimes of excellent quality like those from the Rioja, which had been bottling its fine wines since the end of the 19th century. They were not, however, much drunk except on special occasions and at the more expensive restaurants.

Various factors have contributed to what has been a very remarkable improvement in quality over the last few decades. One of the achievements of General Franco in his latter years was a marked rise in living standards and the creation of a middle class with more sophisticated tastes and the money to indulge them. At the same time, the millions of tourists who started to flood across the Pyrenees began asking for the better wines, and liked what they found.

Hand in hand with this, and starting with Rioja in 1926, the Ministry of Agriculture began the demarcation of the different winemaking areas, laying down strict regulations for the production of better-quality wines sold under a *denominación de origen* (DO) and modernising the cooperatives.

During the last dozen years there has been an increasing realisation among the younger and more enlightened *bodegueros* that Spain's future as a wine producer lies in quality rather than quantity. While the bulk of the wine produced in the vast central plateau is cooperative-made and acceptable enough for everyday drinking, it and dozens of other regions are now – with the help of modern technology – producing characterful and individual growths. Perhaps no other country in Europe makes wine in such a variety of styles: there are the *pétillant* young wines of the north and northwest; a whole gamut of reds, whites and rosés; excellent sparkling wines produced in larger quantity than Champagne; apéritif and dessert wines such as sherry, Montilla and Málaga; and a cupboard full of vermouths and liqueurs. Exports of the better beverage wines have soared in recent years. For example, shipments of Rioja to the UK have increased from 180,000 litres in 1970 to 13 million litres today, and the story is much the same in the US and in northern Europe, indicating the growing appreciation of good value, particularly in the mid-price bracket.

A–Z listings in this volume are arranged within broad geographical areas. This reflects the fact that, in Spain, individual labels and house styles are generally of greater significance than minor geographical areas, and the smaller producers tend not to bottle their wine but to sell to large concerns or direct to local restaurants.

The many *bodegueros* and others who have helped me in the preparation of this new edition are too numerous to mention individually, but I should particularly like to thank Don Bartolomé Vergara of the Asociación de Criadores Exportadores de Sherry and that brilliant oenologist and leading exponent of Spanish wines, Don Miguel Torres Riera. My wife, Maite Manjón, has made a major contribution to the sections on 'Wine and Food', which I hope will add to the enjoyment of visitors to Spain.

How to Read an Entry

Entries are generally of two types: those descriptive of a region or town or of objects or equipment commonly used in Spanish winemaking, and those relating to individual producers (*bodegas*) and their wines. The top lines of entries referring to producers generally gives the following information.

1   The name of the producer.
2   Whether the wine is bottled with a *denominación de origen* (DO) or is a table wine from a specified district (VdlT or VC) – *see* 'Laws and Labels', page 12.
3   The types of wines made by the producer – for example red, rosé, white, sparkling (abbreviated to r, p, w, sp – *see* 'Key to Symbols', page 4).
4   Their general standing as to quality, a necessarily rough-and-ready guide based on the following ascending scale:

    ☆   everyday wine
    ☆☆   above average
    ☆☆☆   excellent quality, highly reputed
    ☆☆☆☆   grand, prestigious, expensive

So much is more or less objective. Additionally, there is a subjective rating; where the stars appear in black rather than in outline (*see* 'Key to Symbols', page 4), this denotes a wine which is in my experience particularly good value within its price range, be it luxury or everyday.

Stars have not been used in the sections covering Montilla-Moriles and Málaga; Sherry; Sparkling Wines; and Spirits, Aromatic Wines and Liqueurs. Here, the producers often make such a vast range of wines or spirits that general judgements become more or less meaningless: one of a sherry

house's *finos* may deserve three stars, while its *oloroso* is of merely two-star quality, and vice-versa. Some guidance to the quality of such wines will be found in the descriptive notes on each producer.
5 Vintage information: which were the more successful of the recent vintages that *may* still be available and which of the younger are ready for drinking and will probably improve with keeping. A more consistent climate places somewhat less importance on vintages than with French wines, and vintages are not given for wines that are made for current consumption.

The text of each of these entries begins with:
1 the town or village in which the *bodega* is located;
2 the province, in parentheses; and
3 where a *bodega* makes demarcated wines, the DO is specified – for example, DO Penedès. This is not repeated for the many wines of Rioja and the sherry region, which all fall under their respective single DOs.

The information under 'Wine and Food' at the end of each section is intended primarily for visitors, and the dishes which are briefly described are those typical of the region. 'International cooking' proliferates in the tourist resorts and large cities. *Nouvelle cuisine* and its successors have left their mark on Spain as elsewhere – often to the good, in lightening heavy dishes. The current trend among sophisticated chefs is to revive traditional dishes and to cook the best prime ingredients in such a way as to bring out their individual flavours to the fullest extent. Recommended hotels are also detailed here.

Where wines are coupled with particular dishes, they are examples of what I myself might choose. However, I do not believe in hard and fast rules about which wine goes with which dish, and suggest that all readers follow their individual preferences.

Suggestions for travelling to and within the regions are made in the introductory paragraphs, and other places to visit appear under the towns in the A–Z listing.

Anatomy of Spanish Wine

Spain has more land under vines than any other country in Europe, but comes third (after Italy and France) in terms of wine production. The reasons for the low yield are various, but include the facts that much of the soil is barren, many of the vines are old and in need of replacement, and the vineyards are often split up among smallholders who have few resources or little technical expertise to draw on.

Criss-crossed by great chains of mountains, Spain is a country of wide geographical contrasts, ranging from the wet and mountainous north to the arid central plateau (with its bitter winters and hot summers) and Andalucía in the south – mild in winter and sun-baked for the rest of the year. It is a pattern giving rise to wines in great variety, and almost every region – apart from the

Atlantic coast in the north – produces wines of sorts. The best of the world's beverage wines are produced along a belt lying between 30° and 50° latitude in both hemispheres, and the best Spanish beverage wines come from Rioja, Penedès, Ribera del Duero, Navarra, Somontano and Galicia, which lie towards the centre of this zone but are somewhat cooler than average because of their altitude. Rioja and Ribera del Duero are predominantly producers of red wines; the Penedès makes both red and white (together with a great deal of sparkling wine) but is better known for its white; Galicia produces elegant and flowery whites.

The great central plateau of La Mancha, which produces a massive 35 per cent of Spain's wines, is classified as semi-arid, and much of the wine is cooperative-made and sold in bulk. Ninety per cent is white and the introduction of cold fermentation has resulted in fresher, lighter wines. The best of the reds are from Valdepeñas, where some are now matured in oak.

The coastal region of the Levante (the Valencian area and Murcia), bordering the Mediterranean to the east of La Mancha, has traditionally produced earthy, full-bodied wines high in alcohol, both red and white, of which the most attractive are the light and fresh rosés from Utiel-Requena. Here, sweeping improvements in technology have resulted in the large-scale elaboration of lighter and very drinkable wines for export.

Andalucía is more or less exclusively a producer of apéritif and dessert wines made in *solera* (*see* page 171-2) by the progressive blending of older and younger wines. Apart from sherry, the best known are the very similar wines from Montilla-Moriles and the classical but fast-disappearing dessert Málagas.

The future looks bright for the Spanish wine industry. With regard to exports, the emphasis was for too long on quantity rather than quality. This has largely been because the heat of the long summers in the central and southerly parts of the country produces very large amounts of sugar in the grapes, and traditional methods of fermentation led to robust wines which are over-strong in alcohol.

With the introduction of earlier picking, stainless-steel vats and the permitting of fermentation at lower and controlled temperatures, the picture is now changing – and changing fast. The Mediterranean countries (after all, the cradle of winemaking in Europe) may yet be at an advantage over the wetter and colder areas of northern Europe.

Further progress will depend on improvement of the vines, either by cloning of the best native varieties – always with a view to quality rather than quantity – or by the acclimatisation of noble varieties such as Cabernet Sauvignon and Chardonnay from abroad. Again, a great deal remains to be done: for example, denser planting of the vines and the provision of supports so as to afford more shade and conservation of water in the soil.

The new emphasis on quality has already resulted in a growing number of wines which can stand comparison with the best from elsewhere. This is particularly true of a new generation of Riojas made with hand-sorted grapes from old vines grown in the best *terroir*. In Spain, these wines have been christened *vinos de alta expresión*, meaning wines made with the utmost care to obtain the maximum concentration and preserve the full flavour of the fruit. Rioja is, of course, far from the only region to make such wines, and a personal choice of the very best from all over Spain for drinking in 2001-2 is listed on page 19.

GRAPE VARIETIES

It would be a Herculean task to list all the grape varieties used in the production of the wines named in this book. Spain claims to have some 600 different varieties – although just 20 cover 80 per cent of the country's vineyards. In Galicia alone there are 136 recognised types of vine. To add to the confusion, the same grape often goes under a different name in different regions of Spain; the Riojan Tempranillo, for example, is the Ull de Llebre in Cataluña and the Cencibel in Valdepeñas.

The main grape varieties of each region are discussed in the general introductions, and the entry for each DO zone names the grapes used for its wines.

Laws and Labels

Since Spain joined the EU, its wine law has been modified to meet the regulations laid down for European wine-producing countries in general. The EU recognises two broad categories: table wine and quality wine. In Spain, as in France, Germany and Italy, these have been subdivided and are, in ascending order of quality: for Spanish table wines, *vino de mesa*, *vino comarcal* and *vino de la tierra*; and for quality wines, *denominación de origen* (DO) and *denominación de origen calificada* (DOCa). *Vino de mesa*, without further qualification, is wine made from grapes grown in unclassified vineyards, or blended. *Vino comarcal* (VC) may be labelled with the area in which it was produced, while *vino de la tierra* (VdlT) corresponds to the French *vin de pays* and is a local wine from an officially demarcated region, which may in due course attain *denominación de origen* (DO) – after an initial stage as *denominación de origen provisional* (DOP). As far as comparisons can be made, Spanish DO wines correspond in quality to either the French VDQS (*vin délimité de qualité supérieur*) or AOC (*appellation d'origine contrôlée*), and to the Italian *denominazione di origine controllata* (DOC). Only Rioja has as yet qualified for the DOCa, which corresponds to the Italian DOCG (*denominazione di origine controllata e garantita*).

The first regions to be demarcated were Rioja in 1926, Jerez in 1933 and Málaga in 1937. The complete list of DOs now runs to:

Abona	Bullas
Alella	Calatayud
Alicante	Campo de Borja
Almansa	Cariñena
Ampurdán-Costa Brava	Cava
Bierzo	Chacolí de Guetería –
Binissalem	(Getariako Txakolina)

Chacolí de Vizcaya – (Bizkaiko Txakolina)
Cigales
Conca de Barberà
Condado de Huelva
Costers del Segre
El Hierro
El Monte
Jerez/Xérès/Sherry y Manzanilla-Sanlúcar de Barrameda
Jumilla
La Mancha
La Palma
Lanzarote
Málaga
Méntrida
Mondéjar
Monterrei
Montilla-Moriles
Navarra
Penedès
Pla de Bages
Plá y Llevant
Priorato
Rías Baixas
Ribeira Sacra
Ribeiro
Ribera del Duero
Ribera del Guadiana
Rioja
Rueda
Somontano
Tacoronte-Acentejo
Tarragona
Terra Alta
Toro
Utiel-Requena
Valdeorras
Valdepeñas
Valle de Güímar
Valle de la Orotava
Valencia
Vinos de Madrid
Ycoden–Daute–Isora
Yecla

Each one of these denominations is controlled by a *consejo regulador*, a regulatory body under the presidency and vice-presidency of delegates appointed by the Ministries of Agriculture and Commerce, and including representatives of the growers, the *bodegas* (winemakers) and shippers. In 1972, the Ministry of Agriculture set up a central body, the Instituto Nacional de Denominaciónes de Origen (INDO), to coordinate and control the activities of the *consejos reguladores* in the field. After the death of General Franco and the restoration of local autonomy to the four provinces of Cataluña between 1978 and 1980, INDO transferred its functions in Cataluña to an agency of the revived Generalitat, the Institut Català de Vi (INCAVI).

All Spanish wines must conform to the procedures and standards laid down in the *Estatuto de la Viña, del Vino y de los Alcoholes*, a lengthy government decree first promulgated in 1970 and applying to Spain as a whole. This detailed document defines the different types of wine and spirits and lays down rules for acceptable and unacceptable methods of viticulture and vinification, for chemical composition, and for the transport, distribution, sale and export of wines.

In addition to complying with the *Estatuto*, wines with *denominación de origen* must also be made in accordance with the further provisions of a *reglamento* issued by the appropriate *consejo regulador*. This defines in detail the geographical area within which a demarcated wine may be made and grown, the permitted grape varieties and the density of plantation, and also sets limits on the amount of must that may be extracted from the grapes. Further stipulations included in the *reglamento* relate to viticulture, methods of pruning, the vinification and maturation of the wine, and its chemical composition, limits being set for alcoholic degree, volatile acidity, sugar content, dry extract and other elements.

The *consejos* maintain control laboratories in the different regions, and when a wine has satisfied its inspectorate there and in the field, the *consejo* authorises the printing of labels to cover the amount involved. Its guarantee often appears on the label in the form of a small emblem or stamp.

To begin with, *cava* (sparkling wine made by the Champagne method) was the subject of a *denominación específica*, that related only to quality and the way in which the wine was produced. In addition to this, the DO Cava – like the others – now defines the areas in which it may be made, in Cava's case in several different regions of Spain (*see* 'Sparkling Wines', page 187). In similar fashion, a *denominación específica* for wines made with the Albariño grape variety has been replaced by the DO Rías Baixas, demarcating the three principal areas where Albariño is grown (*see* 'Galicia', page 91).

Standards of excellence in the different demarcated regions vary greatly, and the largest production of quality wines is in those like Rioja, Jerez and Penedès with long-established reputations for making fine wines. At the other end of the scale, no one could possibly maintain that the wines from the DO Méntrida are in any way comparable with French VDQS or AOC wines. Indeed, the authoritative *Guide to the Wines of Spain*, published by the Club de Gourmets of Madrid, is of the opinion that the region barely deserves denomination and that the consumer will find little joy in its wines. Again, it would seem that some other regions, such as Costers del Segre and Binassalem, have been granted DO status on the strength of one or two prestigious producers. Decisions have clearly been taken with the future potential of the region in mind – and the grant of a provisional DO has often induced producers to modernise equipment and improve their wines – but the magic 'DO' on a label is currently not a reliable yardstick of quality for the consumer. At one time, the famous firm of Miguel Torres was barred from labelling wines made with acclimatised foreign grapes with the DO Penedès, yet the name 'Torres' is the best possible guarantee of quality. The name and reputation of the producer is, in fact, at least as important as DO – and often more so.

Within Spain light wine is sometimes still described as, for example, '3° año' or '5° año', meaning that it was bottled during the third or fifth calendar year after harvest, but all the better wines are now labelled with the year of vintage. The following glossary lists Spanish wine terms that commonly appear on labels.

Glossary

WORDS USED ON WINE LABELS

Abocado Semi-sweet table wine.
Amontillado A style of sherry made by ageing the *fino* wine.
Amoroso A light dessert sherry.

Añejo, añejado por Old, aged by **(4)°ano** bottled in the (fourth) year after the harvest (*see* 'Laws and Labels'). Formerly much used but now virtually discontinued.

Blanco White.

Bodega Literally, a wine cellar, but used to describe a concern which may have grown, produced, shipped or sold the wine. Without further qualification, it normally means that the *bodega* has made and shipped the wine.

Brut Extra-dry, used only of sparkling wine.

Cava a) an establishment making sparkling wines;
b) a term used to describe such wines made by the Champagne method, now the subject of the DO Cava.

Cepa Literally, a vine. Its use on labels is not precise (the word itself is not precise), although it sometimes appears coupled with the name of a grape.

Clarete Light red table wine (but this description is no longer permitted on labels).

Con crianza Used on the back label to indicate the wine has been aged in oak and bottle in accordance with the *reglamento* of the *consejo regulador* (local regulatory body) for a minimum of two years – of which one, in the case of reds, must be in oak casks. Whites and rosés need spend only six months in oak.

Cosecha Vintage; for example: Cosecha 1976.

Cream A sweet sherry or Montilla.

Criado por Matured and/or blended by.

Denominación de origen (DO) The guarantee of the *consejo regulador* (regulatory body) for a demarcated area. It is often printed on the label in the form of a small stamp or drawing.

Dulce Sweet.

Elaborado por Matured and/or blended by.

Embotellado por Bottled by.

Espumoso Sparkling wine.

Fino A pale, dry and delicate sherry or Montilla.

Generoso A fortified apéritif or dessert wine.

Gran reserva Wine of good quality, aged in the case of *tinto* for at least two years in oak cask, followed by a minimum of three in bottle. White or rosé *gran reservas* must be aged for a minimum period of four years, with at least six months in oak.

Gran-vas Sparkling wine made by the *cuve close* method (*see* 'Sparkling Wines', pages 192).

Manzanilla One of the driest of *solera* wines, made at Sanlúcar de Barrameda.

Método tradicional replaced the term *méthode champenoise* as from August 31, 1994.

Oloroso A dark, fragrant, full-bodied sherry or Montilla.

Palo cortado A rare and superior sherry or Montilla, with the nose of an *amontillado* and the body of an *oloroso*.

Pasada, pasado Used to describe old and superior *amontillado* and *fino* sherries.

Raya a) Term used in classifying musts for sherry;
b) a sherry or Montilla resembling *oloroso*, but not of the same quality.

Reserva Wine of good quality. *Tinto* is aged for at least three years in total in oak cask and bottle (and usually for longer) with a minimum one year in cask. White and rosé *reservas* must be aged for at least two years in total in oak cask and bottle, with a minimum of six months in oak.

Rosado Rosé.

Seco Dry.

Semiseco Semi-dry.

Sin crianza Used to denote a young wine that has had little or no maturation in cask.

Solera This denotes (or should denote) that the wine has been aged in a series of butts containing progressively older wine of different vintages (*see* 'Sherry and Manzanilla', page 171-2).

Tinto Red wine.

Vendimia Vintage; for example: Vendimia 1976.

Viña, viñedo Vineyard. Used rather loosely; the name Viña Zaco does *not* necessarily mean that the wine originated exclusively from a vineyard of this name.

Vino Wine (*see also* 'Miscellaneous', below).

MISCELLANEOUS

Agua Water.

Agua de soda Soda water.

Agua mineral Mineral water:
    con gas sparkling,
    sin gas still.

Aguardiente a) Alcohol of not more than 80° strength distilled from vegetable materials;
    b) colloquial name for *aguardiente de orujo*, which is akin to the French *marc*.

Anís Aniseed-flavoured liqueur resembling anisette.

Barrica Small cask (usually 225 litres) used for maturing wine.

Bodeguero The person who owns or runs the bodega.

Café Coffee.

Chacolí A green (young) wine from the Biscay coast. Now the subject of the DOs Chacolí (*see* 'Navarra', page 116-17).

Cold fermentation Fermentation in stainless-steel vats over long periods at low temperatures (*see* 'Anatomy of Spanish Wine', page 10-12).

Comarca Subdistrict.

Coñac Used colloquially of Spanish brandy.

Crema Liqueur:
    de cacao cocoa-based;
    de café coffee-based;
    de menta crème de menthe;
    de naranja Curaçao.

Flor A film of yeasts which grows on the surface of some wines during maturation in *solera* (*see* 'Sherry', page 171-2).

Ginebra Gin.

Hielo Ice.

Horchata Milky-looking non-alcoholic drink made from *chufas* or tiger-nuts.

Leche Milk.
Licor Liqueur.
Limonada Lemonade (fizzy).
Orujo Slang name for *aguardiente*.
Parador State tourist hotel of a good standard, often housed in a building of historic interest.
Ponche A herbalised brandy (*see* page 206).
Queimada A punch made from *aguardiente* (*see* above).
Ron Rum
SA *Sociedad Anónima*, an indication of a public company's limited liability, equivalent to Ltd, plc or Inc.
SAT Private company which was formerly a cooperative.
Sangría Cold wine-cup, made by adding sliced orange and lemon, together with ice and a dash of brandy, to red wine.
Sidra Cider.
Sifón Soda water.
Socio A member of a wine cooperative.
Té Tea.
Vermut Vermouth.
Vino Wine:
  comarcal a wine halfway between plain *vino de mesa* and the better *vino de la tierra* (*see* page 12);
  corriente inexpensive, everyday wine;
  de aguja slightly sparkling, *pétillant*;
  de Jerez sherry;
  de la tierra table wine of superior quality made in a demarcated region without DO (*see* page 12);
  de lágrima sweet wine made from the juice which has emerged from the grapes under the weight of the fruit only, and without mechanical crushing;
  de mesa table wine, either blended or without indication of origin;
  de pasto an ordinary table wine, often light;
  embotellado a better wine, bottled at the *bodega*;
  gaseoso cheap, carbonated sparkling wine;
  generoso an apéritif or dessert wine, such as sherry or Málaga;
  joven/jóvenes young wine/s for immediate drinking, bottled after fining and without ageing in wood;
  rancio an old white wine, maderised and sometimes fortified;
  verde young wine, white or red, with a slight sparkle, prickle or *pétillance*.
Zumo natural Fruit juice:
  de naranja natural juice from freshly crushed oranges.

ORDERING WINES AND DRINKS

May I see the wine list?
La carta de vinos, por favor.

I should like a bottle/half-bottle of .../a carafe/half-carafe of your house wine.
Por favor traiga una botella/media botella de .../una jarra/media jarra de vino de la casa.

Where does your house wine come from?
¿De dónde es el vino de la casa?

Can you recommend a good local wine?
¿Puede usted recomendar un vino bueno de la región?

Yes, I would like a bottle.
Sí, me gustaría una botella.

I should like to drink a red/dry white/sweet white wine.
Me gustaría beber un vino tinto/vino blanco seco/vino blanco dulce.

Would you please chill the wine?
¿Por favor puede usted enfriar el vino?

The waiter, too, will have something to say, and will probably begin by asking if you would like an apéritif:
¿Quieren ustedes un aperitivo?

Yes, I should like a ...
Sí, por favor, un ...

No, thank you.
No, gracias.

After you have ordered the wine, he will ask you whether, as is usual in Spain, you want mineral water:
¿Quieren ustedes agua mineral?

Yes, I should like a bottle/half-bottle of still/sparkling.
Sí, por favor. Me gustaría una botella/media botella sin gas/con gas.

At the end of the meal the waiter will ask you if you want coffee:
¿Quieren tomar café?

Yes, I/we should like black coffee/white coffee/coffee with a little milk.
Sí, por favor, me/nos gustaría café solo/café con leche/café cortado.

Except in expensive restaurants, if you want brandy or a liqueur at the table, you should ask for it:
I/we should like a brandy/liqueur. What sorts do you have?
Me/nos gustaría tomar un coñac/licor. ¿Qué marcas tienen?

And to ask for the bill:
La cuenta, por favor.

Is service included?
¿Está el servicio incluido?

A Spanish Selection for 2001-2

A representative selection of some of the best Spanish wines, red and white: it does not include fortified wines or cava. For details of the wines see the *bodegas* listed in the following regional sections.

WHITE WINES

Albariño de Fefiñanes '98, Palacio de Fefiñanes. DO Rías Baixas.
Chivite Moscatel Vendimia Tarde '98, Julian Chivite. DO Navarra.
Fransola '98, Miguel Torres. DO Penedès.
Guitián Godello '97, Bodegas Tapada. DO Valdeorras.
Palacio de Bornos Vendimia Seleccionada '97, Bodegas de Crianza Castilla la Vieja. DO Rueda.
Viña Tondonia '64, Bodegas López de Heredia. DOCa Rioja.

RED WINES

Alión '94, Bodegas y Viñedos Alión. DO Ribera del Duero.
Aurus '94, Finca Allende. DOCa Rioja.
Barón de Chirel '94, Marqués de Riscal. DOCa Rioja.
Casa Gualda Selección '98, Coop Nstra Sra de la Cabeza. DO La Mancha.
Clos Mogador '97, Clos Mogador. DO Priorato.
Dominio de Valdepusa Syrah '97, Marqués de Griñón. Non-DO. (Castilla-La Mancha.)
Gaudium '94, Marqués de Cáceres. DOCa Rioja.
Grans Muralles '96, Miguel Torres. DO Conca de Barberà.
Lautus '96, Bodegas Guelbenzu. DO Navarra.
Pago de Negralada '96, Abadía Retuerta. Non-DO. (Castilla-León.)
Pagos Viejos '95, Cosecheros Alaveses. DOCa Rioja.
Pesquera '95, Alejandro Fernández. DO Ribera del Duero.
Remelluri '95, Granja Nstra Sra de Remelluri. DOCa Rioja.
Roda I '95, Bodegas Roda. DOCa Rioja.
Torre Muga '94, Bodegas Muga. DOCa Rioja.
Valpiedra '94, Finca Valpiedra. DOCa Rioja.
Viña Ardanza '90, La Rioja Alta. DOCa Rioja.
Viña del Olivo '96, Viñedos del Contino. DOCa Rioja.

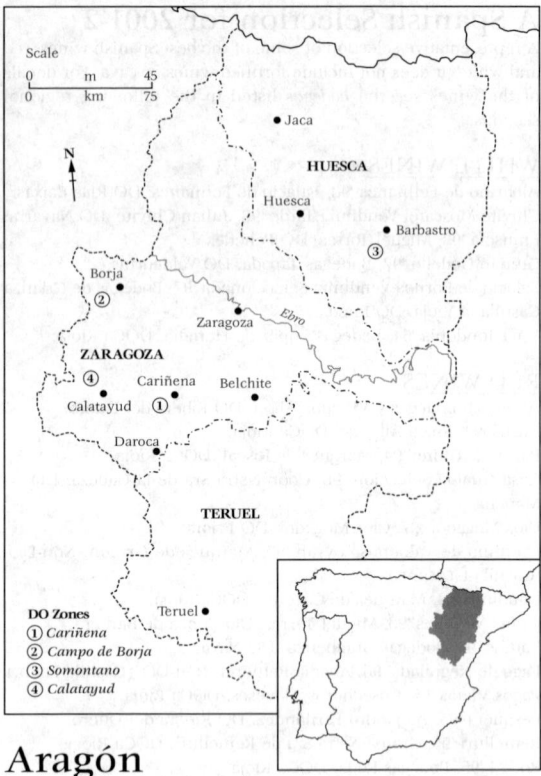

Aragón

With 62,000 hectares of land under vines and an average annual production of 98 million litres of wine, Aragón ranks fifth in order of area and tenth of the Spanish autonomies as regards production. In the past it had been known for sturdy wine that was high in alcohol and extract, much of it sold outside the area for everyday drinking or blending. There have, however, been marked changes in recent years, beginning with the demarcation of new regions and the accompanying modernisation of the cooperatives; the planting of new vine varieties; earlier picking of the grapes so as to lighten the wines; and the emergence of small, sophisticated private firms.

In the early 19th century the best-known of the wine regions, Cariñena, made one of the most sought-after Spanish wines. Later, at the height of the phylloxera epidemic, the Bordeaux firm of Violet maintained a large establishment for shipping them to France. With the land lying mostly between 450 and 650 metres above sea level, and in the harsh climatic conditions of freezing winters, hot summers and strong winds, the vine that does best (and is by far the most prevalent) is the study black Garnacha, though Tempranillo is increasingly being planted for better quality, oak-aged red wines, and there are also small quantities of white grapes such as the Viura, Garnacha Blanca and Alcañón (native to Somontano). Oddly enough, the black Cariñena is much more widely grown in Cataluña (the variety also appears in France as the Carignan). As elsewhere in Spain, small amounts of Cabernet Sauvignon and Chardonnay have been introduced on an experimental scale.

Aragón has four DO zones: Cariñena; the more recently demarcated Campo de Borja and Somontano to the north; and to the west Calatayud, demarcated in 1990.

Alto Aragón, Viñedos y Crianzas del
DO w p r ☆☆→ ☆☆☆ *92, 93, 94, 95, 96*
Barbastro (Huesca). DO Somontano. A young *bodega*, whose fruity, modern-style ENATE wines compete with those from VIÑAS DEL VERO. They include good barrel-fermented Chardonnay ('98), Gewürztraminer ('98), Cabernet, and Cabernet blends.

Aragonesas, Bodegas
DO r p w dr g ☆→☆☆
Fuendejalón (Zaragoza). DO Campo de Borja. Large cooperative making and exporting worthwhile wines, some of them aged in oak, including young red, white and rosé Crucillón; red Don Ramón, Duque de Sevilla and Mosen Cleto *reservas*, all made with 100 per cent Garnacha.

Belchite
VC r w dr ☆
Small area east of CARIÑENA making sturdy reds and whites.

Bordejé, Bodegas
DO r (w g) ☆→☆☆ *98*
Ainzón (Zaragoza). DO Campo de Borja. A family concern dating from 1770 and growing all its own grapes on 100 hectares of vineyards. It is best known for its cherry-red Abuelo Nicolás, made by carbonic maceration, which is not shipped abroad but is delicious when drunk young and on the spot.

Borruel, Bodegas
DO r w dr ☆☆
Ponzano (Huesca). DO Somontano. Small, old-established (1903) *bodega* with 14 hectares of vineyards. Reliable Osca, red, white and rosé. The pick of its wines is the characterful red Barón de Eroles *reserva*, made with a blend of Tempranillo, Moristel and Cabernet Sauvignon.

Borsao Borja, Bodegas
DO r res ★★ *94, 95, 96, 98*
Borja (Zaragoza). DO Campo de Borja. Founded as a cooperative in 1958 and with 1,450 hectares of vineyards and 950 oak *barricas*, this winery is a model of its kind. It makes an excellent and

modestly-priced young Tinto Joven from a blend of Garnacha, Tempranillo and Cabernet Sauvignon, and *crianzas* and *reservas* from the same grapes, sold as Gran Campellas and Señor Atares.

Calatayud
DO r p ☆→☆ ☆

A newly demarcated area situated in the west of Aragón making honest enough wine in a style that is ideal for everyday drinking. The best are the red wines, which are made with 100 per cent Garnacha.

Campo de Borja
DO r ☆

The region takes its name from the small town of Borja in the Ebro Valley west of Zaragoza, the ancestral home of the Borgia family, whose castle still survives. Demarcated in 1977, it now embraces 6,270 hectares of vineyards.

Made mainly from the Garnacha Tinta grape, the traditional wine was a very full-bodied red, more astringent and acidic than the wine from CARIÑENA, and containing an average 15 to 16 per cent alcohol, and sometimes a hefty 18 per cent. For this reason it was often used for blending with less robust growths from other regions, much of it being sold in bulk to concerns in Rioja and Cataluña. Lighter rosés and better oak-aged Tempranillo reds are now being produced.

Cariñena
DO r (w dr sw g) ☆→☆ ☆

A little to the south of Zaragoza, Cariñena – with 19,675 hectares under vine – is the most important wine-producing area in Aragón. The vines grow in calcareous clays and the most dominant varieties are the black Garnacha Tinta (60 per cent) and white Viura (21 per cent).

The traditional wine of Cariñena is the red, of a purplish-ruby colour with a bouquet of violets, 13 to 17 per cent in strength, full-bodied and deep in flavour. Thanks to fermentation in stainless steel, much lighter, more drinkable *jóvenes* are now being made. Cariñena also produces some everyday white wine from the Viura and Garnacha Blanca, and a fortified dessert wine made in a manner similar to that in which Málaga is made (*see* page 103).

Daroca
VC r ☆

Area in the far south of Aragón on the borders of Teruel. It produces sturdy red wines with 13 to 16 per cent alcohol.

Enate *See* Viñedos y Crianzas del ALTO ARAGON.

Lalanne, Bodegas
DO r p w dr res ☆ ☆ 94, 96

Castillo de San Marcos, Barbastro (Huesca). DO Somontano. Small *bodega*, founded by a French family at the time of the phylloxera epidemic in the 19th century, and growing 12 vine varieties on its 32 hectares of vineyards.

Among its highly individual oak-aged wines, produced from Cabernet Sauvignon blended either with Merlot or Tempranillo, are Viña San Marcos rosé and Laura Lalanne red.

Marqués de Aragón
See Vinos y Viñedos del Salón.

Pirineos, Bodega
DO r p w ☆☆ *94, 95, 96, 97, 98*
Barbastro (Huesca). DO Somontano. The large cooperative of Somontano de Sobrarbe was re-equipped in 1990 and renamed Bodega Pirineos, since when it has been making quality wines. The best are the Montsierra range and the oak-aged Señorío de Lazán Reserva.

San Isidro, Bodega Cooperativa del Campo
See Vinos y Viñedos del Salón.

San Valero, Bodegas
DO r (p w dr) ☆→☆☆ *95, 96, 98*
Cariñena (Zaragoza). DO Cariñena. Large former cooperative on the Zaragoza–Teruel road in the village of CARIÑENA. The firm produces the young Don Mendo white, red and rosé in addition to a cold-fermented rosé and oak-aged Monte Ducay, and Marqués de Tosos *crianza* and *reservas*.

Somontano
DO r p w dr ☆☆→☆☆☆
This recently demarcated region, which is located in the province of Huesca in the foothills of the Pyrenees, has 2,086 hectares of land under vine and produces wines completely different from the others on offer from Aragón. Made from a profusion of grape varieties, including the traditional Alcañón, Macabeo (Viura), Garnacha Tinta, Mazuelo and Parraleta, and more recently-introduced Cabernet Sauvignon, Merlot and Chardonnay, the wines were traditionally ruby-coloured, faintly perfumed, light on the palate and slightly acidic, ranging in strength from 11 to 13 per cent alcohol.

At the turn of the century these wines were popular in France, and one of the best of the area's wineries, Bodegas LALANNE in Barbastro, is of French origin. It is a region where, thanks to modern technology and fermentation in stainless steel, a dramatic improvement in standards is under way.

Valdejalón
VdlT r ☆
Large area just west of Zaragoza. The dominant grape variety, Garnacha Tinta, produces wines that are high in alcohol and extract, and are more aligned with the wines of CAMPO DE BORJA than with those of CARIÑENA.

Viñas del Vero
DO r w dr ☆☆→ ☆☆☆ *94, 95, 96, 97*
Barbastro (Huesca). DO Somontano. Founded in 1986, the firm possesses 515 hectares of vineyards and a state-of-the-art winery. Its wines are among the best from the region. There is a lively 100 per cent Chardonnay ('96); a 100 per cent Gewürztraminer ('96); a 100 per cent Riesling; and excellent red wines made with 100 per cent Cabernet Sauvignon, 100 per cent Pinot Noir and a 50/50 blend of Tempranillo and Moristel.

Vinos y Viñedos del Salón
DO r w ★→★★

Maluenda (Calatayud). DO Calatayud. Large cooperative formerly producing only bulk wine, but now making very drinkable red and white Don Aragón table wines, superior 100 per cent Garnacha Marqués de Aragón, and a *reserva* made from a blend of Tempranillo and Garnacha.

Zaragoza
Capital of the medieval Kingdom of Aragón, Zaragoza is rich in historic remains from Roman times onwards, including the Moorish Aljafería, with its figured plasterwork and beautiful *artesondo* ceilings. The city is dominated by the many-domed Basílica del Pilár, looming above the bridge across the River Ebro, which contains the oldest Marian sanctuary in Europe. The festival of El Pilár in October is the most important date in Spain's religious calendar.

WINE AND FOOD
Aragón is sometimes called the *zona de los chilindrónes*, after the famous *chilindrón* sauce made with onions, garlic, tomatoes and peppers, and served with chicken and lamb.

In Aragón, the young lamb from the mountains is excellent. (*Espárragos montañeses* is a delicious dish rather misleadingly named: this 'mountain asparagus' is actually lambs' tails stewed in tomatoes.) South of Zaragoza in the direction of Teruel, the miles of gardens and orchards produce some of the best fruit in Spain: peaches, plums, apricots, apples, cherries and strawberries. The vegetables, too, including the white Aragonese cabbage and cardoon, are first rate.

The sturdy red wines go well with simple dishes and country fare. With a more sophisticated meal, try one of the new, lighter growths from Somontano.

Bacalao al ajoarriero Dried salt cod with garlic, paprika and chopped parsley.

Migas de pastor Breadcrumbs fried until crisp in olive oil, often served as a starter or side dish. Some devotees eat them with hot chocolate or grapes.

Pollo al chilindrón Chicken with *chilindrón* sauce, made from olive oil, garlic, tomatoes and peppers.

Sopas de ajo Garlic soups with bread, eggs and a piquant *sofrito* base are a great speciality of Aragón.
Teresicas Small pastries made with butter, flour and yeast and fried in olive oil.
Ternasco asado Milk-fed kid cooked with white wine, lemon and garlic.

HOTELS
Zaragoza The best hotels in the district are the five-star *Meliá Zaragoza, Palafox; Boston* and *NH Gran Hotel*.

RESTAURANTS
Huesca *Gaby-Casa Blasquico* (at Hecho near Jaca. Gaby Coarasa is a professor of gastronomy and offers some of the best cooking in the province. Inexpensive rooms are also available); *Venta del Sotón* (at Esquedas on the Tarragona road: Imaginative cooking from Alto Aragón).

Zaragoza *Gayarre* (on the road to the airport. Serves Aragonese and Basque cuisine); *Goyesco* (impeccable cooking and extended table d'hôte); *Gurrea* (only one menu, but a choice of ten main dishes and desserts. Excellent).

Balearic Island DO Zones
① *Binissalem*

Other
② *Plá y Llevant*

Canary Island DO Zones
① *Tacoronte-Acentejo*
② *Ycoden-Daute-Isodora*
③ *Valle de la Orotava*
④ *Valle de Güimar*
⑤ *Abona*

Balearics and Canaries

Both these groups of islands, the green and fertile Balearics with their mild, Mediterranean climate and sandy beaches, and the volcanic Canaries, in the wastes of the Atlantic off the coast of North Africa, are favourite tourist resorts for sun-starved northern Europeans. On balance, they consume more wine than they make, so that familiar names from the mainland figure more on their wine lists than the local growths.

Before the depredations of phylloxera there were about 27,000 hectares under vine in Mallorca, the main producer in the Balearics, but in the principal vineyard areas of Binissalem and Plá y Llevant the area has now shrunk to some 1,300 hectares. Tourism aggravated this decline – it proved more profitable to sell the land for holiday villas, and the young people left the villages to work in the hotels of Palma and Pollensa.

The soils of the Balearics are mainly ferruginous clays, and the vines are grown in small plots interspersed with olives and almonds. Most of the grapes are native to Mallorca, the typical varieties being the Manto Negro, Callet, Fogoneu and Fogoneu Francés. Apart from the superior growths of Franca Roja and the tiny *bodegas* of Jaume Mesquida and Miguel Oliver, the wines are reds or rosés made by the cooperatives or small proprietors for current consumption.

In the Canaries, famous for sack in the 16th century, wine production is now mainly confined to the islands of Tenerife, La Palma and Lanzarote. The soils are volcanic and the principal grape varieties are the white Listán Blanco and Malvasía (Malmsey), and the red Listán and Negramoll.

Until recently the few wines with character were the white Malvasías, but since the mid-1980s – as a result of the planting of better vine varieties and the installation of modern equipment in the wineries – some excellent red and white wines are emerging: especially the young reds made by carbonic maceration.

In 1992 there was a single DO, that of Tacoronte-Acentejo, but the number has now leapt to nine. However, because of the small scale of production, demand much exceeds supply and outside the Islands, even in Spain, the wines are virtually unobtainable.

Binissalem
DO r (w dr) ☆→☆☆

Binissalem is the producer of the best Mallorcan wines, although the area under cultivation (some 300 hectares) has shrunk to a fraction of its former size.

The principal red grape is the Manto Negro, producing full-bodied reds of 14 to 16 per cent strength with pronounced bouquet and high extract; also recommended is the native Callet, while the new regulations additionally permit the use of Tempranillo and Monastrell. The main grape for white wines, made in much smaller amounts, is the Moll or Prensal Blanco.

El Grifo, Bodegas
DO r p w dr g ☆→☆☆

La Geria (Lanzarote). DO Lanzarote. Old-established *bodega*; with Bodegas MOZAGA, one of the best in the Canaries. It has long been famous for its 14.5 per cent strength Malvasía El Grifo, but it is now making fresh young reds and whites by cold fermentation.

El Hierro
DO w p r ☆→☆☆

Hierro is the smallest of the Canary Islands, and the newly demarcated region is the only one in Spain to possess just one *bodega* – the local cooperative. It was, however, one of the first in the Canaries to install modern equipment and to eliminate the once common defects of unclean odours, high alcoholic degree, oxidation, etc, and the wines now meet the increasingly improved standards of the other modernised wineries in the Canary Islands.

El Lomo
DO r w ☆☆ 96

Tegueste (Tenerife). DO Tacoronte-Acentejo. Founded in 1990, this is one of the new generation of technologically advanced Canarian *bodegas*. The wines are labelled El Lomo and include a crisp white with 90 per cent Listán Blanco; a fruity red made from a blend of Listán Negro and Negramoll; and an exceptionally fresh and aromatic *maceración carbónica* of 100 per cent Listán Negro.

Felanitx *See* PLÁ I LLEVANT DE MALLORCA.

Flores, Bodegas
DO r ☆☆ *96*

La Matanza (Tenerife). DO Tacoronte-Acentejo. Producers of a young, fruity and deceptively smooth and velvety wine, made with the native Listán Negro, Negramoll and Listán Blanco and containing some 13 per cent alcohol.

Franca Roja
DO r (w dr p) res ☆☆→☆☆☆ *94, 95, 96, 98*

Binissalem (Mallorca). DO Binissalem. The *bodega* was founded in 1931 by the informed and enthusiastic oenologist José L Ferrer and has subsequently been run by his nephews. It is the only concern in Mallorca to export its wines (under the label Franca Roja, the name of the parent company). Its 78 hectares are planted mainly with the indigenous red Manto Negro and Callet, giving rise to smooth and full-flavoured (oak-aged) reds, and the white Moll, from which is made a refreshing, somewhat spicy *blanc de blancs* and a delicious Viña Veritas, fermented in cask.

Fuencaliente *See also* LA PALMA DO.
The main production area in the Canary Island of La Palma. The principal vines, which were unaffected by phylloxera and are grown ungrafted, are the Listán Blanco and Negra, Vijariego and Negramoll, and the typical wine is a dry and full-bodied *clarete*. Winemaking is on the decline, however, and there are now only 1,000 hectares under vines.

Geria, La *See* LANZAROTE DO.

Güímar, Valle de
DO w dr (r) ☆

Newly demarcated region of 606 hectares, lying on the east coast of Tenerife to the south of the DO TACORONTE–ACENTEJO. Best are the fruity white wines grown in the higher vineyards at 1600m above sea level.

Icod
DO w dr ☆

Icod de los Vinos, now part of the new DO YCODEN-DAUTE-ISORA in Tenerife, is traditionally one of the areas in the Canaries best known for its vines, notably Listán Blanco and Malvasía.

Insulares Tenerife, Bodegas
DO r w dr ☆☆ *96, 97, 98*

Tacoronte (Tenerife). DO Tacoronte-Acentejo. Former cooperative selling wines produced individually by 71 of the region's farmers, under the general name of Viña Norte. One of the best is the fresh and fruity young red *vino joven* from Marcos Guimerá Ravina.

Lanzarote
DO w p r g ☆→☆ ☆

The principal vine-growing area in Lanzarote – the most desolate of the Canary islands with its 300 volcanoes, blazing volcanic sands and torrid winds from the Sahara – is La Geria. The vines are sunk into deep pits and surrounded by stone walls to protect them from the wind. The typical wines that result from all this effort are made from a blend of the white Malvasía and Listán and are amber-coloured and high in alcohol.

La Palma
DO w p r ☆

The main production zone is that of FUENCALIENTE at the southern tip of the island.

Las Palmas

The largest town in the Canaries, with a population of 350,000, Las Palmas is dramatically situated on Gran Canaria beneath an extinct volcano, and possesses good beaches, a colourful promenade and a bustling port which provides regular ferry services to the other islands.

Manacor
p ☆

Sizeable vine-growing area near FELANITX in Mallorca, making wines of around nine to eleven per cent alcohol from the Fogoneu grape.

Méndez Siverio, Juan Jesús
DO w p r ☆→☆ ☆

La Guancha (Tenerife). DO Ycoden–Daute–Isora. Founded in 1989, this concern sells wines under the label of Viñatigo. The range includes good whites made with Listán Blanco, one fermented in cask; a rosé; and a fragrant young red produced by carbonic maceration.

Mesquida, Jaume
DO r w dr p ☆☆

Porreres (Mallorca). DO Plá y Llevant. Together with FRANCA ROJA, Miguel OLIVER and Herederos Hermanos RIBAS, Jaume Mesquida is one of the few makers of quality wines in Mallorca. He believes the future of Mallorcan wines lies with acclimatising foreign vine varieties and makes good Cabernet Sauvignons and Pinot Noirs.

Monje, Bodegas
DO r w dr ☆☆

El Sauzal (Tenerife). DO Tacoronte-Acentejo. The young red Monje, made from 80 per cent Listán Negro with a little Listán Blanco and Negramoll, some of it by carbonic maceration, is smooth, full-bodied and fruity: a *vino joven* for early consumption.

Mozaga, Bodegas
DO w sw g ☆→☆☆

La Geria (Lanzarote). DO Lanzarote. Maker of one of the best wines from the Canary Island of Lanzarote, the Malvasía Seco. The grapes are picked when well ripe, lightly crushed and aged in oak for two or three months after vinification. The wine is further aged in bottle in cellars excavated beneath the lava. Also a good Moscatel Mozaga of 17 per cent strength.

Oliver, Miguel
DO r w dr p ☆☆ 95, 96

Petra (Mallorca). DO Plá i Llevant de Mallorca. Miguel Oliver is one of the very few producers to be making worthwhile wines in the Balearics. The wines include a good Chardonnay, a luscious Muscat, and a Manto Negro *reserva* made with 85 per cent Manto Negro and 15 per cent Tempranillo.

Orotava, Valle de la
DO w dr ☆

Small vine-growing area situated between the DOs of TACORONTE–ACENTEJO and YCODEN–DAUTE–ISORA on the north coast of Tenerife. It produces dry white wines very similar to those of ICOD.

Palma de Mallorca

Palma is one of the most beautiful cities of the Mediterranean, with its wide bay and surrounding beaches and the 13th-century cathedral dominating the port.

The narrow streets in the centre are full of elegant shops, good restaurants and old houses with secret, shaded patios. Nowhere in Mallorca is very far from Palma, so it is a good base for visiting the wine areas.

Plá i Llevant de Mallorca
DO r (p w dr) ☆→☆☆

In the southeast of the island, the area around FELANITX has some 2,000 hectares under vines and is the largest of the Mallorcan wine regions. However, only a couple of small *bodegas* produce a wine to match those of FRANCA ROJA in BINISSALEM.

The typical grape is the Fogoneu, usually vinified so as to give rosés of nine to eleven per cent. Most of the wine was made in the cooperative at Felanitx serving the small proprietors; it has, however, now closed down. There are also distilleries in the town producing grape spirit and alcohol.

Ribas, Herederos de
DO r w dr 96

Consell (Baleares). DO Binissalem. An old *bodega* reorganised in 1986, it owns some 50 hectares of vineyards planted with both native and foreign varieties.

The wines, sold as Hereus de Ribas, include a decent white made from a blend of native grapes and Chardonnay, and fruity reds containing a proportion of Cabernet Sauvignon.

Tacoronte-Acentejo
DO r (w dr p) DYA ☆→☆☆

Tacoronte, the first region in the Canaries to be accorded the DO in 1992, is the most intensely cultivated wine area in Tenerife. The 1,300 hectares lie on the mountain slopes to the west of the island and are planted mainly with the red Listán Negro and Negramoll. Since the installation of stainless steel in some of the *bodegas*, the varieties are beginning to make fresh and lighter red wines in the modern style, all of them at the moment young.

Ycoden-Daute-Isora
DO w dr p (r) ☆→☆☆

This new DO at the northwestern tip of Tenerife comprises 650 hectares and includes ICOD de Los Vinos, long known for its wines. It is now one of the most active and innovative wine areas in the Islands with dozens of small, well-equipped new *bodegas*. The best of the wines are the rosés, but there are also reds and whites with good acidity and balance.

WINE AND FOOD
The Balearics, famous for the invention of mayonnaise (from Port Mahón), have a varied regional repertoire. As might be expected, they excel in seafood and rich fish soups. The appetising *coca mallorquina*, traditionally made in outdoor ovens fired by wood, much resembles the Italian pizza; *tumbet* is a variation on ratatouille; most typical of the excellent charcuterie are the delicate white *butifarra* and soft red *sobrasada*; there is a good Mahón cheese; and do not miss the fluffy *ensaimadas*, halfway between bun and pastry, for breakfast.

Apart from basic cooperative-made wine, the local label to look for in the Balearics is FRANCA ROJA. In the Canaries, locally caught fish is excellent and the wines are increasingly interesting. Although the Canaries have a few regional specialities, these do not amount to a cuisine as such; like the wines, you may find it difficult to find them in holiday hotels, where the menus and wine lists are mainland Spanish, if not the international style provided for tourists.

Balearics
Acelgas con pasas y piñones Spanish variety of spinach, paler in colour and sweeter than the English equivalent, boiled and served with *sofrito*, a sauce made with pine kernels, raisins, toasted bread and garlic.

Berenjenas rellenas estilo balear Aubergines stuffed with a mixture of ground beef, chopped ham, onions, eggs, breadcrumbs and garlic.

Butifarra A delicate white pork sausage, eaten uncooked, or in a stew with *mongetes* (haricot beans).

Caldereta de dátiles de mar Chowder made with small, dark sea dates, fished off the coast.

Caracoles con sobrasada Snails cooked together with ham, onions, tomatoes, garlic, olive oil, milk, brandy and white wine. They are usually served with *sobrasada*, the soft and spicy Mallorcan pepper sausage, and green vegetables.

Coca mallorquina The Mallorcan version of pizza, which often contains onion, peppers, tomatoes, anchovies and sardines.

Sopa de pescador formentor Rich fish soup made with garlic, onions, tomatoes, olive oil and parsley.

Tumbet A Mallorcan egg-and-vegetable pie made with potatoes, red peppers, onions, courgettes and tomato sauce.

Canaries

Buñuelos de dátiles Sweet fritters made with flour, orange juice, Cointreau, sugar, eggs and dates.

Gofio A popular form of bread eaten all over the Canaries in country districts, and made in the shape of a big ball from a mixture of flour with water or milk.

Mojo colorado Sauce prepared with olive oil, vinegar, hot paprika, cumin seeds and chillis.

Papas arrugadas New potatoes, boiled in their skins in sea water or much-salted water, then baked in a hot oven and served with *mojo* sauce.

Platanos canarios fritos Fried bananas, Canary style.

HOTELS
Gran Canaria
Las Palmas *Santa Catalina, Meliá Las Palmas, Sol Iberia* and *NH Imperial Palace* (all four-star).

Lanzarote
Teguise *Meliá Salinas* (beautiful views, international food with local dishes in the buffet).

Tenerife
Adeje *Gran Hotel Bahía de Duque* (the best hotel in the Canaries).
Playa de las Américas *Jardín Tropical* (renowned for its cooking).
Puerto de la Cruz *Loro Park Botánico* (set in beautiful grounds and conveniently situated as a base for visiting the *bodegas* in the north of the island); *Tigaiga* (a smaller, family-run hotel with excellent cuisine).

Mallorca
Palma de Mallorca *Son Vida, Meliá Confort, Palas Atena* and *Golf Hotel Arabella* (the best of dozens of hotels in Palma, a prosperous town in which more than half the inhabitants of the Balearics live. There are plenty of hotels in most categories).

RESTAURANTS
Gran Canaria
Agaete *Casa Pepe* (48km from Las Palmas. Home-cooked local dishes with fresh ingredients. Try the *Pescado de la Canaria*).

Lanzarote
Teguise *Meliá Salinas*. See 'Hotels', above.

Tenerife
La Orotava *Los Corales* (good local dishes and wine).
Playa de las Américas *Hotel Jardín Tropical* (its restaurant *El Patio* serves some of the best food and wines in the Canaries).
Tacoronte *Casa del Vino* (local dishes, such as *Solomillo al vino de Tacoronte*, and Tenerife wines); *Los Limoneros* (excellent food, eg *Ensalada de salmón, Angulas y aguacates*).

Mallorca
Inca, near Binissalem *Celler C'an Amer* (one of the best restaurants for typical Mallorcan dishes).
Palma de Mallorca *Koldo Royo* (first class, specialising in locally caught fish).
Portals Nous *Tristán* (20km from Palma de Mallorca; outstanding cuisine, eg *Rape salteado con caracoles de mar y tomillo*, etc).

DO Zones
1. Méntrida
2. La Mancha
3. Valdepeñas
4. Almansa
5. Vinos de Madrid
6. Monéjar

Castilla-La Mancha

Between them, the two Castiles occupy the wide central plateau of Spain. Old Castile, so called because it was the first part of the area to be reconquered from the Moors, stretches north from Madrid. South of the capital the landscape becomes increasingly arid, and the central and southern parts of New Castile are known as La Mancha. What was New Castile is now substantially the autonomy of Castilla-La Mancha, and Old Castile (minus Cantabria) the autonomy of Castilla-León (*see* page 44). Madrid, although listed in this section, is an autonomy in its own right.

The climate is Mediterranean-style, with long, hot summers and low rainfall; for this reason, the grapes contain large amounts of sugar and have traditionally produced earthy wines with high alcohol and little acidity, though cold fermentation and earlier picking of the grapes are changing the picture. Since the land, lying between 500 and 800 metres above sea level, is mainly flat, the vineyards extend in unbroken expanses – in reality, a patchwork of holdings belonging to small proprietors.

This is the land of the cooperatives *par excellence*: there are hundreds in the central region as a whole. Because of its huge size and despite a low yield of about 16 to 18 hectolitres per hectare, the region supplies about 35 per cent of the country's wine output, much of it going to other, less prolific areas for blending and the surplus being used for distillation.

The typical grape is the white Airén (or Lairén), its thick skin affording some protection against the blazing sunshine, of which, on average, there are 200 days in the year. Airén is a favourite with the small proprietors because it produces proportionately three times as much must as the other most important grape of the region, the black Cencibel (known in the Rioja as Tempranillo and in Cataluña as Ull de Llebre or Ojo de Liebre).

Ninety per cent of the wine from the central area is white; but perhaps the best is the red Valdepeñas from the extreme south of La Mancha bordering Andalucía. This is made with a proportion of the black Cencibel and has been famous since the days of the Holy Roman Emperor Charles V (King Charles I of Spain), who had the wine sent across Europe on mule-back during his military campaigns in the Low Countries in the 16th century.

Apart from Valdepeñas, the other DO regions of the area are Almansa, La Mancha, Méntrida, Mondéjar and Vinos de Madrid, as well as the provisional DO Manchuela.

Albali, Viña
DO r w dr (p) ☆☆ 93, 95, 97

A producer of reliable wines, especially the sturdy red from Bodegas Félix SOLIS.

Abellan, Sucesores de Alfonso
DO r p ☆→☆☆

Almansa (Albacete). DO Almansa. One of the three *bodegas* in the DO Almansa to bottle its wines, which are labelled as Señorío de Almansa. The reds are made from 100 per cent Monastrell and some are aged in oak.

Almansa
DO r w dr ☆→☆☆☆

Bordering the Levante and just north of the DO zones of Yecla and Jumilla (see 'Valencia and Murcia', page 177), this region centres on the town of Almansa with its story-book castle.

The soils are chalky, and in its 7,600 hectares of vineyards the predominant grape variety is the black Monastrell (43.5 per cent); the Garnacha Tinta and Tintorera account for another 33 per cent and there is also some white Forcallat, Airén and Bobal. Since the area was little affected by the phylloxera epidemic, 83 per cent of the vines are ungrafted; these produce wines which are high in both alcohol and extract.

The typical wines are deep in colour, full-bodied with little acid and with an alcoholic strength of between 12 to 15 per cent. Their quality depends on the proportion of Monastrell in the blend, but most are sold in bulk for blending. Only three concerns in the region bottle the wines: Hijos de Miguel CARRION, Sucesores de Alfonso ABELLAN and Bodegas PIQUERAS, and those from the latter are outstanding.

Aloque
r ☆→☆☆

The lightest style of VALDEPEÑAS, made with a blend of black and white grapes, usually ten per cent Cencibel and ninety per cent Airén. It's a dry wine, deep-coloured and between 13 to 15 per cent alcohol. Considering their strength, the wines are surprisingly light and fresh in taste, and much drunk in the bars and restaurants of Madrid.

Arganda
DO r w dr ☆☆

One of the subzones of the DO VINOS DE MADRID, and found to the south of the capital. The principal grape varieties grown here are the black Tinto Madrid and Tempranillo, and white Malvar and Jaén – when blended they produce smooth red wines. This area is also home to a pleasant straw-coloured white of 12 to 13.5 per cent alcoholic strength.

The wines were at their most popular during the 17th century, when the court transferred from Valladolid to Madrid. At that time, what is now the airport of Barajas was a flourishing vineyard, producing white wines reputedly more fragrant and delicate than those of Rueda, while Carabanchel, now the site of the great prison, made a luscious Moscatel. Today, the best wines from the area are made by Jesús DIAZ E HIJOS.

Ayuso Bodegas
DO r p w dr ☆☆

Villarrobledo (Albacete). DO La Mancha. Large, well-equipped *bodega*, selling the best of wines under the Estola label. Red Estola, made with 100 per cent Cencibel, is available as *crianza*, *reserva* and *gran reserva*.

Calatrava, Campo de
DO

Subdivision of the DO LA MANCHA, bordering the DO VALDEPEÑAS in the direction of CIUDAD REAL.

Carrión, Hijos de Miguel
DO r ☆→☆☆

Alpera (Albacete). DO Almansa. Small family firm making the smooth and fragrant red Cueva la Vieja, and ageing it for three to four years in large oak vats.

Casa de la Viña
DO r p w dr ☆☆ 96

La Solana (Ciudad Real). DO Valdepeñas. The firm belongs to Bodegas y Bebidas (formerly Savín, *see* page 132) and makes pleasant white, rosé and red wines, ageing its attractive 100 per cent Cencibel *reservas* in oak.

Casa Gualda
See NUESTRA SEÑORA DE LA CABEZA, COOPERATIVA

Castilla-La Mancha Vino de la Tierra

In June 1999 all 600,000 hectares of vineyards in the vast autonomy of Castilla-La Mancha (including the DO regions) producing half of Spain's wine were given V de la T status. This was part of the measures under the Common Agricultural Policy to reinstate 100,000 hectares lost during the droughts of 1991-95.

Castillo de Alhambra
DO r p w ☆☆

Reliable and inexpensive red, white and rosé wines are produced by the VINICOLA DE CASTILLA.

Centro Españolas, Bodegas
DO r p w ☆☆

Tomelloso (Ciudad Real). DO La Mancha. Large, modern winery selling wines under the Allozo and Verdial labels. Ed Flaherty has made a name for himself in Chile and produces some fruity, easy-drinking wines, such as the '96 100 per cent Tempranillo Verdial.

Ciudad Real
Important winemaking town and capital of the province of the same name in LA MANCHA.

Cueva del Granero
DO r p w dr ☆☆

Los Hinojosos (Cuenca). DO La Mancha. The firm owns a sizeable 600 hectares of vineyards, growing Airén, Cencibel, Garnacha and Cabernet Sauvignon. The wines are sold under the label Cueva del Granero.

Dehesa del Carrizal
r ★★★ *92, 94, 95*

Retuerta del Bullaque (Ciudad Real). Non-DO. This tiny *bodega*, with only 13 hectares of vineyard and 400 oak *barricas,* shows the potential of this region. Its 100 per cent Cabernet Sauvignon, currently the '95 *crianza*, is among the best in the country.

Díaz e Hijos, Jesús
DO r ★★

Colmenar de Oreja (Madrid). DO Vinos de Madrid. The red wines from this *bodega* were 'discovered' by CLUVE (Club de Selección de Vinos) and are among the best from the Madrid DO.

La Invencible, Cooperativa
DO r p w dr ☆→☆☆

Valdepeñas (Ciudad Real). DO Valdepeñas. Best of the cooperatives in VALDEPEÑAS. Its light red is particularly attractive.

Los Llanos, Bodega
DO r (p w dr) res ★★ *87, 90, 92, 93, 94, 95*

Valdepeñas (Ciudad Real). DO Valdepeñas. Founded as Bodegas Cervantes in 1875, this was the first concern in Valdepeñas to mature its wines in oak, and Cosecheros Abastecedores, who acquired it in 1972, scored another first in bottling the wines. The *bodega* is equipped with stainless-steel fermentation tanks and possesses no fewer than 12,000 American-oak *barricas*; its mature and fruity Señorio de los Llanos red *reservas* and *gran reservas* are fine wines which will surprise those used to the traditional Valdepeñas, which is made for early drinking. There are also a Pata Negra Gran Reserva made from 100 per cent Tempranillo and a young and flowery white, Armonioso.

Madrid

Madrid lies at the centre of the DO VINOS DE MADRID, a vine-growing district of some interest: and in view of the dearth of accommodation in the wide plains of La Mancha, a stopover in the capital is in any case more or less obligatory for a visit to this region. Nevertheless, its main interest on a wine tour is that its hundreds of restaurants offer the widest possible spectrum of regional wines and cooking from the length and breadth of Spain. Apart from wines, if there for the first time one could hardly leave without visiting the magnificent Prado gallery, the arcaded 16th-century Plaza Mayor or the Palacio Real.

Mancha, La
DO (r) w dr ★→★★

La Mancha, embracing the province of CIUDAD REAL and parts of those of Toledo, Albacete and Cuenca, comprises the larger part of the great central *meseta* of Spain and extends at an average height of some 700 metres from the River Tagus in the north to the Sierra Morena, dividing it from Andalucía, in the south. This is Don Quixote country: an arid, treeless expanse, bitingly cold in winter and mercilessly hot in summer, clothed with unbroken expanses of wheat, olives or vines.

The DO La Mancha, which is located at the centre of the area, is by far the largest in Spain, with 188,000 hectares under vines. The output of wine in 1997-'98, most of it made in cooperatives, was 76 million litres. The subsoil is chalky with a layer of clay above, and by far the most dominant grape, amounting to some 90 per cent, is the white Airén (or Lairén). The typical wines are light yellow in colour, offering a pleasant enough nose but a shortage of fruit, containing very little acid and ranging between 13 to 14 per cent in strength. Because of their somewhat neutral character these wines are supplied in vast quantities to other regions for blending and further huge amounts are distilled. More recently, earlier picking and cold fermentation have resulted in crisper, fruitier wines.

Manchuela
DOP

It was always a puzzle why Manchuela, lying to the east of the DO LA MANCHA and producing bulk wines of no very marked character, was demarcated. The DO was subsequently revoked, but the region is now on probation with a provisional DO.

Marqués de Griñón
r res ☆☆☆→ 87, 88, 92, 93, 94, 95

Malpica de Tajo (Toledo). At the suggestion of Professor Amerine of University of California, Davis the adventurous Carlos Falcó, Marqués de Griñón, embarked on the plantation of Cabernet Sauvignon and Merlot on his estate near Toledo. With advice from the redoubtable Professor Peynaud and the late Alexis Lichine he is making a good Chardonnay, Petit Verdot, a Bordeaux-style Cabernet and an outstanding ('97) Syrah, the likes of which have never been seen in La Mancha.

If the wines first attracted attention because the former *marquesa* was the glamorous Isabel Preysler, it has long since triumphed in its own right and gone from strength to strength since the first vintage in '81, and loses nothing by comparison with good Bordeaux. The wines are, however, at their best within five years of the vintage. The *marqués* also makes in collaboration with Bodegas Berberana (*see* pages 130-1) good Riojas, and red Durius in Ribera del Duero (*see* pages 52-3).

Megía, Luís
DO r p w ☆→☆☆

Valdepeñas (Ciudad Real). DO Valdepeñas. Part Japanese-owned and notable for its size and modern equipment, including plant for continuous vinification and 1.5-million-litre capacity nitrogen-capped *depósitos*. Best wines are the fresh white, Marqués de Castañaga, and the superior red Duque de Estrada, made with 80 per cent Cencibel.

Méntrida
DO r p ☆

Méntrida, with 13,000 hectares of vines and an output in 1997-'98 of 4.4 million litres, is southwest of Madrid in the north of Toledo province. The grapes are 85 per cent Garnacha Tinta, producing robust red wines, deep in colour and 14 to 15 per cent strength. The bulk go for blending and the quality is so nondescript that in Spain it has been suggested that the DO be suspended. Again, the advent of stainless steel and new technology is improving matters.

Navalcarnero
DO r ☆

A little to the south of the capital, this is a subdivision of the DO VINOS DE MADRID. Its dark-red and slightly astringent wines have a following locally and in Madrid, but are apt to oxidise rapidly and lose their freshness because of the high content of Garnacha.

Nuestra Señora de la Cabeza, Cooperativa
DO r ★★→★★★ 96, 98

Pozoamargo (Cuenca). DO La Mancha. Small, well-equipped cooperative making blends of Cencibel (Tempranillo) and Cabernet, and Cencibel and Merlot of unbeatable quality/value. The '98 Selección, 100 per cent Cencibel, was rated by *El País* as one of the 24 best wines from Spain.

Nuestra Señora de Manjavacas, Cooperativa
DO r p w dr ☆→☆☆

Mota del Cuervo (Cuenca). DO La Mancha. Large cooperative producing improved, fresh young wines under the Zagarrón label using temperature-controlled fermentation in stainless steel.

Nuestro Padre Jesús del Perdón, Cooperativa
DO (r p) w dr ★→★★

Manzanares (Ciudad Real). DO La Mancha. A cooperative with a capacity of 40 million litres, bottling its wines under the names of Lazarillo and Yuntero: good dry whites, and reds made with 100 per cent Cencibel, some cask-aged.

Piqueras, Bodegas
DO r res ★★→★★★ 93, 94, 95

Almansa (Albacete). DO Almansa. This small family *bodega* makes some of the best red wines from La Mancha, using Cencibel, Monastrell and Garnacha grapes. They include the Castillo de Almansa *crianza* and *reserva*, and Marius *gran reserva*.

Rodríguez y Berger
DO w dr sw (r p) ☆

Cinco Casas (Ciudad Real). DO La Mancha. Large, private firm making fresh young wines by temperature-controlled fermentation in stainless steel.

San Martín de Valdeiglesias
DO r ☆

Subzone of the DO VINOS DE MADRID lying between MENTRIDA and Cebreros (*see* 'Castilla-León', page 44). Its sturdy red wines, made from a blend of Garnacha Tinta, Tinto Navalcarnero and white Albillo grapes, resemble those from Cebreros.

Sánchez Rustarazo, Bodegas
DO r ★★

Valdepeñas (Ciudad Real). DO Valdepeñas. Founded in 1900, this family concern makes some of the most honest VALDEPEÑAS, ageing some of them, such as its Solar de Hinojosa, in oak casks.

Solís, Bodegas Félix
DO r res w ★★ 93, 95, 97

Valdepeñas (Ciudad Real). DO Valdepeñas. Best known for its sturdy and reliable red VIÑA ALBALI, aged in oak and made with 100 per cent Cencibel.

Tinajas

These large amphora-shaped vessels are made of the local clay and derived from the Roman *orcae*. Standing three metres high and with an approximate capacity of 1,600 litres, they have traditionally been used in LA MANCHA, Málaga and Montilla–Moriles for fermenting wines, and are now used for maturing wines in VALDEPEÑAS.

Tinajas have been progressively replaced by much larger cylindrical receptacles of cement reinforced with steel rods, and by stainless-steel tanks.

Toledo

Rising dramatically above the River Tagus, Toledo – with its superb medieval cathedral and collections of paintings by its adopted son, El Greco – is by far the most interesting place to visit in LA MANCHA.

Valdepeñas

Town in the south of the province of CIUDAD REAL, long famous for its red wines, which has given its name to the local DO and is the headquarters of the *consejo regulador*. There are *bodegas* to be found in almost every street, in the form of courtyards with a high, blank wall pierced by a high arch and double doors. Many are now disused, but the town, an unpretentious place of low houses and sunbaked streets, still boasts establishments of all sizes currently making wine.

Valdepeñas

DO r (w dr) ★★

The demarcated region lies in the most southerly part of the province of CIUDAD REAL and possesses 28,245 hectares of vineyards. The soil is a mixture of gravel, clay and chalk, and the average annual rainfall is only 400 millimetres. Although the typical wines are red, 93 per cent of the grapes are white Airén, the balance consisting of the black Cencibel (or Tempranillo) and Garnacha Tintorera. The red wines often contain a proportion of Airén, but such is the amount of colour and extract in the black grapes that, in spite of the small proportion used, the wines emerge bearing a deep ruby colour.

The tradition was to make and mature the wines in earthenware TINAJAS, from which they were usually sold young in their first or second year. The *tinajas* have largely been replaced by stainless-steel tanks, allowing for temperature-controlled fermentation. Again, it was not normal practice to age the wines in oak, because Airén musts oxidise easily and, until recently, little wine was made with a large proportion of the scarcer and more expensive Cencibel.

There are now a number of *bodegas*, notably CASA DE LA VIÑA, LOS LLANOS and Bodegas Félix SOLIS, making red *crianza* and *reserva* wines from 100 per cent Cencibel and successfully ageing them in 225-litre oak *barricas*. The Airén contributes a fragrant nose to the finished wine, but also leads to low acidity; the colour, body and fruity flavour come from the Cencibel. Alcoholic strength lies between 12.5 and 14 per cent. Valdepeñas also makes white wines similar to those of the DO LA MANCHA.

An increasing number of the *bodegas* in the DO Valdepeñas bottle their wine – but it must be said that some of the best and freshest examples come unnamed from the jugs of bars and restaurants in Madrid.

Villarrobledo

Villarrobledo, off the road from MADRID to Albacete, was the source of much of the clay for making TINAJAS.

Vinícola de Castilla

DO r p w dr sw ★★→★★★ *94, 95, 96, 97, 98*

Manzanares (Ciudad Real). DO La Mancha. This huge, ultra-modern *bodega* with a storage capacity of 15 million litres was one of the showpieces of the dispossessed RUMASA group (*see* page 148). The *bodega* is well-known for its well-made and reasonably priced Gran Verdad, Castillo de Manzanares and Castillo de Alhambra wines (red, white and rosé). It also makes superior Señorío de Guadianeja 100 per cent Cencibel and 100 per cent Cabernet Sauvignon ('86) *gran reservas* from grapes grown in its own vineyards.

Vinos de Madrid

DO r ☆→☆☆

Newish DO in the immediate vicinity of Madrid, with 11,466 hectares of vineyards, long known for its sturdy red wines. It comprises the subzones of NAVALCARNERO, ARGANDA and SAN MARTIN DE VALDEIGLESIAS.

Visán

DO r (w dr) ☆☆

Santa Cruz de Mudela, Valdepeñas (Ciudad Real). DO Valdepeñas. The firm makes pleasant white and red wines, selling them under the labels of Castillo de Calatrava, Castillo de la Mancha and Castillo de Mudela. Some of the reds are aged in oak.

WINE AND FOOD

With its roasts, its nourishing *potajes* (thick soups) and *cocidos* or *ollas* (stews), the cooking of New Castile is in many ways similar to that of Old Castile, though, because of its more limited resources, more austere. Drink a good red Valdepeñas with meat dishes (alternatively, treat yourself to a bottle of the Marqués de Griñón's Cabernet Sauvignon or Syrah) and a La Mancha white with lighter fare.

Atascaburras Rabbit stewed with garlic.
Bizcochos borrachos Sponge cakes in the shape of rings then soaked in wine or liqueur.
Caldereta de cordero Lamb ragout prepared with tomatoes and peppers.
Callos a la madrileña Tripe, Madrid style; highly spiced and a model to other countries' tripe dishes.
Ensalada manchega Salad containing dried cod and tuna, hard-boiled egg, olives and onions.
Espárragos de Aranjuéz South of Madrid Aranjuéz, with its royal palace, produces some of the most luscious fresh asparagus (and the best strawberries) in Spain.
Gallina en pepitoria Stewed fowl with almonds.

Lágrimas de aldea A stew of pork, potatoes, black pudding or *chorizo*.
Marmita de verduras A vegetable hot-pot.
Miel con hojuelas Pancakes with honey.
Migas Fried breadcrumbs, often served with fried eggs.
Mojete A vegetable dish resembling ratatouille.
Morteruelo Highly spiced regional version of liver pâté.
Perdices estofadas Partridge stewed in white wine with chopped ham and seasoning.
Pisto manchego A vegetable dish somewhat like ratatouille with scrambled eggs.
Queso frito Wedges of cheese, dredged in egg and breadcrumbs before being fried.
Queso manchego Best known of Spanish cheeses, made in large rounds from ewes' milk, either fresh or matured in olive oil.
Tortilla a la magra An omelette made with strips of cooked fillet of pork.
Tortilla española A thick and substantial potato omelette, sometimes including onion.

HOTELS

Madrid *The Ritz Hotel* is one of the most perfect in Europe. The best guides to Madrid's countless other hotels and to its restaurants are the Spanish publication *Gourmetour* and the red *Michelin* Spain and Portugal.

Toledo *María Cristina*, *Doménico*, *Alfonso VI* and the *Hostál del Cardenál*, and the four-star *Parador Conde de Orgaz*, poised on a hill above the city.

Valdepeñas *Meliá El Hidalgo* (outside the town to the north, on the N IV towards Madrid).

RESTAURANTS

Almagro *Parador de Almagro* (historic *parador* in a fascinating old town. Try aubergines in spicy sauce; rabbit stewed in white wine).

Madrid A vast range. For the ultimate in sophisticated cooking and wines, *Zalacaín* and *Jockey* are outstanding. Among the many others, a few personal favourites are: *El Cenador del Prado*; *Café de Oriente*; *Cabo Mayor* (Cantabrian cooking, fish); *Lhardy* (one of the oldest and most traditional); and *Viridiana* (which has the most interesting wine list in Madrid).

Manzanares *Parador de Manzanares* (a gastronomic oasis).

Toledo *Asador Adolfo*. Reliable cooking and an extensive wine list.

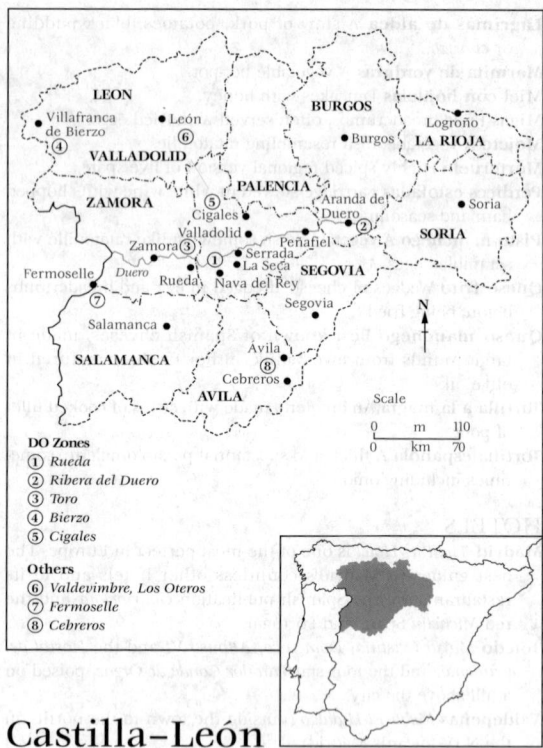

DO Zones
① Rueda
② Ribera del Duero
③ Toro
④ Bierzo
⑤ Cigales

Others
⑥ Valdevimbre, Los Oteros
⑦ Fermoselle
⑧ Cebreros

Castilla–León

Old Castile and the ancient Kingdom of León, united in 1230, are the very heart of Catholic Spain. It was their monarchs who planned and carried through the counter-offensive against the Moors; and the very names of their cities – Avila, Segovia, Salamanca, Burgos, Valladolid and León – seem to echo the 'slow old tunes of Spain'. They now form the autonomous region of Castilla–León. (The former province of Santander is now the autonomy of Cantabria, *see* page 116.)

Apart from the enclave of Cebreros in the Sierra de Gredos near Avila, only the northern area, especially around the River Duero basin, produces wines in any quantity. The land is often bleak and arid, bitterly cold in winter and fiery-hot in summer; in areas such as Toro the annual rainfall amounts to only 300 millimetres. In some districts, once famous for their wines, production has declined disastrously because of the difficulty of cultivating vines in such conditions. Nevertheless, Castilla–León produces worthwhile wines in great variety, notably the stylish reds from the Ribera del Duero, the refreshing whites from Rueda and the light reds of Cigales and Bierzo. The wines from León and Toro have improved notably with modern methods.

There is a profusion of vine varieties, but among the best and most typical are the black Tinto Fino (also known as the Tinto del País or Tinto Aragonés), a variant of the Tempranillo grown in the Ribera del Duero; the white Verdejo, native to Rueda; and the Prieto Picudo, a black grape with a white pulp, used for making rosés in León. The white 'Jerez' or Palomino is also widely grown, but its musts are not of the same quality as in its native habitat in the south of Spain. In one remote district of León there are even hybrids resulting from the direct crossing of American and native vines, but they are frowned upon by the authorities as containing a toxic alkaloid, the ill-famed *malvina*, and wines of this type may not be exported.

As in most parts of Spain, a great deal of the wine is made in cooperatives; but perhaps nowhere else have these small proprietors making wine for consumption in the immediate locality survived in greater numbers. In districts such as Los Oteros and Valdevimbre near León, the serried peasant *bodegas*, which are dug deep into the ground and have mounded earth roofs, look like prehistoric earthworks.

There are five *denominaciónes de origen*: RUEDA, instituted in 1980, RIBERA DEL DUERO (1982), TORO (1987), and the even more recently demarcated BIERZO and CIGALES.

Abadía Retuerta
r ★★★→★★★★★ 96, 97, 98

Sardón de Duero (Valladolid). Non-DO. This is one of the most modern *bodegas* in Spain, with 204 hectares of vineyard and 3,100 oak *barricas*. Under the direction of the oenologist from Château Ausone, it is making exceptional 100 per cent Tempranillo; Tempranillo/Cabernet Sauvignon/Merlot; and Tempranillo/Cabernet Sauvignon. The *crianza* '96, made from 100 per cent Cabernet Sauvignon and aged for two years in *barrica*, is superb.

Agrícola Castellana Sociedad Cooperativa
DO w dr am ★→★★

La Seca (Valladolid). DO Rueda. This large and well-regulated cooperative in the TIERRA DE MEDINA was founded in 1935 and now has a storage capacity of eight million litres.

The cooperative makes both the traditional *flor*-growing RUEDA from a blend of Verdejo and Palomino, ageing it either in *solera* or in glass carboys in the open, and also fresh, young wines made from 100 per cent Verdejo. Typical of the first type are the Campo Grande *fino* and Dorado 61, both sherry-like in flavour and of about 15 per cent strength. Its pleasant light wines are sold as Azumbre, Pampano and Veliterra. The Cuatro Rayas, made from 100 per cent Verdejo, is light-greenish in colour, dry, fragrant, fruity and pleasantly astringent.

Alión, Bodegas y Viñedos
DO r ☆☆☆ 92, 93, 94, 95

Peñafiel (Valladolid). DO Ribera del Duero. Since discontinuing the three-year-old VALBUENA, VEGA SICILIA has developed this second *bodega* to make red wines with 100 per cent Tempranillo. The results are impressive; the wines are vigorous and good for short- to medium-term laying down.

Alta Pavina, Bodegas
r ☆☆ 94, 95, 96, 98

La Parrilla (Valladolid). Castilla y León. Non-DO. This small *bodega* makes good 100 per cent Cabernet Sauvignon and Tinto Fino, both oak-aged, spicy, dark and dense. Also variable Pinot Noir.

Antaño, Bodegas
DO w dr (r) ☆☆

Rueda (Valladolid). DO Rueda. Ambitious new *bodega* started by Madrid restaurateurs, making clean and fruity white Viña Mocen, and red Viña Cobranza made from a blend of Tempranillo and Cabernet Sauvignon in VT Medina del Campo.

Bañeza, La
r ☆

La Bañeza is an area to the west of the city of LEON and part of the undemarcated COMARCA DE LEON. It was formerly widely known for its *claretes de aguja* (light red wines with slight sparkle), but little wine is now made except in primitive subterranean cellars for local consumption.

Basa
w ★★

Brand name for Verdejo white from Rueda, made by gifted young oenologist Telmo Rodríguez of La Granja Remelluri in Rioja.

Benavente
VC r ☆

Like LA BAÑEZA, Benavente once made good *claretes* with a slight sparkle, but many of its vineyards have now been abandoned.

Bierzo
DO r w p ☆→☆☆☆

Bierzo, in the northwest of the province of León bordering Galicia, of which the new DO Bierzo forms part, is ideal for the production of quality wines. Its 3,622 hectares of vineyards thrive in a climate which could be described as halfway between the dry heat of Castilla–León and the rain and humidity more typical of Galicia.

Vines are thickest on the ground around Villafranca and Ponferrada, and the most dominant vine varieties are the black Mencía and Alicante, and the white Palomino.

The fragrant and fruity red wines age well in cask, developing a good ruby colour, and are smooth and silky, with not more than 12 per cent alcohol. The whites, which average 10.5 to 11.5 per cent, are fruity, flowery on the nose and better balanced than the traditional acidic wines of Galicia. There are also excellent rosés, produced mainly from the Mencía grape and having a refreshing residual acidity.

The temptation has always been to sell the wines to Galicia and Asturias, where they find a ready market. The cooperatives of Cacabelos and Villafranquina bottle worthwhile and representative wines (see Sociedad VINOS DEL BIERZO); but perhaps the most sophisticated wines from the region are the 100 per cent Godello whites and red Mencía from PRADA A TOPE.

Bornos, Palacio de
See Bodegas de Crianza CASTILLA LA VIEJA.

Callejo, Bodegas Félix
DO r p ☆☆→☆☆☆ *91, 95, 96*
Sotillo de la Ribera (Burgos). DO Ribera del Duero. Young *bodega* making fruity, well-structured reds from 100 per cent Tinto Fino.

Casar de Valdaiga
DO r p w dr ☆☆
Label for the wines made by PEREZ CARAMES in the DO BIERZO. The fruity red is well worth looking out for.

Castilla la Vieja, Bodegas de Crianza
DO r w p ★★→★★★
Rueda (Valladolid). DO Rueda. *Bodegas* founded by local growers to elaborate their wines in the best possible fashion, ageing some in oak. Founded by Antonio Sanz and now run by Ricardo Sanz (*see also* Vinos SANZ) it makes first-rate Palacio de Bornos whites, including a barrel-fermented 90 per cent Verdejo Rueda Superior ('98); 100 per cent Sauvignon Blanc ('98); a red non-DO Almirantazgo de Castilla; and an excellent sparkling non-DO Palacio de Bornos Brut.

Cebreros
VdlT r p ☆
Situated in the province of Avila in the Sierra de Gredos west of Madrid, Cebreros produces wines from the black Garnacha and Tinto Aragonés and the white Albillo.

Robust and heady *tintos* and *rosados* with a minimum of 13 per cent alcohol, they are much in demand for everyday drinking in Madrid and the surrounding area.

Cigales
DO r ☆→☆☆
The 2,712 hectares of the recently demarcated Cigales are planted with white Palomino, Verdejo and Albillo, and black Garnacha, Tinto del País and Tinto Madrid. Its *claretes*, famous since medieval times, may no longer be labelled as such thanks to the wisdom of Brussels; they are made by mixing the black and white grapes, destalking them and fermenting them *en blanc*. Light red wines of this type were, from time immemorial, the most popular in the taverns of VALLADOLID, but what now passes for a light red Cigales is more likely to be a blend of red wine from Zamora with a white from the central plains of La Mancha.

Because much of the wine is made in archaic subterranean *bodegas* for local consumption, and the production of good Cigales was more or less limited to two sizeable private concerns – those of Pablo Barrigón Tovar and Bodegas FRUTOS VILLAR – demarcation of this small region was delayed. The large and modernised cooperative at Cigales makes an excellent Torondos rosé.

Con Class, Bodegas
DO w ☆☆→☆☆☆ *DYA*

La Seca (Valladolid). DO Rueda. A catchpenny name, but this newish, go-ahead *bodega* is making exciting wines from Verdejo/Viura and Sauvignon Blanc, especially the Rueda Superior ('98).

Condado de Haza
DO r ☆☆☆ *94, 95, 96, 97*

Pesquera de Duero (Valladolid). Do Ribera del Duero. Alejandro FERNANDEZ'S new *bodega*, producing a pure Tinto Fino aged in oak. Akin to PESQUERA, the first vintages are winners.

Conde de Siruela
DO r ☆☆☆

Good red Ribera del Duero wines from Bodegas FRUTOS VILLAR.

Dehesa de los Canónigos, Bodega
DO r res ☆☆→☆☆☆ *92, 94, 95, 96*

Pesquera de Duero (Valladolid). DO Ribera del Duero. The grapes from the vineyards of this young firm in the Ribera del Duero were formerly sold to VEGA SICILIA. It is now making its own stylish and concentrated, if dauntingly expensive, Tinto Fino reds.

Dominio de Pingus
DO r ☆☆☆→☆☆☆☆☆ *99*

DO Ribera del Duero. Tiny *bodega* with 4.5 hectares of 60-year-old vines, recently founded by Danish winemaker Peter Sisseck. Its excellent, concentrated wines have already achieved cult status and are expensive to a degree, but there is an affordable second wine named Flor de Pingus.

Durius
r w dr ☆☆

Refreshing white and vigorous young red wines recently introduced by the Marqués de Griñón (*see* page 39). The red is made by Bodegas Berberana (*see* page 130-1) from a blend of 65 per cent Tinto Fino from Ribera del Duero and 35 per cent Tinto de Toro from TORO, before ageing for 24 months in American oak.

Fariña, Bodegas
DO r res ★★→★★★ *92, 94, 95, 97, 98*

Casaseca de las Chanas (Zamora). DO Toro. The best-known *bodega* of the recently demarcated TORO, making dark, spicy red wines with heavy fruit: Colegiata is unoaked, while the Gran Colegiata is aged in cask.

Fermoselle
VdlT r ☆

Fermoselle lies between the basins of the two rivers Duero and Tormes in the southwest corner of the province of Zamora, almost within a stone's throw of the Portuguese border. Its granite and schistous soils, and its blistering summers and low rainfall, resemble those of the Upper Douro. That its wines, though in some ways resembling the Portuguese, are not their equal, is probably because the dominant grape, Juan García, is not of the same quality as the varieties grown in Portugal.

During the 18th century Fermoselle produced an annual one million litres of wine, and the place seems to be hollow with disused cellars hewn from the granite. Now, however, it is difficult to find the authentic full-bodied red wine, with its strange resinous (but not unattractive) nose and flavour, because most of it is sold in bulk for blending.

Fernández, Alejandro
DO r res ☆☆☆☆☆ 92, 93, 94, 95, 96, 97

Pesquera de Duero (Valladolid). DO Ribera del Duero. The *bodega* was founded in 1970. Its wines, intensely fruity in the very best manner of the RIBERA DEL DUERO, improved dramatically with the installation of stainless steel and new-oak barrels. Since the PESQUERA wines were 'discovered' by the foreign press and Robert Parker put them on a par with those of Château Pétrus, prices, prestige and exports have leapt. The Janus *gran reserva* is made only in exceptional years. *See also* CONDADO DE HAZA.

Frutos Villar, Bodegas
DO r p w dr ☆→☆☆

Cigales (Valladolid). DO Cigales. The largest outfit in Cigales, making the reliable Viña Calderona *rosado*.

The company also makes very drinkable red Muruve and Gran Muruve in TORO, and has further outposts in Rueda and in Ribera del Duero, where it makes good CONDE DE SIRUELA *crianzas* and *reservas*.

Grandes Bodegas
DO r res ★★ 94, 95, 96, 98

Roa de Duero (Burgos). DO Ribera del Duero. Founded in 1986, the *bodega* has begun making wines from grapes grown only in its own vineyards. Good-quality and affordable Marqués de Velilla *crianza* and *reservas*.

Grupo Sindical de Colonización No 795
VdlT r (p w dr) ☆→☆☆

Cebreros (Avila). Makers of El Galayo, available in different styles and perhaps the best of these sturdy wines.

Ismael Arroyo
DO r res ★★→☆☆☆ 91, 92, 93, 94, 95, 96, 98

Sotillo de la Ribera (Burgos). DO Ribera del Duero. Small *bodega* with 16 hectares of vineyard and 1,000 oak *barricas*, well-known for its reliable and well-structured wines sold under the labels of Mesoneros de Castilla and Valsotillo.

León

Situated high on the Castilian plateau, the old city of León, capital of the medieval kingdom, is the centre of an increasingly im-portant wine-producing area. The Gothic cathedral, with its airy flying buttresses and magnificent stained-glass windows, is one of the finest in Spain.

León, Comarca de
r p w dr ☆→☆☆

The name is used to describe the wine-producing area to the southeast of the city of León. It comprises, in order of importance, the following subdivisions: VALDEVIMBRE, LOS OTEROS, LA BAÑEZA, LEON, Tierra de Campos, Valderas, La Antique, Payuelos and RIBERA ALTA DEL CEA.

Los Curros, SAT
DO w dr r ★★→★★★

Rueda (Valladolid). DO Rueda. Former cooperative making the fresh and flowery Viña Cantosán from 100 per cent Verdejo – the house white at Madrid's famous Zalacaín restaurant. The *bodega* also bottles the rich and oaky non-DO YLLERA, made by a sister establishment in Boada de Roa in RIBERA DEL DUERO.

Marqués de Riscal *See* VINOS BLANCOS DE CASTILLA

Mauro, Bodegas
r res ☆☆→☆☆☆ 94, 95, 96, 97

Tudela de Duero (Valladolid). Small, private *bodega* whose round and fruity reds from the Tinto Fino are made by Mariano García of VEGA SICILIA fame. They do not currently carry the DO RIBERA DEL DUERO, as some of the fruit is grown outside Ribera del Duero.

Mauro Toro
r ☆☆☆ 97

Tudela de Duero (Valladolid). It is a new departure for Bodegas Mauro to make Toro wines and the operation has been mounted by Mariano García, former oenologist of VEGA SICILIA. The first wine – non-DO, like the other Mauro wines – is San Roman '97, which is splendidly fruity and concentrated, and tannic in the way of a Toro.

Morales, Bodega Cooperativa de
DO r ★★

Morales de Toro (Zamora). DO Toro. The cooperative is situated just east of the town of Toro and makes wines of great character and outstanding value. The basic Moralinos, made from 100 per cent Tinta de Toro, is big and hearty. There is also a supple and fruity Niña Bajoz *crianza* and a densely fruity Moralinos Garnacha.

Nava del Rey
Largest of the townships in the TIERRA DE MEDINA southwest of VALLADOLID, and part of the DO RUEDA.

Oteros, Los
VdlT r p w dr ☆→☆☆

Los Oteros, east of the LEON–BENAVENTE road, is second in importance of the subdivisions of the Comarca de LEON. The major grape is the Prieto Picudo, grown in clay soils. Much of the wine is made in tiny peasant *bodegas*, constructed by digging deep into the ground, installing the simplest of beam presses, mounding up the soil on top and leaving a chimney for the escape of carbon dioxide. The typical wine made in such cellars is a *clarete* (which may no longer be described as such under EC regulations) of ten to 13.5 per cent, but methods are so archaic that on occasion the volatile acidity is so high the wine tastes of raspberry vinegar. *See also* VALDEVIMBRE.

Pago de Carraovejas
DO r ☆☆☆ *91, 92, 93, 94, 95, 96*

Peñafiel (Valladolid). DO Ribera del Duero. New *bodega* with 60 hectares of vineyards, planted between 1988 and 1991 with Tinto Fino and Cabernet Sauvignon. Currently earning a reputation for some of the region's most stylish and densely fruity wines.

Palacio de Bornos *See* Bodegas de Crianza CASTILLA LA VIEJA

Peñafiel
Township in RIBERA DEL DUERO surmounted by a magnificent 12th-century castle, beneath which Bodegas PROTOS maintains cellars for maturing its wines. Another part of its medieval legacy is the extraordinary jousting ground and the houses surrounding it.

Peñalba López, Bodegas
DO r (p) ★★→★★★ *91, 92, 94, 95, 96*

Aranda de Duero (Burgos). DO Ribera del Duero. Fast-expanding family firm with its own vineyards, making and ageing in oak good fruity TORREMILANOS reds from the Tinto Fino grape, more Rioja-like than most.

Pérez Caramés
DO w dr r ☆☆

Villafranca de Bierzo (León). DO Bierzo. This is the largest of the producers in BIERZO, making wine in the northwest corner of the province. It produces some very creditable wines under the labels of Casar de Santa Inés and Casar de Valdaiga.

Pérez Pascuas, Bodega Hermanos
DO r (p) res ☆☆☆ *90, 91, 92, 94, 95, 96, 97*

Pedrosa de Duero (Burgos). DO Ribera del Duero. This tiny and scrupulously kept family *bodega* makes fruity and complex VIÑA

PEDROSA red wines and a magnificent Pérez Pascuas Gran Selección, rated by *Club de Gourmets* magazine as among the best in Spain.

Pesquera
r ☆☆☆ *89, 91, 92, 93, 94, 95, 96, 97*

Famous wines from Alejandro FERNANDEZ.

Prada a Tope
DO (w dr p) r res ★★ *94, 96, 98*

Cacabelos (León). DO Bierzo. Tiny modern *bodega* installed in the Palace of the Señorío de Canedo, where the individualistic José Luís Prada makes small amounts of some of the best Bierzo wines, including a white Godello and reds with the local Mencía grape.

Protos, Bodegas
DO r rs ☆☆→☆☆☆ *91, 92, 94, 95, 96, 97*

Peñafiel (Valladolid). DO Ribera del Duero. This *bodega*, which was formerly a cooperative, was one of the first in Spain to age its wines in oak. Its storage capacity runs to 1.2 million litres and it has 2,300 American-oak casks for maturing the wines, which average 12.5 per cent alcohol. The youngest wine is the *crianza*, with a deep, plummy colour: fresh and tasting of blackberries. The *reserva* spends two years in oak *barricas*; and there are also Protos *gran reservas*, aged for much longer in cask and bottle. The wines, much improved by a new oenologist, are shipped to the UK and Germany and have been much admired by connoisseurs for their clean, fruity nose, deep flavour and long finish.

Ribera Alta del Cea
VC r

Small winemaking area between LEON and Palencia, formerly producing red wines from hybrids obtained by directly crossing European and American vines. Since the wines contained small amounts of a toxic alkaloid (*malvina*), they were blended with others from the area. The district now makes pleasant light red wines from a blend of Mencía, Prieto Picudo and Palomino.

Ribera de Burgos
DO r ☆→☆☆

Part of the DO RIBERA DEL DUERO, centred on Aranda de Duero. The predominant grape varieties are the Tinto del País, Tinto Madrid, Jaén, Valenciano, Albillo, Tinto Aragonés and the Tempranillo. The area's typical wines are the light reds formerly known as *claretes* or *claros*, most of which are made by small proprietors or in cooperatives. Some of the best of them are produced by the Bodegas Santa Eulalia in La Horra and bottled as CONDE DE SIRUELA.

Ribera del Duero
DO r ☆☆→☆☆☆

Demarcated in 1982, this region – together with Rioja and Cataluña – produces some of the best red wine in Spain. It borders the River Duero for a distance of 110 kilometres, with a maximum width of 30 kilometres, from Tudela de Duero near VALLADOLID to just east of El Burgo de Osma, and borders an area of 12,577 hectares. This is one of the fastest-growing and most fashionable wine-growing areas in the country, with *bodegas* mushrooming and finance flowing in from Madrid. Prices for the wines are correspondingly high.

The larger and central part of the region lies within the province of Burgos; there are small areas within the provinces of Soria to the east and Segovia to the south, but the best of the wines are made around PEÑAFIEL and Valbuena in the province of Valladolid. In these areas the vines grow on chalky, pine-fringed slopes bordering the Duero, and the predominant grape is the Tinto Fino or Tinto Aragonés, a variant of the Riojan Tempranillo, whose musts are particularly suitable for maturation in oak. This area is famous for the legendary VEGA SICILIA but many excellent *bodegas*, such as Alejandro FERNANDEZ and Bodegas Hermanos PEREZ PASCUAS, have now come to the fore.

Rueda
DO w dr am ★★

This small region to the southwest of VALLADOLID, with an area of 6,001 hectares, has long known as the TIERRA DE MEDINA and takes its name from the village of Rueda, which, with NAVA DEL REY, LA SECA and SERRADA, is a main centre for making the wines.

The predominant grape varieties are the native white Verdejo, Viura and Palomino, grown in calcareous clays. More recently, Sauvignon Blanc has been introduced in small amounts from France. The district is demarcated only for white wines, for which it has been famous since the 17th century. The traditional Rueda, amber-coloured and of some 15 per cent strength, is a *flor*-growing white matured either in loosely stoppered glass carboys or in *solera*, and tasting like a rough sherry. More recently, and following the lead of the MARQUES DE RISCAL, which has built a large modern winery near Rueda, the region has been producing fresh and attractive cold-fermented white wines, made mainly with the Verdejo.

Sanz, Vinos
DO r p w dr am res ★★ DYA

Rueda (Valladolid). DO Rueda. Large family *bodega* founded in 1870, and headquarters of the Sanz dynasty of Rueda. It makes wines in various styles, including Sanz Rueda Superior and Sanz Sauvignon, and also undertakes the vinification and maturation of wines for a variety of other concerns.

Seca, La
Small village and winemaking centre in the DO RUEDA.

Señorío de Nava, Bodegas
DO r p r ☆☆→☆☆☆ 89, 91, 94, 96, 97, 98

Nava de Roa (Burgos). DO Ribera del Duero. Controlled since 1986 by VINOS DE LEON, the firm owns 140 hectares of vineyard planted with Cabernet Sauvignon, Merlot and native varieties. The Don Alvaro rosé, made from 100 per cent Tinto Fino, is one of the best and freshest from the region, and there are good Señorío de Nava *crianzas* and *reservas*. The *bodega* won a gold medal for its wines at the 1993 Vinexpo in Bordeaux.

Serrada

Another of the winemaking villages of the small DO RUEDA. Much of the house wine in the bars and restaurants of VALLADOLID is sold as 'Serrada'.

Tierra de Medina

Traditional name for what is now the DO RUEDA. Before the phylloxera epidemic of 1909 there were 90,000 hectares under vines, but this is now reduced to 24,000 hectares, of which the DO Rueda occupies 6,000 hectares.

Tierra del Vino

Vine-growing area near TORO, at one time famous for its strong red wines, but now virtually abandoned.

Toro

DO r ☆☆

This newly demarcated region to the east of Zamora, with 15,000 hectares under vines, of which 3,018 qualify for DO, is one of the most parched in Spain, having an annual rainfall of only 300 millimetres.

In strength and body its red wines are rivalled only by those from Priorato (*see* 'Cataluña', page 74), Jumilla and Yecla (*see* 'Valencia and Murcia', pages 181 and 184-5) and were formerly among the most prized in Spain, being much drunk by the students and academics of Salamanca University. The principal vine varieties are the Tinta de Toro and Tinto de Madrid, together with some Garnacha.

Not so long ago, winemaking methods were primitive and the wines overstrong. But something of a technological revolution is now under way, spearheaded by concerns such as Bodegas FARIÑA, and with new *bodegas* multiplying, including branches of MAURO and FRUTUS VILLAR.

Torremilanos

DO r ★★→★★★ *91, 92, 94, 95, 96*

Name of the light, well-made red wines from Bodegas PEÑALBA LOPEZ in the RIBERA DEL DUERO.

Valbuena

DO r ☆☆☆ *89, 90, 91, 92, 93, 94, 95*

Made by the heavyweight VEGA SICILIA with the same grape varieties, but sold when five years old. It is best drunk at about ten years and some prefer it to its elder brother. The three-year-old has been discontinued.

Valdevimbre
VdlT r ☆→☆☆☆

This is the largest of the Comarca de LEON subdistricts, and with the neighbouring LOS OTEROS there are 3,900 hectares under vines. Its light-red wines, known as *claretes*, can be aromatic, light and fruity. They are traditionally made by adding bunches of Prieto Picudo to the must during secondary fermentation, so prolonging it and giving the wine a refreshing prickle. In some of the more primitive *bodegas*, the proprietors try for the same result by adding fizzy lemonade!

Some of the best of the wine is bottled by the Cooperative Vinícola Comarcal under the label of Señorío de Valdes Artesanal. *See also* VINOS DE LEON.

Valduero, Bodegas
DO r res (w) ★★→★★★ 90, 92, 94, 95, 96

Gumiel del Mercado (Burgos). DO Ribera del Duero. Founded in 1984, the *bodega* has a reputation for good and good-value *reservas*.

Valladolid
Home to a famous university and once the capital of Spain, Valladolid is a good base for visiting the RIBERA DEL DUERO, RUEDA, TORO, BIERZO and CIGALES. The superb 15th-century Colegio de San Gregorio houses the National Museum of Polychrome Sculpture, with its outstanding collections of sculptures and paintings.

Vega de la Reina, Vinos
r (w dr) res ☆☆ 89, 91, 94, 98

Rueda (Valladolid). Only the characterful white wine made from Verdejo and Viura rates DO, because the region is not demarcated for reds. However, the *bodega* was famous for its reds, which were complex and oaky in the style of Rioja *gran reservas* of old; but the style has changed under Mexican control and the wines are now more reminiscent of those from RIBERA DEL DUERO.

Vega Sicilia, Bodegas
DO r ☆☆☆→☆☆☆☆☆ 64, 66, 67, 69, 70, 72, 73, 74, 75, 76, 79, 80, 82, 83, 85, 86 *Reserva Especial*

Valbuena de Duero (Valladolid). DO Ribera del Duero. Vega Sicilia is a name to conjure with in Spain, where its wines, all red, are strictly rationed and supplied only for state functions and to the best hotels and restaurants. The estate of some 900 hectares, with 200 under vines, borders the river in the RIBERA DEL DUERO, east of VALLADOLID, at a height of 765 metres.

As far back as 1864 select French vines were acquired from Bordeaux and acclimatised in its chalky, pine-fringed vineyards. They have subsequently been replanted with the same three varieties, Cabernet Sauvignon, Merlot and Malbec, whose musts are blended with those of the native Tinto Aragonés and white Albillo. The *bodega* believes in vinifying and maturing its wines very slowly; only the must which separates naturally after light crushing is used, and after vinification the Vega Sicilia is matured for not less than four years in oak (and often much longer) with three more in bottle. The *bodega* also makes a five-year-old red VALBUENA. The wines, of 13.5 per cent alcohol or more, are full-bodied, deep in colour, complex and intensely fruity, with a fragrant nose, compounded of oak and fruit, and a long finish. Some experts have criticised Vega Sicilia for the degree of volatile acidity, preferring the VALBUENA, with its shorter period in cask. *See also* Bodegas y Viñedos ALION.

Viña Pedrosa
r ☆☆☆ 89, 90, 91, 92, 94, 95, 96, 97
Fruity red RIBERA DEL DUERO from Bodega Hermanos PEREZ PASCUAS.

Vinos del Bierzo, Sociedad
DO r res (p w) ☆☆→☆☆☆
Cacabelos (León). DO Bierzo. The red Guerra *reservas* from this large cooperative, made with 100 per cent Mencía and aged in oak, are soft and well-balanced with hints of coffee and spices.

Vinos Blancos de Castilla
DO w dr ★★→★★★ DYA
Rueda (Valladolid). DO Rueda. The *bodega* was constructed – with advice from Professor Peynaud of Bordeaux University – by the Rioja firm of MARQUES DE RISCAL, which did not, at the time, market a white wine. Its capacity is two million litres: the wines are cold-fermented in stainless-steel tanks and made with 90 per cent Verdejo, but Peynaud found that they improved through blending with a little Viura and by maturing for a few months in oak casks. Fresh and fruity, they are sold under the label of the Marqués de Riscal, most of the output going for export. More recently the *bodega* has introduced a fresh and outstanding young 100 per cent Sauvignon Blanc, and a first-rate, characterful Marqués de Riscal Reserva Limousin, which is matured in oak.

Vinos de León-VILE, Bodegas
VdlT r p w dr ★→★★ 92, 94, 95, 96
Armunia (León). Long known as VILE, a somewhat unfortunate abbreviation, this large private consortium owns a modern winery with a capacity of 12 million litres and 2,500 casks for maturing the wines. The group has vineyards of its own, but buys most of the grapes – mainly Prieto Picudo, Tempranillo, Mencía, Tinto del País and Garnacha for the red and rosé wines, and Verdejo and Palomino for the white – from independent proprietors in VALDEVIMBRE and Los OTEROS. Its crisp, young red and white wines have proved very popular in the UK. Among its more select and older wines are the red Catedral de León and good, full-bodied Don Suero and Palacio de los Guzmanes *reservas*.

Yllera
r ★★ 92, 95, 96
Good-value RIBERA DEL DUERO red from LOS CURROS, but not with DO status because it is bottled in Rueda.

WINE AND FOOD

If one had to name the type of dish most typical of Castilla–León it would be the roasts; of lamb, suckling pig and kid, and the baby milk-fed lamb, or *lechazo*, is at its best around Valladolid. However, the region has much else to offer: partridge from the mountains, trout from the cold streams and the rib-warming *cocidos* made from chickpeas and local varieties of pork sausage.

Arroz con cordero Rice combined with tomato sauce and stewed lamb, finished in the oven to crisp the top. The dish matches a light red or rosé with a little residual acidity, such as Vinos de León's Castillo de Coyanza, or Calderona from Bodegas Frutos Villar.

Besugo al ajoarriero Sea bream in a sauce made with olive oil, garlic, onions, parsley and vinegar. A fresh, young Rueda: for example, Verdejo Pálido.

Cabrito asado Roast kid.

Cachelada leonesa Potatoes boiled with seasoning and *chorizo* sausage, from which they take the cheerful orange colour and spicy flavour.

Cochinillo asado Roast milk-fed suckling pig of a tenderness and succulence rarely found in Britain or the US, where the piglets are killed when they are older. A fine red *reserva* such as Valbuena, Pesquera or Vega Sicilia – if you can find it.

Cocido castellano A substantial stew made of chickpeas, brisket, marrow bones, ham bones, black pudding, *chorizo*, pork, potatoes and green vegetables. Go the whole hog and wash it down with a sturdy Cebreros!

Cordero asado/lechazo Roast lamb/milk-fed baby lamb, often cooked in a baker's oven. A good red, such as Torremilanos.

Jamón de Guijuelo Cured *páta negra* ham, from semi-wild pigs.

Judías blancas a la castellana Stew of haricot beans, tomatoes, onions, garlic and seasoning. Try the local red house wine.

Leche frita Squares of a stiff custard, dredged in beaten egg and breadcrumbs and fried crisp in hot olive oil.

Lentejas zamoranas Lentils stewed with black pudding, onions, paprika, garlic, parsley and seasoning.

Liebre en su salsa Hare, marinated in white wine and garlic, cooked in an earthenware dish with onions, carrots, turnips, nutmeg and red wine. The sauce is thickened with the liver. A full-bodied red, such as Gran Colegiata from Bodegas Fariña.

Mantecadas Small cakes made with butter, flour and eggs and baked in paper cups.

Pantortillas de Reinosa Fluffy pancakes made from puff pastry flavoured with *anís* and eaten cold.

Pisto castellano A vegetable dish resembling ratatouille, with potatoes, bacon and often with eggs.

Rebozos zamoranos Small cakes made with flour, eggs and lemon.

Ropa vieja Meat from a *cocido* served with a sauce made of fresh peppers, aubergines and tomatoes.

Tomates rellenos Tomatoes stuffed with olives, anchovies, rice and peppers.

Truchas a la montañesa Trout cooked in white wine with bay leaves and onions. A white wine with a hint of oak, such as Marqués de Riscal Limousin.

HOTELS

León You need stir no further than the memorable *Hotel San Marcos*, housed in a splendid 16th-century monastery, to sample a good range of wines from the Comarca de León and Bierzo in its sophisticated restaurant.

Sierra de Gredos The *Parador de Gredos* is a former hunting lodge of King Alfonso XIII, set high in the mountains among pine forests, and a delightful place to stay.

Valladolid The best hotels are the four-star *Olid Meliá*, *NH Ciudad de Valladolid*, and the somewhat old-fashioned *Felipe IV*.

Zamora A pleasant stopping place in this historic old town, especially if you are en route for Galicia, is the *Parador de los Condes de Alba y Aliste*, with its magnificent Renaissance courtyard.

RESTAURANTS

Aranda de Duero *Mesón de la Villa* (serves good charcuterie and regional dishes).

Burgos *El Asador de Aranda 'Papamoscas'* (the best place to eat lamb).

León *Independencia*; *Hotel San Marcos* (regional dishes and a selection of local wines); *Regia* (local fare and Bierzo wines in a 13th-century house near the cathedral).

Palencia *Lorenzo*; *Casa Damián* (both restaurants, run by the same family, are worth the stop when approaching Valladolid from Burgos or Santander).

Peñafiel *Asador Mauro* (roast suckling pig and baby lamb, regional wines); *El Molino de Palacios* (housed in an old mill, especially good for roasts).

Valladolid *Mesón Panero*; *La Fragua*; *La Criolla*; *La Parrilla de San Lorenzo* (all offer well-cooked Castilian dishes and a selection of regional wines).

DO Zones
① *Ampurdán-Costa Brava*
② *Pla de Bages*
③ *Alella*
④ *Penedès*
⑤ *Tarragona*
⑥ *Priorato*
⑦ *Terra Alta*
⑧ *Conca de Barberà*
⑨ *Costers del Segre*

Cataluña

The resourceful and industrious Catalans claim that they make wines in a greater variety of styles than any other region of Spain, pointing to the fine table wines from the Penedès; the sparkling wines (described under 'Sparkling Wines', pages 187–97), which account for 90 per cent of Spanish production; the maderised *rancio*; and the old *solera*-made dessert wines of Tarragona, which so resemble Málaga or sweet *oloroso* sherry. All these, plus some of the best brandy in the country and a gamut of vermouths and liqueurs, both indigenous varieties and foreign brands made under licence, give substance to that claim.

Comprising as it does the provinces of Gerona (Girona), Barcelona, Lérida (Lleida) and Tarragona, with an area about the size of the Netherlands or Belgium, Cataluña's landscape is rugged and broken – it has been described as a flight of stairs rising from the coastal plains of the Mediterranean towards the peaks of the Pyrenees and its associated spurs to the south. In the more mountainous areas the slopes must be terraced to allow a foothold for the vines, a system still employed in upland areas such as Priorato, and you need not leave the *autopista* from Barcelona through Penedès to see disused terraces. Many of these were constructed during the late 19th century, when every available patch of ground was pressed into service to supply wine to a France desolated by phylloxera – at that time the epidemic had not yet reached Spain.

Patterns of agriculture date from the times of the Kingdom of Aragón, which was among the most powerful medieval states of the Mediterranean, when James the Conqueror (1213–76) turned over the territories recaptured from the Moors to working farmers, instead of handing over large estates to the nobility, as happened in Castile. The tradition of the small peasant farmer was reinforced by the institution of the *Rebassa Morta*, which provided for a landowner to lease part of his land to smallholders for the plantation of vineyards in exchange for half of the produce. To this day, the great bulk of the wine is made in cooperatives from fruit supplied to them by small farmers, and even the large and well-known private firms buy more grapes than they grow in their own vineyards, and purchase large amounts of cooperative-made wine for further elaboration in their *bodegas*.

Until recent decades the emphasis was on bulk rather than quality, and the emergence of wines rivalling those of Rioja in quality is a comparatively new phenomenon. This has largely been a matter of climate. Vineyards are thickest on the ground in the coastal regions of Penedès and Tarragona, with their Mediterranean climate and hot summers. When the grapes were fermented by traditional means, temperatures often rose to 30°C or more, and much of the fruity nose and flavour were lost during a fast and furiously tumultuous fermentation. The first stainless-steel vats with provision for cooling were introduced about 1960, and they are now extensively used. This has revolutionised the Catalan wine industry. Given suitable soils and the excellent quality of the fruit, there is now nothing to prevent the production of wines as good as those from more northerly European regions; indeed, Cataluña has one advantage over the traditional producers of fine wines such as Bordeaux, Burgundy and the Rhine, namely the reliability of its weather conditions. In Cataluña the winters are not too severe and the summers uniformly sunny and hot, though still tempered by breezes from the Mediterranean. Harvests are good in 90 per cent of the years.

Grape Varieties

Although Torres and increasing numbers of other *bodegas* have very successfully acclimatised noble vines from France and Germany, most of the wine is made from native grapes. The most important varieties are as follows.

WHITE
Macabeo Known as Viura in Rioja and widely grown in Spain, Macabeo produces pale-coloured, fruity, well-balanced wines, resistant to oxidation and well-suited to cold fermentation.

Xarel-lo A native of Cataluña, known in Alella as Pansà Blanca, its wines are of medium alcoholic strength, though over-acidic in the relatively rare years when it does not fully ripen. It is one of the grapes much used for making sparkling wines in Penedès.

Parellada (or Montonec) Grown exclusively in the higher areas of Penedès Superior and Conca de Barberà, its musts are low in alcohol (nine to 11 per cent) and high in acidity. Again much used for making sparkling wines, it is the Parellada which gives the exceptionally fresh and fruity bouquet to still wines such as the Torres Viña Sol.

Garnacha Blanca Also grown in Rioja, it is extensively cultivated in Terra Alta and the Campo de Tarragona, yielding wines high in alcohol with little acid.

Malvasia This is the well-known Malmsey, of Greek origin but grown for centuries in Spain. Its musts are fruity and medium strength and (as also in Madeira, where Malmsey is the name given to the sweetest wine) when fortified and aged gives rise to dessert wines like those of Sitges.

Pansé Grown in the Campo de Tarragona, Conca de Barberà and the Ribera d'Ebre, it matures late and prolifically, but the wines are coarse and high in alcohol.

Pedro Ximénez Much grown in Andalucía, where it is used for sweet wines, and in Montilla, where it makes dry, Pedro Ximénez is grown in small amounts in Priorato and Terra Alta, where its musts are mixed with those from other varieties.

BLACK

Cariñena Originally a native of Aragón, Cariñena produces wines of 11 to 12 per cent strength, robust, rich in colour and extract, but without a very distinctive nose.

Garnacha Peluda A mutant of the Garnacha Tinta, cropping more regularly but otherwise with similar characteristics.

Garnacha Tinta Another native Spanish grape, very widely grown in Rioja and other parts of Spain. Its wines are high in alcohol (11 to 14 per cent), full-bodied, fruity and deep in colour, but oxidise rapidly, turning a brick-red when aged in wood.

Monastrell A native grape, also widely grown in the central regions of Spain. The yield is small, but its wines are deep in colour, of considerable elegance and mature well.

Ull de Llebre (Ojo de Liebre) The well-known Tempranillo of Rioja or Cencibel of Valdepeñas, which produces wines of 11 to 13 per cent strength, with good acid balance, a distinctive fruity nose and good ageing properties.

Sumoll Once widely cultivated in Penedès, it produces aromatic but very tart wines and is now being phased out.

In addition to these native grapes, foreign grapes are increasingly grown in the area, and the following varieties have been authorised by various *consejos reguladores*. Red: Cabernet Sauvignon, Cabernet Franc, Merlot, Pinot Noir; white: Chardonnay, Chenin Blanc, Sauvignon, Gewürztraminer, Riesling, Muscat d'Alsace.

Cataluña now possesses nine *denominaciónes de origen*, of which control has passed from the Instituto Nacional de

Denominaciónes de Origen (INDO) to Institut Català de Vi (INCAVI), an agency of the Generalitat, the autonomous governing body of Cataluña. The areas, together with production figures for 1997-98, are: Penedès (26,350 hectares, 54.6 million litres); Alella (525 hectares, 65,600 litres); Tarragona (10,992 hectares, 48.2 million litres); Priorato (900 hectares, 982,500 litres); Ampurdán-Costa Brava (2,475 hectares, 5.3 million litres); Conca de Barberà (6,000 hectares, 8.4 million litres); Terra Alta (8,171 hectares, 14.8 million litres); Costers del Segre (3,886 hectares, 5.9 million litres); and the new Pla de Bages (500 hectares, 948,000 litres).

In addition, a new DO Cataluña was instituted in November 1999 which embraces all the above *denominaciós*; but producers must choose between registering for one of the smaller, more specific DOs or the general one, which permits them to make wine with grapes – or a combination of grapes – from any of the DOs already in place.

Vintages, as has been explained, are remarkably consistent, and the only really poor one in recent decades was in '72. The following chart for the Penedès gives some idea of the variation.

Year	Red Wines	White Wines
'76	*very good*	*good to very good*
'77	*good to very good*	*very good*
'78	*very good*	*good*
'79	*fair to good*	*good*
'80	*good*	*good*
'81	*excellent*	*very good*
'82	*very good*	*very good*
'83	*good*	*good*
'84	*excellent*	*good*
'85	*good*	*good*
'86	*fair*	*good*
'87	*excellent*	*good*
'88	*very good*	*excellent*
'89	*good*	*fair*
'90	*very good*	*very good*
'91	*excellent*	*excellent*
'92	*good*	*good*
'93	*very good*	*excellent*
'94	*good*	*very good*
'95	*excellent*	*excellent*
'96	*very good*	*very good*
'97	*very good*	*very good*
'98	*very good*	*excellent*

If you have a car, it is not difficult to plan a visit to the Catalan winemaking areas, since four of them (Ampurdán-Costa Brava, Alella, Penedès and Tarragona) lie along the axis of the A17 *autopista* from the French border to Barcelona, and its southward extension (the A7) to Tarragona and Valencia. Costers del Segre is near Lérida (Lleida). Conca de Barberà, Priorato and Terra Alta, in the hills of the hinterland, are less easy to reach and require fairly time-consuming side trips, but there are notable con-solations in the rugged and well-wooded countryside, the hill-top castles and in the great monasteries of Montserrat and Poblet, which are so closely associated with the development of viti-culture in the region. Cataluña also boasts the pleasant coastal resorts and the splendid cliff scenery of the Costa Brava; and it would be a single-minded devotee of wines who did not pause in Barcelona to visit Gaudí's astonishing cathedral of La Sagrada Familia or its magnificent museums and galleries, or in Tarragona to see the remarkable Roman remains.

Large *bodegas*, such as Miguel Torres, are happy to welcome visitors without an appointment, arranging guided tours and instructive tastings. Even in the smallest cooperative you will be able to taste and buy the wine, and will receive a friendly welcome – *if* you can muster enough Spanish to communicate. If in doubt about your reception, ask the porter at the hotel to telephone beforehand. Catalan food, meanwhile, is interesting and varied, though sometimes more than substantial in country hotels and restaurants.

The Catalans take their regained autonomy seriously. Under Franco it was forbidden to speak in Catalan; now it is a point of pride to do so. Most signs and place-names are now in Catalan, which is a separate language and not a dialect, although the Castilian equivalent is generally added. This also applies to menus, although these sometimes appear exclusively in Catalan in smaller restaurants. The waiter or proprietor will, however, always explain in Castilian.

Albet i Noya
DO w dr (p) r res ☆☆→☆☆☆ *93, 94, 95, 96, 97, 98*
Sant Pau d'Ordal (Barcelona). DO Penedès. Best-known Spanish producer of organic wines, growing a range of grapes in its 50 hectare vineyard. The best wines are labelled Colleccio and made from 100 per cent Chardonnay, Xarel-lo, Syrah, Tempranillo and Cabernet Sauvignon.

Alella
DO (r p am) w dr sw ☆☆→☆☆☆
The tradition of winemaking in this small region dates from Roman times, but it is now threatened by urban expansion from Barcelona towards the south. Despite a surprising extension of the DO zone in 1989, of the 1,400 hectares that were under vine in 1967 only 525 survive, producing mostly white wine. The grape varieties approved by the *consejo regulador* are: for white wines, Xarel-lo (or Pansà Blanca), Pansà Rosada, Garnacha Blanca, Chardonnay and Chenin Blanc; and for the reds, Tempranillo (Ull de Llebre), Garnacha Tinta and Garnacha Peluda, and there are experimental plantations of foreign varieties, notably Chardonnay.

Many of the vineyards, all of them small and few exceeding 1.5 hectares, are owned by professionals dedicated to preserving the wine industry. The vines are planted on granitic slopes sheltered from the prevailing east wind, one of which – with a northerly aspect – produces wine of high acidity. The wine from the other, more southerly slope is rather sweeter and lower in acidity.

Alella Vinícola, Can Jonc
DO (p) w dr s/sw ☆☆ *DYA*

Alella (Barcelona). DO Alella. This well-equipped former cooperative, founded in 1906 and with a capacity of 500,000 litres, makes much of the wine from ALELLA. It is sold as Alella Legítima in hock-type bottles under the brand name of Marfil ('ivory'). There are four types: a fruity dry white wine made from 100 per cent Pansà Blanca; a hundred per cent Chardonnay; a semi-sweet made from 100 per cent Pansà Blanca; and a fruity rosé containing 60 per cent Garnacha Tinta and 40 per cent Pansà Rosada.

Altar wine

Altar wine, made without chemical additives especially for the celebration of Holy Communion, is a speciality of Tarragona – particularly of DE MULLER, supplier to popes Pius X, Benedict XV, Pius XI, Pius XII and John XXIII. It is often made with Macabeo from the CAMPO DE TARRAGONA, alcohol being added to the musts to make a sweet white *generoso* of 15 per cent strength. Recently De Muller, which runs a special *bodega* with stained-glass windows, has been making drier wines to suit a younger generation of priests. It is exported all over the world in resin-coated steel drums.

Alvaro Palacios
DO r ☆☆☆ 93, 94, 95, 96, 97

Gratallops (Tarragona). DO Priorato. Within ten years this gifted emigré from the Rioja has begun making some of the most fashionable and expensive red wines in Spain, with grapes from his tiny 9.5 hectare vineyard. They include Finca Dofí, L'Ermita and Les Terrases.

Amadis
r res ☆☆☆ 95, 96, 97

Much sought-after red Priorato from the small and sophisticated Rotllan Torra.

Ampurdán, Cavas del
DO r p w sp ★→★★

Perelada (Girona). DO Ampurdán-Costa Brava. Situated in the village of Perelada near Figueres, on the verges of the Pyrenees, this is the sister ship of the well-known CAVA concern of the Castillo de Perelada (*see* page 195).

The Cavas' worthwhile still wines include the three-year-old red Tinto Cazador, Perelada Rosado and a dry white Pescador. The white Cresta Azul is made in *cuves closes* pressurised to only a quarter of the normal extent and it was this concern that produced a *cuve close* sparkler, the subject in 1960 of the celebrated 'Spanish champagne' case, brought by the French Champagne companies in England and known in France at the time as 'the Second Battle of the Marne'.

Ampurdán-Costa Brava
DO r p w dr ☆→☆☆

Known as *Empordà-Costa Brava* in Catalan, this is a fairly recently demarcated region, abutting the Pyrenees in the province of Girona and inland from the holiday coast. A problem for the growers here is the prevailing north wind, the *tramontana*, which blows 100 days in the year, at velocities of up to hurricane force. For this reason the vines are staked.

The area under vine is 2,475 hectares and the main vine varieties are the black Garnacha Tinta and Cariñena, and the white Macabeo and Xarel-lo. Seventy per cent of the wine, made mostly in cooperatives, is rosé, but the region is now producing a fresh young *vi novell* in the manner of Beaujolais Nouveau.

Anoia, Comarca de
VC r (p)

Winemaking area bordering PENEDES to the west.

Bach, Masía
DO r p w dr sw res ☆☆→☆☆☆ 92, 93, 94, 95, 96

Sant Esteve Sesrovires (Barcelona). DO Penedès. Shortly after the First World War a couple of elderly bachelor brothers from Barcelona, who had made a fortune by supplying uniforms to the Allied armies, built a flamboyant, Florentine-style mansion in PENEDES and started a small winery. It grew, like Topsy, and when it was taken over by the great sparkling-wine firm of Codorníu (*see* page 190), it embraced vast cellars and 8,500 oak casks with a total capacity of 3.1 million litres. The *bodega* maintains its high reputation and makes good Cabernet Sauvignon wines, a fresh, young Extrísimo Seco white and Magníficat containing 60/30 per cent Albariño and Chardonnay and 10 per cent Sauvignon Blanc. The wine with which it made its name is the luscious, oaky Extrísimo, one of the best white dessert wines from Spain.

Baix Ebre-Montsià, Comarca de
VC (r) w dr

Winemaking area lying in the extreme south of the province of Tarragona, bordering the Ebro delta.

Barcelona
Barcelona, the capital of Cataluña and second city of Spain, takes its name from the Carthaginian general Hamilcar Barca, but was founded long before his time, probably by the Phoenicians. Apart from being an excellent base for visits to the wine areas of Cataluña, it is a metropolis of outstanding interest. Do not miss the old city, with its Roman remains, its Gothic cathedral, the Palace of the Generalitat (the governing body of Cataluña), and the flower-decked Ramblas; or again, the many buildings by that master of Art Nouveau, Antonio Gaudí, foremost among them the extraordinary unfinished cathedral of La Sagrada Familia. There are many museums and galleries, including those devoted to primitive art, Picasso and Miró.

Once every two years, in mid-March, Barcelona is of special interest to gastronomes, when it mounts the Salón Internacional de la Alimentaria, one of the largest international wine and food fairs, with exhibits from every Spanish wine firm of consequence. It is a city long famous for its high culinary standards, and in recent years especially its restaurateurs have been among the most innovative in Spain.

Barril, Masía
DO r (g) ☆☆→☆☆☆ 87, 91, 93, 94, 95, 96

Bellmunt del Priorat (Tarragona). DO Priorato. The tiny family firm makes authentic PRIORATO wines, dense in colour and concentrated in fruit and alcohol – the '83 was 18° – by strictly traditional methods. It also produces a herbal white apéritif wine and delicious sweet RANCIO. The firm has recently been bought by the Rovira family of Cavas Hill and its style of wines is changing.

Bombonas
These large, loosely stoppered pear-shaped glass carboys are used for making the traditional, sherry-like Catalan RANCIO (*rancí*) wine in an open-air CAMPO DE AÑEJAMIENTO.

Campo de Tarragona
DO r w dr sw ☆

Large subdenomination of the DO TARRAGONA occupying much of the centre of the province and embracing the towns of REUS, Valls, and TARRAGONA itself. Its vineyards are the most extensive of the Tarragona region, but in recent years farmers have found that hazelnuts are a more profitable crop, and the plantations, which amount to some 70 per cent of arable land in certain areas, have been making severe inroads. Most of the wines are sturdy whites made from the Macabeo (Viura) and Xarel-lo, known locally as the Cartuxà, but the Cooperativa de Valls makes small quantities of a smooth, ruby-coloured wine from the Ull de Llebre (Tempranillo) and Trepat – however, the whole production is preempted by the Mossos d'Esquadra, the security force of the Catalan Generalitat.

Campo de añejamiento
Name given to the open-air plots where the maderised RANCIO, known in Catalan as *vi rancí*, is made in BOMBONAS by a method corresponding to that of a rough and ready *solera* (*see* Sherry, page 171-2). *Campos de añejamiento* are also to be found in other parts of Spain, as in La Seca near Valladolid (*see* 'Castilla-León', page 53).

Can Ràfols dels Caus
DO r w dr ☆☆☆ 89, 90, 91, 94, 96, 97

Avinyonet del Penedès (Barcelona). DO Penedès. This small firm, established in 1980, makes first-rate wines – its '84 Gran Caus Tinto came fifth among the Cabernets at the 1986 Vinexpo in Bordeaux. Made from Cabernet Sauvignon, Cabernet Franc and Merlot, it spends seven months in cask and twenty in bottle, and is a big, fruity wine with masses of extract. The white Gran Caus Blanco, a blend of Chardonnay, Chenin Blanc and Xarel-lo, is clean and buttery. Also less expensive Petit Caus Blanco and Tinto and a good Extra Brut Reserva *cava* containing 40 per cent Chardonnay and 60 per cent Xarel-lo. Best is Caus Lubis 100 per cent Merlot ('94, '95).

Castillo de Perelada, Cavas del
DO r p w dr res ☆☆→☆☆☆☆ 90, 93, 94, 96

Perelada (Girona). DO Ampurdan Costa Brava. Better-known for its *cavas* (*see* 'Sparkling Wines', p 187), the Castillo also makes some worthwhile red, rosé and white wines. Best is the red Gran Claustro ('95), made from Cabernet Sauvignon, Cariñena and Merlot.

Castell del Remei
DO r p w dr res ☆☆→☆☆☆☆ 88, 89, 90, 91, 93

Penelles (Lleida). DO Costers del Segre. Old-established firm with its own vineyards in the extreme west of Cataluña, near Lleida. It was taken over by the Cusiné family in 1982, who embarked on extensive replanting of the vineyards with Sauvignon Blanc, Chardonnay, Cabernet Sauvignon and Merlot, and also modernised the *bodega*, replacing most of the 6,000 old oak casks. The wines include good white 100 per cent Chardonnay and 100 per cent Sauvignon Blanc Castell de Remei, an excellent Gotim Bru *reserva* made from Tempranillo and Cabernet Sauvignon, and a fresh young 100 per cent Merlot.

Clos de l'Obac
r res ☆☆☆☆☆ 92, 93, 95

Prestigious red Priorato from COSTERS DEL SIURANA.

Clos Mogador
DO r res ☆☆☆→☆☆☆☆☆ 92, 93, 94, 95, 96

Gratallops (Tarragona). DO Priorato. All the wine from this tiny *bodega* owned by René Barbier (no connection with Freixenet) is made from grapes grown on its 20 hectares of vineyard. The *reserva*, containing 40 per cent Garnacha, 40 per cent Cabernet Sauvignon and 20 per cent Syrah, is deep, complex and elegant and made to last for decades.

Conca de Barberà
DO (r p) w dr

This hilly region, bordering PENEDES to the west, was first demarcated by INCAVI (Institut Català de Vi) and recently by INDO (Instituto Nacional de Denominaciónes de Origen). In 1997-'98 its 6,000 hectares of vineyards produced 8.4 million litres of wine, most of it white and for everyday drinking – though standards are improving with the construction of hi-tech wineries – made from Parellada and Macabeo (Viura) grapes. Its Parellada grapes are also much in demand for making the *cavas* of SANT SADURNI D'ANOIA. A little red and rosé is also made from the Ull de Llebre, Sumoll and Trepat, but until recently the only concern to bottle any wine (in REUS, outside the region) was the great cooperative combine, the UNION AGRARIA COOPERATIVA. *See also* Bodegas CONCAVINS.

An interesting development in the region has been the purchase by Miguel TORRES of the 12th-century castle of Milmanda and its surrounding vineyards, after investigation had shown that the soils were exceptionally well-suited for growing Cabernet Sauvignon and Pinot Noir; the plantations also supply Chardonnay for the exceptional MILMANDA, vinified and matured in cask.

Conca de Tremp, Comarca de la
VC r w dr (p)

Area to the far northwest of Cataluña in the province of Lleida, better known for its hydroelectric schemes than its wine. The better wines are made by Bodegas Valeri Vila, which produces red, white and rosé Castell d'Orcau.

Concavins, Bodegas
DO w dr (p) r ☆☆

Barberà de la Conca (Tarragona). DO Conca de Barberà. This former cooperative sells its well-made wines as Castillo de Montblanc and Via Aurelia. It is best-known abroad for its red and white Santara, made by Hugh Ryman, who is no longer associated with the firm.

Conde de Caralt
DO r p w dr sw res ☆☆→☆☆☆ 90, 91, 92

Sant Sadurní d'Anoia (Barcelona). DO Penedès. Long known for its sparkling wines made by the Champagne method, this old family firm is now part of the Freixenet group, sharing premises with Segura Viudas (*see* 'Sparkling Wines', page 197) and RENE BARBIER. Apart from sparkling wine it now produces a range of sound still wines: Conde de Caralt Tinto, Rosado, Blanco Seco, Blanco Suave. The light and soft red *reservas*, containing a proportion of Cabernet Sauvignon and with a hint of cedarwood at the end, are wines of considerable sophistication. *See also* Sparkling Wines, page 187.

Conti, Celler Oliver
DO r ☆☆→☆☆☆

Capmany (Girona). DO Ampurdán-Costa Brava. New estate in the Ampurdán producing a single, high quality Bordeaux blend (Cabernet Sauvignon/Cabernet Franc/Merlot) in soft Graves style.

Costers del Segre
DO r p w dr res sp ☆☆→☆☆☆

Demarcated in 1988, the region comprises four small separate subzones around the city of Lleida: Artesa to the northeast, Valls de Riu Corb and Les Garrigues to the southeast and Raimat to the west. It was undoubtedly because of the successful development of the 3000-hectare estate of RAIMAT by the Raventós family of Codorníu and the growing prestige of its wines, inside and outside

Spain, that the region was demarcated. The total area under vines is 3,886 hectares and production of wine in 1997-98 was 5.9 million litres. A large quantity of the grapes goes to Raimat and to SANT SADURNÍ D'ANOIA for making *cava*; the other two wineries of note in the region are CASTELL DEL REMEI and the small cooperative of L' Olivera.

Costers del Siurana
DO r (w dr sw) res ☆☆☆☆ 92, 93

Gratallops (Tarragona). Carles Pastrana was one of the originators of a new generation of handcrafted Priorato wines made in tiny dedicated *bodegas*. His Clos de l'Obac and Miserere, made from a blend of Garnacha, Cabernet Sauvignon, Merlot, Cariñena and other grapes, remain among the most sought-after. There is also an intriguing sweet Dolç de l'Obac containing Garnacha, Cabernet Sauvignon and Syrah.

COVIDES
DO r w p sp res ★★→★★★

Sant Sadurní d'Anoia (Barcelona). DO Penedès. Large former cooperative making good Duc de Foix white and equally attractive Cabernet Sauvignon, Cabernet/Tempranillo, as well as first-rate Duc de Foix cava.

Dalmau Hermanos
DO r w dr sw am gen ☆→☆☆

Tarragona. DO Tarragona. The firm began blending and exporting wines as long ago as 1830, and, like many of the large houses in Tarragona, it is mainly concerned with bulk shipments abroad. It does, however, bottle some of its better wines exclusively for the home market, notably the Selecto Blanco Seco, Costa Dorada Blanco Suave and Añejo Selecto Tinto.

De Muller, SA
DO r p r g sp ★→★★★

Reus (Tarragona). DOs Tarragona, Terra Alta, Priorato, Cava. Famous old Tarragona firm and long-term supplier of altar wines to the Vatican, and which has recently moved its headquarters and *bodegas* to REUS. If its Solimar table wines are not up to Penedès standards, it makes an attractive young Moscatel Oro dessert wine, while its fortified and *solera*-made wines – reminiscent of very old and round *olorosos* and Málagas – are outstanding. They include Priorat Dom Joan Fort tinto, Solera 1865; Priorat Dom Berenguer Tinto, Solera 1918; and Aureo Semidulce, Solera 1954.

Falset, Comarca de
DO r w dr ☆

Subdenomination of the DO TARRAGONA to the southwest of the region. Its cooperative-made wines are high in alcohol, the reds velvety and with agreeable astringency, and the sturdy whites soon tend towards maderisation.

Fransola
w dr ★★★ *98*

Marvellously fresh and fruity white wine from Miguel TORRES, containing 85 per cent Sauvignon Blanc and 15 per cent Parellada.

Gandesa, Cooperativa Agrícola
DO (r) w dr sw res ☆→☆☆

Gandesa (Tarragona). DO Terra Alta. Founded in 1919, this is the oldest of the cooperatives in the recently demarcated region of TERRA ALTA and now has a capacity of 2.8 million litres. It bottles 25 per cent of its wines, selling the whites under the labels of Antic Castell and Garidells, and the reds as Garidells and Varvall. In 1938, during the Spanish Civil War, the cooperative found itself in the firing line, but this was not allowed to interfere with production. A year later the remains of two of General Franco's Moorish guards were found in one of its vats!

Gran Coronas Mas La Plana
DO res ☆☆☆☆ *88, 89, 93, 94, 95*

The famous varietal from Miguel TORRES, which in its '70 vintage was declared the best Cabernet Sauvignon in the world at the 1979 Gault-Millau 'Olympiad'.

Hill, Cavas
DO r p w dr s/sw sw res sp ★★→★★★ *88, 89, 91, 93, 94, 95, 96*

Moja-Vilafranca del Penedès (Barcelona). DO Penedès. The Hill family emigrated from England in 1660, planting a vineyard and establishing a *bodega* which was much expanded by Don José Hill Rose in 1884. The firm now makes wines by the Champagne process and a range of still wines, including good whites Blanc Bru, Chardonnay and semi-sparkling Timon, also excellent red Gran Civet and Gran Toc *reservas*. Masía Hill is one of Penedès' best young Tempranillos. *See also* 'Sparkling Wines', page 192.

INCAVI

Following the death of General Franco and the restoration of local autonomy to the four provinces of Cataluña between 1978 and 1980, the Instituto Nacional de Denominaciónes de Origen (INDO) transferred control of the demarcated regions and oenological stations in Cataluña to an agency of the revived Generalitat, the Institut Català de Vi. Under the energetic direction of the late Jaume Ciurana, it demarcated the new regions of CONCA DE BARBERA, TERRA ALTA, COSTERS DEL SEGRE and PLA DE BAGES, and subdivided the DO TARRAGONA.

León, Jean
DO r w dr res ☆☆☆ *89, 90, 91, 93, 96*

Plà del Penedès (Barcelona). Founded in 1962 by a Los Angeles restaurateur of Spanish descent and bought by Miguel TORRES in 1995, this tiny *bodega* was one of the first to plant foreign vines in Penedès and, unusually for Spain, grows all its own grapes. The vineyards extend to 60 hectares, planted mainly with Chardonnay and Cabernet Sauvignon. The annual production amounts to 10,000 bottles of Chardonnay, 200,000 of Cabernet Sauvignon and a little Merlot, the bulk exported to the US and a little available in Spain. All are excellent wines. The Chardonnay ('97), fermented in cask, is round and buttery. To begin with the reds were huge, fruity and tannic, but have become lighter in style.

Marfil
w dr (p) ★★→★★★

Brand name (it means 'ivory') for the fresh young white and rosé wines from ALELLA VINICOLA.

Marqués de Alella
DO ★★→★★★ *DYA*

Fresh *cava* and elegant white Alella wines from PARXET.

Marqués de Monistrol
DO r p w pt dr res ★★→★★★ *92, 94, 95*

Sant Sadurní d'Anoia (Barcelona). DO Penedès. Old family concern first taken over by Bass-Bacardi and now belonging to Arco Bodegas Unidas (Berberana, *see* page 130-1). It has made excellent sparkling wine since 1882 and still wines since 1974. The best are the refreshing and incipiently *pétillant* young Blanc de Blancs (40 per cent Parellada, 40 per cent Macabeo, 20 per cent Xarel-lo), bottled only two months after the grapes are picked; the Blanc en Noirs; a fruity rosé; a good Cabernet Sauvignon/Tempranillo and a fragrant, first-rate Merlot. *See also* 'Sparkling Wines', page 193.

Mas Borás
DO res ☆☆☆☆ *89, 90, 93, 94*

This magnificent 100 per cent Pinot Noir from Miguel TORRES outclassed all the Burgundies at the 1988 Gault-Millau 'Olympiad'.

Mas Martinet Viticultors
DO r res ☆☆☆☆ *92, 93, 94, 95, 96, 97*

Falset (Tarragona). DO Priorato. The Pérez Ovejero family has been in the vanguard of making high-quality, estate-grown Prioratos. Here, Garnacha is enhanced with Cabernet Sauvignon, Merlot and other grapes, of which the intense, juicy and well-structured Clos Martinet is a leading example.

Mascaró, Cavas
DO r p w dr ☆☆→☆☆☆ *90, 91, 92*

Vilafranca del Penedès (Barcelona). DO Penedès. Makers of a lemony, fresh Viña Franca white as well as an excellent Anima Cabernet Sauvignon. *See also* 'Sparkling Wines', page 193, and 'Spirits, Aromatic Wines and Liqueurs', page 205.

Milmanda
DO w dr ☆☆☆☆ *96, 97, 98*

This beautiful Chardonnay from Miguel TORRES takes its name from the castle of Milmanda below the monastery of POBLET, where the grapes are grown. Vinified and matured in small oak casks, it is one of Spain's best white wines.

Mollet de Perelada, Cooperativa de
DO r p w dr gen ★→★★

Perelada (Girona). DO Ampurdán-Costa Brava. Simón Serra, the French-trained oenologist of this sizeable cooperative with a storage capacity of some 2.8 million litres, is making very fresh red, white and rosé *vi novell* after the style of Beaujolais Nouveau, of which the most attractive is perhaps the red.

The cooperative also makes a very full and fruity dessert wine from Garnacha Blanca grapes, fermented with their skins for a few days before the addition of grape spirit, and small quantities of a good sparkling wine.

Montserrat, Monastery of

On the northwest fringe of PENEDÈS, the imposing monastery of Montserrat is an essential stop for any visitor to the area. The precipitous hill to which it clings, with its massive outcrops of rounded, weather-worn rock, is extraordinary enough to have inspired Wagner's *Parsifal*, and appropriately enough the splendid boys' choir is the oldest musical conservatory in Europe. In medieval times its vineyards, along with those of POBLET, were among the most important in Cataluña. The Virgin of Montserrat, whose blackened wooden image is preserved in the monastery, is the patron saint of Cataluña, and the monastery, which was founded in the 11th century, is the object of mass pilgrimages. Its huge restaurants have panoramic views across PENEDÈS.

Olivella Sadurní
DO w dr p r ★★

Subirats (Barcelona). DO Penedès. Old family firm housed in new *bodega*. Wines include a Prima Lux made with Xarel-lo and Chardonnay, and Prima Nox and Prima Vesper reds, the first a 100 per cent Cabernet, the second a Cabernet/Merlot blend.

Parxet
DO w dr ★★→★★★ *DYA*

Santa María de Martorelles (Barcelona). DO Alella. Founded in 1920 as a *cava* producer, Parxet began making still wines in 1981. It owns 200 hectares of vineyards, mostly Pansà, and makes its new-style white wines by cold fermentation in stainless steel without ageing in oak. Its MARQUÉS DE ALELLA Clásico, 100 per cent Pansà Blanca, is light and clean with delicate fruit. The Marqués de Alella Seco, made with additional Macabeo and Chenin Blanc, is aromatic and lively and there is a light and delicious Marqués de Alella Chardonnay. *See also* 'Sparkling Wines', page 194.

Penedès
DO r p w dr s/sw sw am g res ★→★★★★★

Penedès, with its 26,350 hectares of vineyards, is a limestone region southwest of Barcelona best known for its sparkling wines, but the best of its still wines rival those of Rioja. The region slopes upwards from the Mediterranean coast to a height of 700 metres in the hills of the interior. The temperate climate and adequate rainfall are ideal for growing grapes. There are three subregions: the hotter Bajo Penedés near the coast is best suited for black grapes; the Medio Penedès, at an average altitude of 200 metres, produces some 60 per cent of the wine from the area as a whole, much of it made from the white Xarel-lo and Macabeo and used for sparkling wines; and the typical grape of the cooler and hillier Penedès Superior is the white Parellada, used both for the dry, fragrant and refreshing white wines and also for sparkling *cavas*, which are widely produced in the area.

The *consejo regulador*, whose standards are rigorous, approves the following native varieties: the white Macabeo (or Viura), Xarel-lo, Parellada (or Montonec) and Subirat-Parent; and the black Cariñena, Monastrell, Garnacha Tinta, Samsó and Ull de Llebre (or Tempranillo). Cabernet Sauvignon, Chardonnay and a variety of other foreign noble grapes, first acclimatised by Miguel TORRES, are also permitted. Owing to the favourable climate, vintages are remarkably consistent, the best of the last two decades being, for the white wines: '86, '88, '90, '91, '93, '94 and '96; and for the reds '87, '88, '90, '91, '93, '94, '96, '97 and '98. The only really disastrous year in the last three decades was '72.

The best base for visiting Penedès is VILAFRANCA DEL PENEDES where there is one of the best wine museums in the world. Many visitors prefer to stay in one of the comfortable hotels of the pleasant, relatively unspoilt coastal resorts of SITGES, which is just half-an-hour's drive from Vilafranca, or in BARCELONA, an hour away by the *autopista*.

Piñol, Vinos
DO w dr & sw r ☆☆

Batea (Tarragona). DO Terra Alta. Small firm, one of the few in Terra Alta, making worthwhile white and red wines under the labels of L' Avi Arrufi and Nuestra Señora del Portal.

Pla de Bages
DO ☆→☆☆

New Catalan DO centred on Manresa, northwest of Barcelona. Best of its *bodegas* is SAT Masies d'Avinyo, maker of good white and rosé wines and a first-rate Cabernet Sauvignon, and the small Ramón Roqueta. There is also a large cooperative, Cellers Cooperativa d'Artés, making drinkable Artium table wines.

Poblet, Monastery of

Famous Cistercian monastery dating from the 12th century in the hills of CONCA DE BARBERA, and the burial place of the kings of Aragón and Cataluña. During the Middle Ages it was the abbeys and monasteries that fostered viticulture and, along with those of the monastery of MONTSERRAT, the vineyards of Poblet were important in keeping winemaking traditions alive in Cataluña. It has magnificent arched wine cellars.

Pontons

Superior vineyard area at a height of 700 metres in the PENEDES, developed by Miguel TORRES for growing the native Parellada and the Riesling, Gewürztraminer and Chardonnay from the cooler climes of northern Europe. Hailstorms are dispersed by rockets charged with silver iodide. The results are so promising that other producers are moving into the area.

Porrón (Catalan Porró)

This conical-shaped glass drinking vessel with spout and handle, now sold in debased form in souvenir shops, has been used for centuries in Cataluña. When in use, the spout does not touch the lips, so that the *porrón* enables a party of drinkers to enjoy their wine without the need for glasses.

Priorato (Catalan Priorat)

DO r (w dr) am ☆→☆☆☆

A small, mountainous enclave, with 900 hectares of vines and its own DO, within the much larger DO TARRAGONA. The name, 'priory', derives from that of the ruined monastery of SCALA DEI.

The grapes are grown in small plots or on terraces in the volcanic soils of the steep hillsides: decayed lava with a high silica content which, in combination with the hot summer sun, produces good, very full-bodied wines with high alcohol content. Authorised grapes for the red wines are the Garnacha Tinta, Garnacha Peluda Cariñena, Cabernet Sauvignon, Merlot and Syrah; and for the whites, the Garnacha Blanca, Macabeo (Viura) and Pedro Ximénez.

The traditional wine is red, almost black in colour with a huge amount of extract, containing up to 18 per cent alcohol. It was formerly much in demand for blending. Another speciality was a golden-yellow RANCIO. With modern methods of fermentation in stainless steel, the wines, while still preserving their rich, brambly taste, have been lightened and now average around 13.5°.

Until fairly recently there were only three wine operations which bottled and labelled the wines: Cellers de SCALA DEI, Masía BARRIL and VINICOLA DEL PRIORAT. Five other small *bodegas* are now making choice and expensive wines: COSTERS DE SIURANA (Clos de l'Obac and Miserere); ROTLLAN TORRA (AMADIS); MAS MARTINET VITICULTORS (Clos Martinet and Martinet Bru); René Barbier Fill (CLOS MOGADOR) and ALVARO PALACIOS. The region is now becoming the fastest-growing in Spain, with 60 new producers moving in and grape prices rocketing. New producers yet to release their wines include TORRES, FREIXENET, PINORD and the ROVIRA family.

The best base for visiting Priorato is the important wine city of TARRAGONA, on the coast.

Puig y Roca, Cellers

DO w dr r ☆☆→☆☆☆ 93, 94, 96

El Vendrell (Tarragona). DO Penedès. New firm with a fair reputation and international grapes, making estate-grown wines: most noteworthy are a barrel-fermented Augustus Chardonnay and an intense and fruity Augustus Merlot.

Rabassa Morta

The historic form of land tenure in Cataluña was that a proprietor leased land to a farmer on condition he planted it with vines, and that the former should share the produce with the farmer, whose right to cultivate the land expired only with the death of the first-planted vines. After phylloxera (from 1876) and replanting with grafts, the life of the vines became much shorter, and the institution fell into disuse. It is now usual for small farmers to own their land.

Raïmat
DO w dr r res ★★★ *89, 90, 91, 92, 94, 95, 96*

Raïmat (Lleida). DO Costers del Segre. Winemaking in the area had declined until the sparkling wine company of Codorníu (*see* page 190) bought the castle of Raïmat and its 3,000-hectare estate. With advice from Davis University in California, 1,400 hectares have been irrigated and planted with selected native vines, together with Cabernet Sauvignon, Chardonnay, Merlot and Pinot Noir. A brand-new winery has been built into the side of a hill, and as a result Raïmat is now making some of the most attractive wines from Spain. They include white Raïmat Casal, made from a blend of Chardonnay, Macabeo and Xarel-lo, and first-class Raïmat Chardonnay ('97); a red Abadía made from a blend of Cabernet Sauvignon, Tempranillo and Merlot; wines made with 100 per cent Merlot, 100 per cent Tempranillo and 100 per cent Pinot Noir; and, perhaps most attractive of all, a Raïmat Cabernet Sauvignon made with 85 per cent Cabernet and 15 per cent Merlot, aged in oak and bottle, with strong varietal characteristics and overtones of coffee and tobacco.

Rancio (Catalan Rancí)

A maderised or oxidised white wine, popular in various parts of Spain, but particularly so in Cataluña. *Rancios* vary enormously in character and quality, from the tart and sour product of a peasant *bodega* or local cooperative, where the wine is left to oxidise without sufficient hygiene, to the perfected wines of DE MULLER in Tarragona. These are sweetened with *mistela* (a must in which fermentation has been checked by the addition of alcohol) or *arrope* (boiled-down must), and aged in *solera* (*see* 'Sherry and Manzanilla', pages 171-2). They can be magnificent, resembling in their different styles very round and old *oloroso* sherries. Another type is made in large glass carboys, known as BOMBONAS, and left partially unstoppered and open to the sun and wind, as at Miguel TORRES, whose fortified Dry Solera is very palatable and distinctly sherry-like. What all *rancios* have in common is a deep golden-yellow colour, a sherry-like nose, more or less marked, and a high degree of alcohol.

Raventós i Blanc, Josep María
DO w dr ☆☆→☆☆☆☆ *98*

DO Penedès. Maker of a good 100 per cent Chardonnay and El Preludi Macabeo/Xarel-lo/Parellada/Chardonnay. *See also* SPARKLING WINES, page 196.

René Barbier
DO r p w dr sw res ☆☆ *91, 93, 96*

Sant Sadurní d'Anoia (Barcelona). DO Penedès. This company, like CONDE DE CARALT, with which it shares cellars at the *cavas* of sparkling-wine firm Segura Viudas near Sant Sadurní d'Anoia in PENEDES, is part of the Freixenet group (*see* 'Sparkling Wines', page 191). Its Kraliner is a lively and fresh young white wine, and there are good reds made with a blend of Cabernet, Tempranillo and Garnacha. The *bodega*, which has invested heavily in new oak, also makes a 100 per cent Cabernet Sauvignon.

Reus
Important wine town with 80,000 inhabitants, west of TARRAGONA. It is here that the great cooperative combine, the UNION AGRARIA COOPERATIVA, has its central site for blending, maturing and bottling wines from outlying cooperatives. There are also many private firms engaged in elaborating both wines and vermouth.

Ribera d'Ebre
r w dr ☆

Subdenomination of the DO TARRAGONA, adjoining the DO TERRA ALTA in the far southwest of the province of Tarragona. The wines are like those of FALSET but rather more acidic. Some good dessert wines, especially those from its leading *bodega*, Pedro ROVIRA. This is one of the largest concerns in the DOs Tarragona and Terra Alta, a family firm that has just been taken on by Market Access Europa, which continues to sell its Viña Mater and other wines.

Rotllán i Torra
DO r w sw ☆☆☆ *95, 96, 97*

Torroja del Priorat (Tarragona). DO Priorato. Small family winery with 24 hectares of vineyard and 280 oak *barricas*. Their Reserva and Balandra are dark and traditional; Amadis and Tirant, aged in French oak and incorporating small amounts of Merlot, Syrah and Cabernet Sauvignon are more spectacular. Also a sweet Moscatel/Pedro Ximénez.

Roura
DO w dr p r ☆☆→☆☆☆ *94, 95, 96*

Alella (Barcelona). DO Alella. Third and most recent of the *bodegas* in Alella, making good 100 per cent Chardonnay and Sauvignon Blanc, 100 per cent Merlot and Cabernet Sauvignon/Tempranillo.

Rovira, Pedro
One of the largest – and the most prominent – concerns in the DOs Tarragona and Terra Alta, this family firm has just been taken over by Market Access Europa.

San Miguel de las Viñas, Cofradía de
Catalan order of *tastevins*, celebrating its functions at the historic old castle of San Martí, near Vilafranca del Penedès. Its light-

hearted inauguration ceremony, which is conducted to the strains of a band in traditional costume, includes drinking from a PORRON and distinguishing blindfold between a white and a rosé wine – which is much more difficult than it sounds – on pain of continuing the tasting indefinitely.

San Sadurní de Noya (Catalan Sant Sadurní d'Anoia)

Township in the east of PENEDES towards Montserrat, where most of the cavas making sparkling wines are situated. Now that firms such as MARQUES DE MONISTROL, CONDE DE CARALT, RENE BARBIER and Freixenet are diversifying, it has also become a centre for making still wines. *See also* 'Sparkling Wines', pages 196-7.

Sangre de Toro
r ★★

Sound and big-selling Tempranillo/Cabernet Sauvignon from Miguel TORRES.

Sant Cugat del Vallés, Monastery of

Located between BARCELONA and MONTSERRAT, Sant Cugat – with its beautiful Romanesque cloisters – was one of the great religious houses that did so much to foster viticulture. Among its monuments is a deed recording the gift of a vineyard to the monastery in 927.

Santamaría, Cellers
DO r (p) res ★★→★★★

Capmany (Girona). DO Ampurdán-Costa Brava. Small family concern with a history of winemaking going back to 1767. Made with a blend of Cariñena and Garnacha, its Gran Recosind is ruby in colour, full-bodied, soft, fruity and long on the finish.

Santara
DO w dr r ☆→☆☆ *DYA*

Brand name for big-selling, very drinkable Chardonnay, Cabernet and Cabernet Sauvignon/Merlot, formerly made for CONCAVINOS in the CONCA DE BARBERA by flying winemaker Hugh Ryman.

Scala Dei, Cellers de
DO r res (w dr p) ☆☆☆ *91, 93, 94, 96, 97, 98*

Scala Dei (Tarragona). DO Priorato. Housed in an ancient stone building near the ruined monastery and run since 1974 by the Peyra family, the Cellers are equipped with stainless-steel fermentation vats, underground *depósitos* coated with epoxy resin, oak *barricas* and a modern bottling line allowing for the topping-up of bottles with carbon dioxide.

The *bodega* makes a fresh but alcoholic rosé, a young red Novell, now called Negre Scala Dei and containing 85 per cent Garnacha and 15 per cent Cabernet Sauvignon, and a superb Cartoixa Scala Dei – this is aged in oak and bottle, is deep and complex in flavour, and has 13.8 per cent alcohol. It also makes the only white wine from the region, a 100 per cent Garnacha

Blanca aged for six months in oak. Prices are climbing since Robert Parker gave the Novell '94 ('terrific purity... knock-out, lusty, rich finish') 89 points.

Scala Dei, Monastery of

When visiting the *bodega* it is worth walking the ten minutes to the great roofless monastery, choked with trees and aromatic vegetation, a victim of Mendizábal's anti-clerical reforms of around 1830. According to legend, it was founded when angels were seen ascending and descending a ladder into the heavens, and the theme of the ladder is embodied in the seal of the *consejo regulador* for PRIORATO. There are now plans to restore the ruin.

Serra, Jaume

DO r w dr (p) res ☆☆

Vilanova i la Geltrú (Barcelona). DO Penedès. Formerly one of the only three producers in ALELLA, the firm has transferred to PENEDES. Good dry *pétillant* Albatros and Cabernet Sauvignon rosés (DYA); easy-drinking Cristalino *cava*. Other wines to be avoided.

Sitges

The *Subur* of the Romans, Sitges, on the coast south of BARCELONA, is now a pleasant and relatively unspoilt seaside resort with a palm-fringed promenade, though bursting at the seams in summer. Its famous dessert wine, made by allowing Malvasía and Moscatel grapes to wrinkle on the branch before picking, with the addition of grape spirit to the must and long maturation in oak, is now made only in minuscule amounts.

Sitges celebrates a harvest festival in early September, with a harvest queen, decorated floats, the solemn pressing and blessing of the first fruits, and a fountain flowing with free wine.

Tarragona

The imperial *Tarraco* of the Romans, Tarragona is a city rich in historic remains, including massive walls built by the Romans on a much earlier foundation of monolithic blocks, an aqueduct and forum, and a fine Gothic cathedral. It is an important wine city specialising in the blending of wines, both from the surrounding region and other parts of Spain, and their bulk export. It is most reputed for the Tarragona *clásicos*, sweet dessert wines, both red and white, containing up to 23 per cent alcohol. It was a cheap *clásico*, sold as Tarragona and also known by the less complimentary names of 'poor man's port' and 'red biddy', which was once so popular in English pubs.

Another important activity in the town is the production of vermouths and liqueurs.

Tarragona

DO r w dr am ☆→☆☆

Tarragona (10,992 hectares under vines; an output in '97/'98 of 48 million litres) is divided into the subregions of CAMPO DE TARRAGONA, FALSET and RIBERA D'EBRE. Its beverage wines, made mainly in co-ops, tend to be sturdy and high in alcohol; though very suitable for blending, they lack the delicacy of those from PENEDES to the north.

Terra Alta
DO r w dr ☆→☆☆

The newly demarcated Terra Alta, with 8,171 hectares under vine, lies in mountainous country in the extreme southwest of Cataluña, bordering the province of Teruel. It makes robust but characterful wines, white and red, the best from the Celler Cooperativa GANDESA and Vinos PIÑOL. Now that modern equipment has been installed, the wines are becoming lighter.

Torres, Miguel
DO r p w dr s/sw sw g res ★★→ ★★★★ *87, 88, 89, 90, 91, 92, 93, 94, 95, 96*

Vilafranca del Penedès (Barcelona). DO Penedès. The Torres family has been making and selling wine in PENEDES since the 17th century. It is now the most reputed firm in Cataluña to make still wines, exporting all over the world – exports to the US alone top 1.8 million bottles annually – and is still very much a family concern.

Miguel Torres Riera, with a French degree in oenology, has been responsible for introducing a variety of foreign vines to PENEDES, grown in addition to native vines on the firm's 1,300 hectares, where the quality of the fruit has been improved by clonal selection of the vines and careful evaluation of the soils for the most suitable varieties. In common with almost all Spanish *bodegas*, the firm also buys grapes from independent farmers. Foreign varieties include the white Chardonnay, Gewürztraminer, Riesling, Sauvignon Blanc; and the red Cabernet Sauvignon, Cabernet Franc, Petit Syrah and Pinot Noir. Those vines that are accustomed to a cooler habitat are grown on sites in the hills of the hinterland.

Torres has been responsible for many technical innovations and was the first winery in Spain to introduce temperature-controlled fermentation in stainless steel. Typical of the cold-fermented whites are the dry, fresh and fruity Viña Sol (100 per cent Parellada); Gran Viña Sol (85 per cent Chardonnay, 15 per cent Parellada); the marvellously fruity single-vineyard Fransola made from 85 per cent Sauvignon Blanc and 15 per cent Parellada; the Waltraud Riesling and luscious semi-dry Esmeralda, made with Gewürztraminer and Moscatel d'Alsace. MILMANDA, a Chardonnay of exceptional quality, is fermented and aged in traditional fashion in small French-oak casks.

The red wines spend less time in oak casks – usually one to two years – and correspondingly more time in bottle than most traditional Riojas, and they are therefore less oaky in nose and flavour. Both the fruity and full-bodied Sangre de Toro and Gran Sangre de Toro are made with native grapes; Coronas contains 86 per cent Tempranillo and 14 per cent Cabernet Sauvignon, and Gran Coronas 85 per cent Cabernet Sauvignon and 15 per cent Tempranillo. Viña Magdala contains 70 per cent Pinot Noir, and the award-winning Gran Magdala and single-estate Mas Borás are made with 100 per cent Pinot Noir.

Recent introductions are the light and fruity Las Torres Merlot for summer drinking, and the Grans Muralles, a full-bodied red made from a blend of the native Monastrell, Garnacha Tinta, Garró and Samsó. The pride of the Torres stable – velvety, smooth, intensely fruity and long in finish – is GRAN CORONAS MAS LA PLANA Black Label, made with selected Cabernet Sauvignon. It is now history that at the Gault-Millau 'Olympiad' in Paris in 1979, the '70 vintage was judged by a short head to be better than the less fully developed '70 Château Latour. Torres also makes excellent brandies (*see* page 207) and an orange liqueur; has acquired vineyards and a winery in Chile; and makes wine in California and China.

Trobat, Bodegas
DO w dr r p g ★★ 90, 92, 94, 96

Garriguella (Girona). DO Ampurdán-Costa Brava. This small firm makes the fresh, delicious rosé served by the Hotel-Restaurant Ampurdán in Figueres, and also produces a Blanc de Blancs, a trio of red wines and a good 100 per cent Garnacha dessert wine.

Unión Agraria Cooperativa
DO r p w dr sw res ☆→☆☆

Reus (Tarragona). This vast combine, founded in 1962, handles wines from all the cooperatives in the province. It sells large quantities of wine to private firms for further elaboration and bottling. More select growths are matured in the central cellars at Reus, and then bottled and sold under their own label. Among its many labels are the red and white Tarragona Unión; red, white and rosé Yelmo; the dry, semi-dry and rosé Collar Perla, Collar Zafiro and Collar Rubí; and also *reservas*.

Vallformosa, Masía
DO r p w dr g res ☆☆→☆☆☆ 89, 90, 92, 94, 95, 96

Vilobí del Penedès (Barcelona). DO Penedès. A family firm producing fresh white and rosé wines, and good red *crianzas* and *reservas*, which are made both with native grapes and Cabernet Sauvignon. *See also* 'Sparkling Wines', page 197.

Ventura, Jané
DO w dr p ☆☆☆ 91, 92, 93

El Vendrell (Tarragona). DO Penedès. Small family firm making a fresh, flowery, well-structured white wine from Xarel-lo and Parellada; a distinguished rosé from Tempranillo and Garnacha; a really first-rate red ('94) from 90 per cent Cabernet Sauvignon and 10 per cent Tempranillo; and sparkling wines (*see* page 197).

Vilafranca del Penedès
Vilafranca, a small town off the *autopista* between BARCELONA and TARRAGONA, is the centre of the still-wine industry in PENEDES and the home of many of its best-known *bodegas*. It also makes some sparkling wine by the Champagne process and is the headquarters of the Spanish offshoots of Cinzano and Cointreau. Apart from the *bodegas*, the great point of interest is the wine

museum, installed in a 13th-century palace of the kings of Aragón, and one of the best in the world. The exhibits begin with tableaux illustrating winemaking from ancient times onwards. There are numerous examples of Greek, Carthaginian and Roman amphorae. The main hall houses every type of agricultural implement, press and barrel, many originating from old *bodegas* in the region; there are also pictures and drawings, drinking glasses and PORRONES. The visit ends in a small bar, where local wines may be sampled. The museum is the headquarters of the old-established *Academia de Tastavins de Sant Humbert*, a wine fraternity devoted to maintaining traditions and quality of Penedès wines. Closed Monday.

Vinícola del Priorát
DO r w dr p ☆☆ 96, 97

Gratallops (Tarragona). DO Priorato. The Catalan Government closed the seven small village cooperatives in PRIORATO in 1990 and constructed this brand-new plant with stainless-steel vats and up-to-date facilities, with a capacity of 750,000 litres. It numbers some 400 members with 480 hectares of vineyards, makes good white Mas de L' Alba and rosé Clos Gebrat, together with an excellent L' Arc Cabernet blend, and a fruity and full-bodied Onix, made from Garnacha and Cariñena.

WINE AND FOOD

Cataluña has a long-established tradition of gastronomy. The raw materials, especially fish, shellfish and fresh vegetables, are first rate.

There are five famous sauces: *alioli* (the aïoli of Provence), and the piquant *picada*, *chanfaina*, *sofrito* and *romesco*. Appetites are hearty, and in the smaller regional restaurants even the soups and starters are meals in themselves.

Some of the restaurants found in places such as BARCELONA and the province of GIRONA are among the most sophisticated in Spain.

Anec amb figues Duck with figs.

Bolets Field mushrooms, often cooked on a charcoal grill with garlic and parsley. Torres Viña Sol, or other dry white.

Botifarra catalana A white sausage, resembling *boudin blanc*, which is eaten raw, cooked on its own or used in other dishes.

Brandada de bacalla Creamed salted cod.

Calcotada Made only in the spring, this is spring onions sliced in half and grilled over a wood fire. They are served with a sauce resembling *romesco*. Marqués de Monistrol Vin Natur Blanc de Blancs or other light dry white.

Conill con cargols Young rabbits stewed with snails, herbs, cinnamon, almonds and biscuit crumbs. One of the lighter reds from René Barbier, Hill, Conde de Caralt, Torres.

Costellas amb allioli Grilled ribs of lamb served with *alioli*. A medium-bodied red such as Raïmat Tempranillo.

Crema catalana The local variation on cream caramel or 'flan', made with egg yolks, milk and cinnamon and topped with a brittle layer of caramel. Bach Viña Extrísimo.

Ericos de mar gratinados al cava Sea urchins *au gratin* with *cava*.

Escudella i carn d'olla This most typical of Catalan dishes is served in two parts: first the *escudella*, a meaty soup with pasta; and then the *carn d'olla*, a rich stew containing veal, chicken, pork, blood sausage, egg, breadcrumbs and vegetables. A full-bodied red, such as Cartoixa Scala Dei or the less potent red Bach Viña Extrísima.

Espinacs a la catalana Boiled spinach with pine kernels and raisins. Try one of the lighter *rancios*.

Favas a la catalana Vegetable dish containing fresh broad beans, *botifarra negra* (Catalan black sausage) and belly of pork, together with spring onions, fresh mint, bay leaf and parsley. Marqués de Monistrol rosé or Trobat Rosado.

Llagosta a la catalana Stewed lobster with onions, carrots, garlic, herbs, parsley, saffron, pepper, sweet paprika, chocolate, nutmeg and brandy. This obviously calls for a wine of character such as the Torres Milmanda Chardonnay.

Mel y mató Fresh cream cheese with honey. Torres San Valentín or other sweet or semi-sweet wine.

Menja blanc A dessert of ground almonds, cream, kirsch and lemon. Ideally, De Muller Moscatel Oro.

Oca amb peres Roast goose with pears.

Pa amb tomàquet Catalan country-style bread rubbed with fresh tomatoes, oil and salt. It appears at the beginning of the meal and is sometimes served with slices of cured ham. Any full-bodied Mediterranean-type dry white.

Panellets A dessert made either with almonds, sugar and eggs, or with pine kernels in the form of a marzipan.

Parrillada de prix amb salsa romesco Mixed grill of fish served with the typical Catalan *romesco* sauce and mayonnaise.

Perdiu a la catalana Partridge with herbs and lemon. Marqués de Monistrol Gran Reserva or Raïmat Cabernet Sauvignon.

Pollastre en chanfaina Chicken stewed with aubergines, green peppers, tomatoes, wine and herbs, and served with croûtons. Cavas Hill Castell Roc or other light red.

Postre de música Mixed plate of almonds, raisins, hazelnuts, walnuts, figs or other dried fruit.

Rap a la Costa Brava Anglerfish cooked with fresh peas, red pimientos, mussels, saffron, garlic, parsley and white wine, with a little lemon. Cavas del Ampurdán Pescador.

Salchichón de Vic A salami, for which the mountain town of Vic, in the Pyrenees near the French frontier, is famous.

Sarsuela de mariscs Literally a 'variety show', this famous dish is a mixture of shellfish and firm white fish in a sauce of saffron, garlic, white wine and parsley. With such seafood, Spaniards often drink red wine. The choice is between a good medium-bodied red, such as a Conde de Caralt or René Barbier Tinto, or a dry white like the Jean León Chardonnay with sufficient character to stand up to the rich flavours.

Sopa de musclos catalana A soup made with mussels and flavoured with tomatoes, *aguardiente*, garlic, parsley and cinnamon. Torres Dry Solera, a dry sherry or Montilla, or a spicy white from Valencia, Jumilla or Alicante.

Sopa de pilotes Chicken broth containing small meatballs and flavoured with cinnamon, garlic and chervil. Dry sherry.
Suquet Catalan fish and potato soup.
Truita de botifarra i mongetes A hearty omelette of Catalan sausage served with haricot beans, first boiled and then fried. Perelada Tinto Cazador or other honest-to-goodness red.

HOTELS
Barcelona Of its many hotels, the best are Arts and Husa Ritz; reasonably priced establishments with high standards are the *Colón*, near the cathedral, the *Regente*, the old-fashioned and thoroughly traditional *Oriente* and new *Rivoli* in the Ramblas.
Sant Sadurní d'Anoia A new two-star hotel, the *Sol*, is four kilometres out on the Vilafranca road, with a good restaurant.
Sitges A good base for visiting Penedès, the best hotels are the four-star *Meliá Gran Sitges*, the three-star *Calípolis* and the *Antemare*.
Tarragona A good base for visits to the outlying regions; the most comfortable hotels are the four-star *Ciutat de Tarragona* and *Imperial Tarraco*, and three-star *Lauria*.
Vilafranca Two modern four-star hotels are the *Domo* and *Alta Penedès*.

RESTAURANTS
Barcelona is full of good restaurants. Recommendations include: *Jaume de Provença* (especially for Catalan and *cuisine naturelle* dishes); *Neichel* (the leading, most sophisticated Barcelona exponent of *cuisine naturelle*); *Reno* (recently taken over, but happily this classical Barcelona establishment maintains its high standards); *Vía Veneto* (stylish surroundings in *belle époque* style); *Florián* (small restaurant, inventive cooking and attractively priced young wines); *Botafumeiro* (good fish and seafood).
Cambrils (near Tarragona) *Can Bosch*; *Casa Gatell*, both specialising in fish and seafood.
Figueres *Ampurdán* (in the Hotel Ampurdán outside Figueres; highly sophisticated restaurant started by Josep Mercader, founder of the new Catalan cuisine); *Hotel Durán* (good Catalan food and a long list of Ampurdán wines).
Lleida *Forn del Nastasi*; *Sheyton*.
Platja d'Aro *Big Rock* (first-rate restaurant in an old hilltop mansion and run by one of Cataluña's leading chefs, Carles Carmós).
Rosas/Roses *El Bulli* (fish/seafood, one of Spain's best restaurants).
S'Agaro *La Gavina* (sophisticated international cooking in this most elegant and expensive of Costa Brava hotels).
Sant Feliú de Guixols *Eldorado Petit* (the famous chef Luís Cruanyas has returned to his origins).
Sitges *Maricel* (menu de degustación); *Mare Nostrum* (fish, especially *sopa de pescadores*).
Tarragona *Merlot*; *Barquet*; *Les Coques*.
Vilafranca del Penedès *Airolo*; *Casa Joan*. Outside, on the road to Sitges: *Celler de Penedès* (a simple restaurant with typical, substantial Catalan fare). Just to the north, at San Martí Sarroca, is *Ca L' Anna* (outstanding regional cooking).

Extremadura and the Southwest

Extremadura lies between the two Castiles and Portugal in the southwest of Spain. It suffered from mass depopulation after the expulsion of the Moors in the 13th century, and again in the 16th, when the Extremeños joined in the conquest of the New World.

It remains an empty and sparsely populated area, and in its high *sierras*, clothed with cork-oak, beech and chestnut, sheep are more numerous than humans. Cultivation of vines is somewhat sporadic, the most densely planted area being the new DO of the Ribera del Guadiana in the province of Badajoz, comprising the subzones of Ribera Baja, Ribera Alta, Tierra de Barros, Matanegra, Cañamero and Montánchez. Here, summers are hot and rainfall low, with an annual average of only 411 millimetres. The principal grape is Cayetana Blanca with an astonishingly high yield, 36 hectolitres per hectare, of a neutral white wine of low acidity. Of the annual output of some 1.2 million litres, much goes to Jerez, Asturias and Galicia for blending; the remainder is consumed locally or distilled.

There are two small areas in Extremadura – Cañamero and Montánchez – that produce *flor*-growing wines of marked individuality; but to taste them you will have to visit the region. Although often ignored by foreign tourists it is of great scenic and historical interest, with its forgotten towns of Medellín and Trujillo, the birthplaces of Cortés and Pizarro, the splendid monastery of Guadalupe and, above all, Mérida, with its little-known and marvellous Roman monuments.

The other vine-growing area in the far southwest is the demarcated region of Condado de Huelva, again with nostalgic associations, since it was from Palos, near the city of Huelva, that Columbus first sailed for the Americas. It is known for decent white table wines but more especially for *generosos* in the various sherry styles, which would be more familiar if they had not for many years now been sent to Jerez de la Frontera for blending.

It is difficult to list more than a handful of *bodegas* which actually bottle the wine, since so much of it, especially from Extremadura, is made by small proprietors for consumption in local bars and restaurants, or sold in bulk by the cooperatives for blending outside the region.

Almendralejo

The main wine town of the demarcated region of Ribera del Guadiana in the province of BADAJOZ. Its dusty main street is crowded with *bodegas* and distilleries.

Badajoz

A province of Extremadura which flanks the Portuguese frontier and lies between the provinces of CACERES to the north and CONDADO DE HUELVA to the south. The principal vine-growing area is TIERRA DE BARROS.

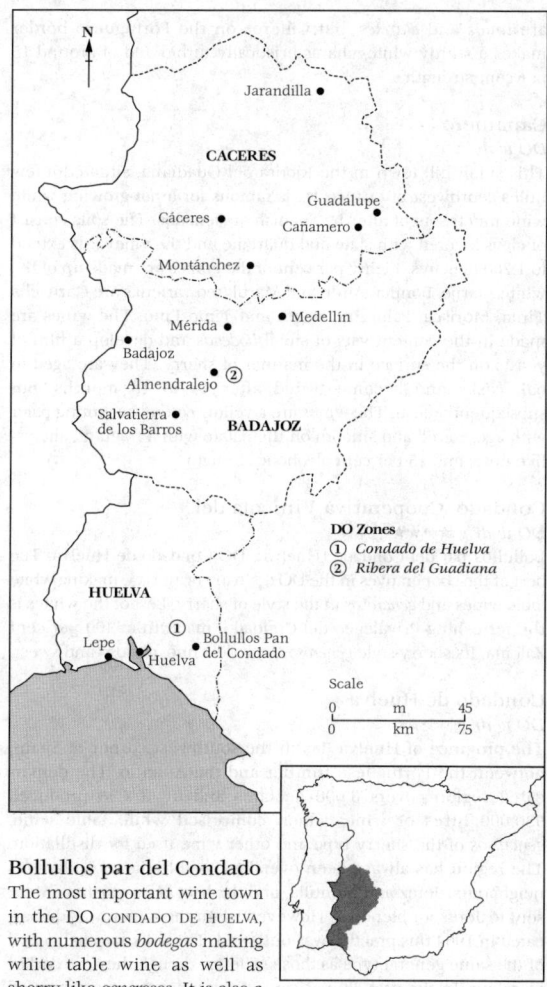

Bollullos par del Condado

The most important wine town in the DO CONDADO DE HUELVA, with numerous *bodegas* making white table wine as well as sherry-like *generosos*. It is also a centre for distilling the *holandas* used for making brandy (*see* 'Spirits, Aromatic Wines and Liqueurs', page 203).

Cáceres
r w dr

Province of Extremadura bordering Portugal and to the north of Badajoz, whose most characterful wines are CAÑAMERO and MONTÁNCHEZ. The other winemaking areas are those of Miajados, west of GUADALUPE, and Jerte, Hervás, Cilleros and Ceclavin, which are scattered around the historic old towns of JARANDILLA and Plasencia in the north of the province. In the main, their wines are *tintos* and *claretes*, but Cilleros on the Portuguese border makes a sturdy white, characteristically turbid and of around 15 per cent strength.

Cañamero
DO w dr ☆☆

This small hill town in the Ribera del Guadiana, situated a few miles southwest of GUADALUPE, is famous for a *flor*-growing white wine much sought after by Spanish aficionados. The soils consist of clays layered with slate and quartzite and the vineyards extend to 1,200 hectares. Eighty per cent of the grapes are made up of the white Alarije, Bomita, Airén and Marfil; red varieties are Garnacha Tinta, Morisca, Palomino Negro and Tinto Fino. The wines are made in the cement vats of small *bodegas* and develop a film of yeasts on the surface in the manner of sherry. They are aged in oak casks and become turbid after 14 to 18 months, but subsequently clear. The wines are a yellow colour, becoming paler with age; round and smooth on the palate with a fragrant, sherry-like nose, and 15 per cent alcoholic strength.

Condado, Cooperativa Vinícola del
DO w dr g ★→★★

Bollullos par del Condado (Huelva). DO Condado de Huelva. The best of the cooperatives in the DO CONDADO DE HUELVA, making white table wines and *generosos* in the style of sherry. Best of the whites is the refreshing Privalegeo del Condado, made from 100 per cent Zalema. Its sherry-style *generosos* include a fino, oloroso and sweet.

Condado de Huelva
DO w dr g ☆→☆☆

The province of Huelva lies in the southwest corner of Spain, between the Portuguese frontier and the Atlantic. The demarcated region covers 6,000 hectares and in '97/'98 produced 930,000 litres of wine, which comprised white table wine, *generosos* of the sherry type and other wine used for distillation. The region has always been overshadowed by its more famous neighbours, Jerez and Montilla, and the best of its *generosos* were sent to Jerez for blending. However, when the region was demarcated in 1964 this practice was outlawed. The soils are chalky and of the same general type as those of Jerez, though they are darker in colour. In the past, 90 per cent of the vineyards were planted with the white Zalema, but this is being replaced by Palomino, Mantúa, Garrido Fino, Pedro Luís and Pedro Ximénez.

The *solera*-made *generosos* are of the same general types as those of Jerez – *fino, amontillado, oloroso* – but lack the finesse of the best sherry. The white table wines, now being cold-fermented, are acceptable enough for holiday drinking but have no great distinction.

Condado de Niebla
Ancient domain of the Guzmán Counts, who occupied it after its reconquest from the Moors, and now the heart of the vine-growing area of the province of Huelva.

Guadalupe

High in the mountains northeast of Mérida, the little town of Guadalupe clusters around a monastery founded by Alfonso XI in 1340, in thanksgiving for his victory over the Moors at Salado. It later became the shrine of the Conquistadores and was enriched by generations of princes and grandees; among its many treasures is a magnificent series of paintings by Zurbarán. The bars of Guadalupe are the best place to sample the *flor*-growing CAÑAMERO; it is also the house wine at the comfortable *parador*.

Hijos de Francisco Vallejo
DO g ☆☆

Bollullos par del Condado (Huelva). DO Condado de Huelva. Family firm making honest wines of the *generoso* type.

Huelva *See* CONDADO DE HUELVA

INVIOSA, Bodegas
DO w dr r res ☆→☆☆ 93, 94, 96

Almendralejo (Badajoz). DO Ribera del Guadiana. Established in 1980, this concern makes the best wine from the TIERRA DE BARROS, but not from native grapes. The cold-fermented white Lar de Barros is made from Macabeo, and both the red Lar de Barros and the full-bodied and spicy Lar de Lares *gran reserva* are made from a Riojan blend of Tempranillo, Garnacha and Graciano. INVIOSA also makes an excellent Bonaval *cava* from Macabeo and is one of the few concerns in the Extremadura to export its wines.

Jarandilla
r ☆

The *claretes* from Jarandilla, in the north of the province of Cáceres, were once rated among the best in Spain, and were the prime favourites of the Emperor Charles V during his last years at the nearby monastery of Yuste.

Lar de Barros, Lar de Lares
DO r w ☆☆ 93, 94, 96

Names of the wines from INVIOSA, the best in Extremadura.

Lepe

Small town west of HUELVA near the Portuguese frontier. Its wines, the precursors of sherry, were mentioned by Chaucer.

Martínez Payva, Bodegas SAT
DO w dr r ☆→☆☆ 92

Almendralejo (Badajoz). DO Ribera del Guadiana. One of the few concerns in Extremadura to achieve national distribution for its wines. The range includes two 100 per cent Cayetana whites; one of which – the De Payva – is fermented in barrel, and a very drinkable red De Payva made from a blend of Tempranillo, Mazuelo and Graciano.

Medina, Bodegas
DO r p w dr ☆☆

Puebla de Sancho Pérez (Badajoz). DO Ribera de Guadiana. Family firm founded in 1931 with 66 hectares of vineyards. It makes a large range of wines, red, white and rosé, the best being the red Jaloco and Marqués de Badajoz, both made from blends of Cabernet Sauvignon, Tempranillo and Garnacha.

Mérida

Once the tenth city of the Roman Empire, Mérida, in the north of Badajoz, is the best placed and most interesting town from which to visit the winemaking areas of Extremadura. Its Roman remains, including a theatre, a circus, an amphitheatre and a triumphal arch, as well as bridges, aqueducts and tessellated pavements, are among the most impressive in Europe.

Montánchez
DO Ribera del Guadiana r w dr ☆→☆☆

This small village, high in the hills above MERIDA, is remarkable for making a red wine which grows a *flor* in the manner of sherry. All the wines are aged in earthenware *tinajas* (see 'Castilla-La Mancha', page 40) for about a year after vinification, when the yeasts appear on the surface. They emerge slightly turbid with a pronounced and aromatic sherry-like nose, and the 'red' is more orange in colour. Between 13 to 14.5 per cent strength, they are usually drunk as apéritifs in the bars of Mérida.

Ruíz Torres, Bodegas
w dr ★★

Cañamero (Cáceres). The only *bodega* of any size to make and bottle the individual *flor*-growing white wine of CAÑAMERO. Non-DO, it may be sampled at the Parador or in the bars of nearby GUADALUPE. It also makes red *crianzas* and *reservas* from Cabernet Sauvignon, Cencibel and Monastrell.

Ribera del Guadiana
DO w dr r ★→★★

Newly demarcated DO with headquarters at Almendralejo, comprising the subzones of Ribera Baja, Ribera Alta, TIERRA DE BARROS, Matanegra, CAÑAMERO and MONTANCHEZ. It currently covers 6,483 hectares of vineyard and 34 bodegas.

Salas, Bodegas
DO g ☆☆

Bollullos par del Condado (Huelva). DO Condado de Huelva. Bodegas Salas is a family concern which makes some of the best of the sherry-like wines of the region.

SOVICOSA
DO w dr p ☆→☆☆ *DYA*

Bollullos par del Condado (Huelva). DO Condado de Huelva. This *bodega*, belonging to the Sanlúcar firm of José Medina y Cía (see

'Sherry and Manzanilla', pages 166-7), makes fresh young Viña Odiel from 100 per cent Zalema, the traditional and predominant grape of the region, which is among the best of its type.

Tierra de Barros
DO Ribera del Guadiana r w dr ☆→☆☆

The Tierra de Barros, centring on ALMENDRALEJO in the province of BADAJOZ, has the somewhat dubious distinction of making the cheapest wine in Spain, even 'exporting' some of it to La Mancha! Some 75 per cent of the grapes are Cayetana Blanca, producing dry white wines, neutral in character, without much acidity and of 12 to 13.5 per cent, whose main use, apart from current consumption, is for blending. The village of Salvatierra de los Barros on the verge of Portugal does, however, make small amounts of an aromatic and intensely coloured red wine, highly prized by Spanish connoisseurs.

Viña Extremeña
DO w dr p r ☆☆

Almendralejo (Badajoz). DO Ribera del Guadiana. Founded in 1970 this family firm owns 1,000 hectares of organically cultivated vineyard. Standards are high and it exports its wines on some scale. Among the labels are Palacio de Monsalud, Monasterio de Tentudia, Viña Extremeña and Corte Real.

WINE AND FOOD

When General Junot sacked the monastery of Alcántara in 1807 and ordered its medieval manuscripts to be used for making cartridges, one was salvaged and sent to the famous chef Escoffier, who commented that 'it was the only positive advantage which France reaped from the [Peninsular] War'. It contained the first directions for the use of truffles, still abundant in the region, and for making *pâté de foie gras*. Its pheasant, Alcántara style remains a classic recipe, but today the region is perhaps best known for its remarkable charcuterie – *chorizo* (pepper sausage), *jamón serrano* (cured ham) and the rest.

As regards the wines, the difficulty is to find the local growths in the better hotels and *paradors*, which offer the standard list of Riojas. Nevertheless, the house wine at the *parador* in Guadalupe is a thoroughly typical white Cañamero; in hotels and restaurants generally, the carafe wine (when available) will probably be a sturdy red or white from Almendralejo.

Boquerones en adobo Fresh anchovies, marinated in olive oil, vinegar, garlic, parsley and seasoning and eaten raw.

Cochifrito Lamb cooked and served in an earthenware dish with onions, garlic, paprika, freshly ground pepper, parsley and lemon juice.

Coliflor al estilo de Badajoz Cauliflower, boiled and divided into florets, dredged in egg and breadcrumbs and then fried crisp in olive oil.

Frito típico extremeño Kid fried with garlic, parsley, black pepper and bay leaves.

Huevos a la extremeña A sauce is first prepared with olive oil, onions and fresh tomatoes, then boiled potatoes, *chorizo*, ham and seasoning are added. Eggs are then broken on the top and the dish finished in the oven.

Huevos serranos Large tomatoes, halved, scooped out and stuffed with chopped ham, topped with fried eggs and sprinkled with grated cheese, before being browned to perfection in the oven.

Riñonada A dish made with a mixture of lambs' kidneys and sweetbreads.

Solomillo de cordero Lamb marinated with salt, pepper, olive oil and red wine, and cooked slowly with the marinade in a casserole.

HOTELS

Guadalupe The comfortable *Parador Nacional Zurbarán* faces the monastery and is housed in a 15th-century hospice for pilgrims.

Mérida The four-star *Parador Nacional Vía de la Plata* is an historical convent and offers good regional wines and cooking.

RESTAURANTS

Badajoz *Aldebarán* (sophisticated cooking, elegant ambience); *La Toja* (Galician and seafood).

Cáceres *Atrio* (excellent regional cooking).

Guadalupe *Hospedería del Real Monasterio* (typical dishes at moderate prices).

Huelva *Las Candelas* (sophisticated cooking, extensive wine list); *Las Meigas*.

Jarandilla de la Vera *Parador Nacional Carlos V*.

Mérida *Parador Nacional Vía de la Plata* (the Parador has won various gastronomic awards for its cooking); *Nicolás*; *El Encinar* (good hotel restaurant).

Puebla de la Reina (south of Mérida) *Mesón de la Jara Casa Andrés* (it is worth the detour to visit this small restaurant with its atmospheric ambience and typical Extremeñian fare).

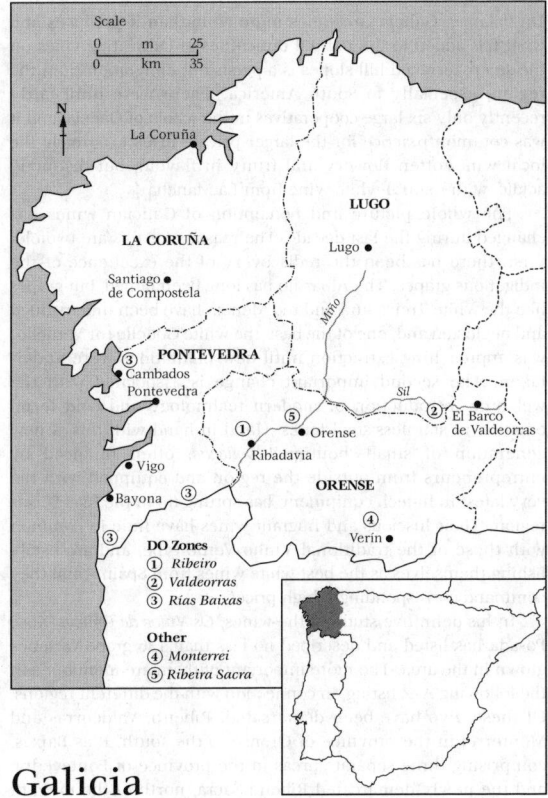

Galicia

Galicia, in the far northwest of Spain, bounded to the south by Portugal and to the west and north by the Atlantic, comprises the provinces of La Coruña, Lugo, Pontevedra and Orense, of which only the two last produce significant amounts of wine. With its green hills, its chestnut forests, its unspoilt sandy coves and wide *rías* (deep salt-water inlets like fjords), it is a romantic part of Spain. Its wines, too, will appeal to wine romantics.

The granitic soils and wet climate are similar to those of northern Portugal, and traditional methods of viticulture, especially in the more westerly coastal districts, are strikingly similar; with high-climbing vines being trained away from the damp ground on chestnut stakes, or grown in the form of a pergola along wires stretched from granite pillars. The wines often undergo a prolonged secondary or malolactic fermentation, which leaves them with a subdued and refreshing *pétillance*. Since many of the grape varieties are the same or akin to those of the Vinho Verde area of Portugal, there is a strong family resemblance between the wines from both sides of the River Miño (or Minho).

On balance, Galicia consumes more wine than it produces and what has added to the natural difficulties of cultivating vines on the steep, terraced hill slopes is a persistent emigration from the region, especially to South America. There were until fairly recently only six large cooperatives in the whole of Galicia, and it was common practice for the larger private firms to 'stretch' the local wine, often flowery and fruity in flavour, but distinctly acidic, with neutral white wine from La Mancha.

The whole picture and perception of Galician wines has changed during the last decade. The reasons for this are twofold. First, there has been the rediscovery of the excellence of the indigenous grapes. The Albariño has long been famed, but grapes like the white Treixadura and red Mencía have been undervalued and neglected and, one of the best, the white Godello (or Verdello) was approaching extinction until new plantations were undertaken. The second important change is associated with the welcome introduction of modern technology and cold fermentation in stainless-steel tanks. Hand in hand with this, a new generation of small 'boutique' *bodegas*, often financed by entrepreneurs from outside the region and equipped with the very latest in hi-tech equipment, has sprung up in the Rías Baixas region. Their luscious and fragrant wines have little in common with those of the traditional Vinho Verde type, and are establishing themselves as the best white wines from Spain – and they command correspondingly high prices.

In his definitive study of the wines, *Os Viños de Galicia*, Xosé Posada has listed and described no less than 136 grape varieties grown in the area. The more important of them are mentioned in the following A–Z listing, in connection with the different regions. Of these, five have been demarcated: Ribeiro, Valdeorras and Monterrei in the province of Orense to the south, Rías Baixas, comprising three separate areas in the province of Pontevedra, and the newly demarcated Ribeira Sacra, north of the town of Orense and partly in the province of Lugo.

The best and most characterful wines are made with the white Albariño, sometimes with the addition of a smaller proportion of Treixadura or Loureira, from the zones of the Val do Salnés, O Rosal and the Condado de Tea. In Monterrei, the most easterly region, the vines are grown low, *a la castellana*, as in most other parts of Spain, and are pruned and trained by the method of *poda en vaso* ('goblet-shape'). Its wines, mostly red and of some 14 per cent strength, resemble those of León more closely than those from the more westerly regions of Valdeorras and Ribeiro, where the vines are grown higher and the wines are lower in strength and often *pétillant*.

Adegas das Eiras
DO w dr ☆☆☆ *DYA*

O Rosal (Pontevedra). DO Rías Baixas. In addition to the ALBARIÑO, this *bodega* is making some very imaginative use of revived grape varieties such as the Loureira and Caiño. Its labels are Abadía de San Campo and Terras Gauda.

Agro de Bazán
DO w dr ☆☆☆

Villanueva de Arosa (Pontevedra). DO Rías Baixas. Small but select winery, with 13 hectares of vineyard planted exclusively with Albariño. The wines are sold as Granbazán, a regular Verde in a green bottle and an Ambar made from free-run juice, which gives it exceptional fragrance. There is also a Limousin, one of the few from the region matured for a year in oak – but *see* BODEGAS DEL PALACIO DE FEFIÑANES.

Albariño
This most famous of Galician grapes, sometimes said to have been introduced to the region from the Rhine by the Benedictine monks from Cluny, is similar to the Portuguese Alvarinho. Such is the quality of its white wines, crisp and flowery with overtones of apple, pear or peach, that in the first place (in 1980) a *reglamento* was promulgated covering wines made from the grape, irrespective of their origin. This was replaced in August 1988 by the DO RIAS BAIXAS, covering the three areas where the ALBARIÑO is most prevalent.

Alanis, Bodegas
DO w dr ☆☆ *DYA*

Barbantes-Estación (Orense). DO Ribeiro. This Galician outpost of the giant Bodegas y Bebidas makes a trio of good white wines from Treixadura and Torrontés: Xanandro; Gran Alanis (plus Palomino) and San Trocado.

Amandi
DO r ☆

According to tradition, the *claretes*, made exclusively from the Mencía grape and produced by winemakers in this small village in the new DO Ribeira Sacra, were once favourites with Caesar Augustus, who drank them with his spiced lamprey.

Cambados
Small seaside town to the northwest of Pontevedra, and the only place of any size in the VAL DO SALNES. Cambados celebrates an annual *Fiesta del Albariño* on the first Sunday of August, at which the wines are judged by expert tasters and are also available to the public.

Chaves, Bodegas
DO w dr pt ☆☆→☆☆☆ *DYA*

Barrantes-Cambados (Pontevedra). DO Rías Baixas. A small family operation with its own vineyards and a *bodega* equipped with modern stainless-steel fermentation and storage tanks, as well as refrigeration equipment for precipitating tartrates.

Most of the *bodega*'s annual 30,000 bottles of good *pétillant* ALBARIÑO are only available in local hotels and restaurants, but its Castel de Fornos was one of the very first Albariño wines available in the United Kingdom.

Condes de Albarei
DO w dr ☆☆☆ *DYA*
Cambados (Pontevedra). DO Rías Baixas. Flowery 100 per cent ALBARIÑO from the VAL DO SALNES, made by Bodegas Salnesur, which was founded in 1988.

Cosecheros del Vino del Ribeiro
DO r w dr ☆
Ribadavia (Orense). DO Ribeiro. Bottlers of representative RIBEIRO wines under the labels of Ouro, Agarimo and Campo Hermoso.

Fefiñanes, Bodegas del Palacio de
DO w dr ☆☆☆
Fefiñanes (Pontevedra). DO Rías Baixas. For decades before the present vogue for young, cold-fermented wines emerged, the most famous of ALBARIÑOS – now labelled as Fefiñanes – was produced by the Marqués de Figueroa, in a tiny *bodega* occupying a wing of the historic palace of Fefiñanes, found on the outskirts of CAMBADOS. The wines were aged in oak casks for several years. The *bodega* is now making young, modern-style Albariño wines plus a 100 per cent Albariño *crianza*, aged in cask for six months and in bottle ('97).

Fillaboa, Granxa
DO w dr ☆☆☆ *DYA*
Salvatierra de Miño (Pontevedra). DO Rías Baixas. This is one of the newer small Galician *bodegas* (established in 1986). Its modern equipment helps in making one of the very best of the ALBARIÑO wines.

Gallega, Bodegas
r w dr ☆
Los Peares (Lugo). Emigration and the tricky terrain of the steep valleys of the Miño and Sil mean wine production in this area of Lugo has greatly declined. This *bodega's* Tres Ríos, once produced locally, is now a blend of wines from León and La Mancha.

Godeval SAT
DO w dr ★★
El Barco de Vadeorras (Orense). DO Valdeorras. A small *bodega*, sited in the ancient monastery of Xagoaza, was founded in 1986 by a group devoted to the revival of the traditional white Godello grape. It makes wine only from the Godello, its best being the clean and extremely fresh Viña Godeval.

Guitián Godello
DO w dr ☆☆☆ 97, 98
Rubiá de Valdeorras (Orense). DO Valdeorras. Made by Bodegas Tapada, these splendidly fruity, fragrant and complex 100 per cent Godello wines, rated among the very best whites in Spain, typify the renaissance of native grapes in Galicia. The barrel-fermented type has the slight edge.

Jesús Nazareno, Bodega Cooperativa
DO r w dr ★→★★

El Barco (Orense). DO Valdeorras. Aside from bulk wine, this cooperative bottles large amounts of very drinkable dry reds and whites, without *pétillance* and sold as Valdeorras Tinto, Valdeorras Blanco and Moza Fresca. It also makes a superior Viña Abad Gran Vino Godello ('98) from the best traditional grapes.

Lagar de Cervera
w dr ☆☆☆
See LAGAR DE FORNELOS.

Lagar de Fornelos
DO w dr ☆☆☆ DYA

O Rosal (Pontevedra). DO Rías Baixas. A subsidiary of La Rioja Alta (*see* page 146), this small firm makes a first-rate 100 per cent Lagar de Cervera ALBARIÑO, which is pale-straw in colour, light, refreshingly acidic and highly aromatic.

Lapatena, Bodegas
Non-DO w dr r (sp) ★→★★

Santa Cruz de Arrobaldo (Orense). This huge, innovative *bodega* was built in glass and marble and opened in 1990. It buys from local farmers and makes fresh, juicy white wines (best is the Fin de Siglo, a blend of Palomino, Torrontés and Treixadura) and characterful reds, plus sparkling wine and *aguardiente*.

Martín Codax
DO w dr ☆☆☆ DYA

One of the best of ALBARIÑOS from an innovative cooperative, Bodegas de VILARIÑO-CAMBADOS.

Miño, Condado de *See* Condado de TEA

Miño, River

The Miño, rising in the centre of Lugo province, is the principal river of Galicia, flowing south through Orense and finally forming the northern border of Portugal, where it is known as the Minho.

Monterrei
DO r p w dr ☆

Small wine area and recently restored DO in the south of Orense, centred on the valley of the River Támega and bordered by Portugal. It is subdivided into the districts of VERIN, Monterrei, Castrelo and Oimbra. Sheltered by the Sierra de Larouco, vines grown low *a la castellana* produce the strongest of Galician wines, of up to 14 per cent strength. About 70 per cent of the wine is red from the Alicante Negro, Garnacha, Tintorera (Mencía), Tinta Fina, Tinta de Toro and Monstelo. The main white grapes are Godello, Doña Blanca and 'Xerez' (Palomino). The most important producer is the Cooperativa de MONTERREI. Adegas Ladairo make good white wine and red *jóvenes*.

Monterrei, Cooperativa de
DO r p w dr ☆

Verín (Orense). DO Monterrei. The cooperative was founded in 1963 and was, until recently, the only concern in the region of Monterrei – in the south of Galicia near the Portuguese border – to bottle its wines. It makes fresh young red, rosé and white wines labelled simply as Monterrei, and also a two-year-old Castillo de Monterrei.

Morgadío, Bodega
DO w dr ☆☆☆ DYA

Creciente (Pontevedra). DO Rías Baixas. Outstanding 100 per cent Albariño Morgadío: it is clean, flowery and intense with a long finish.

Moure, Adegas
DO w dr r ☆☆☆ 97, 98

Escairón (Lugo). DO Ribeira Sacra. This *bodega* is the flagship of the new DO. It makes an excellent white Abadía da Cova ('98) Albariño, with 85 per cent Albariño and 15 per cent Godello, and a 100 per cent red Mencía, clean, fruity and well-balanced.

Orense
Orense is the most southerly of the provinces of Galicia, bounded by Pontevedra to the west and Portugal to the south. It embraces the demarcated regions of RIBEIRO and VALDEORRAS as well as MONTERREI and some smaller areas. Orense itself is not the most attractive of Galician towns, and it is more pleasant to stay in VERIN or on the coast.

Pazo
(r p) w dr ★→★★DYA

One of the biggest-selling and most frequently encountered branded Galician wines; made by Bodega Cooperativa del RIBEIRO.

Pazo de Barrantes, Bodegas
DO w dr ☆☆☆ DYA

Ribadumia (Pontevedra). DO Rías Baixas. First-rate Albariño from the late Conde de Creixell of the Riojan Marqués de Murrieta.

Pazo de Señorans
DO w dr ☆☆☆ DYA

Meis (Pontevedra). DO Rías Baixas. New small *bodega* (founded in 1980) producing a fresh and fruity estate-grown ALBARIÑO. Made by the president of the *consejo regulador*, it is now one of the most consistent of all Albariños.

Pontevedra
Province in the southwest of Galicia, bordered by the River Miño and Portugal to the south and by the Atlantic to the west. Its green and hilly coastline is deeply penetrated by the picturesque *rías*, on one of which stands the port of Vigo. It is in this region that

the famous ALBARIÑO grape and the high-climbing vines, trained on wires stretched between granite pillars, come into their own. All three subzones of the DO RIAS BAIXAS lie within this province.

Queimada *See* 'Spirits, Aromatic Wines and Liqueurs', page 206

Rías Baixas
DO w dr (r) ☆→☆☆☆

Instituted in 1988, the DO replaces a provisional measure of 1980 applying to the ALBARIÑO grape rather than the area of production. It covers the three subzones of the VAL DO SALNES, focusing on the town of CAMBADOS, and O ROSAL and the Condado de TEA, lying back from the coast along the River Miño on the Portuguese frontier. Their combined area is 10,197 hectares, of which 1,960 are demarcated. Production in 1996-'97 totalled seven million litres.

Ribeira Sacra DO

A new DO in the north of Galicia, lying between the Rivers Sil and Miño. At present it comprises some 1,500 hectares of vineyard of very varied soil types. The permitted grape varieties are: the white Godello, Albariño, Treixadura, Torrontés, Doña Blanca and Loureiro; and the red Mencía, Brancellao and Merenzao. The leading *bodega* is Adegas MOURE.

Ribeiro
DO r p w dr pt ☆→☆☆

The most productive vine-growing area in Galicia, situated in the west of the province of ORENSE in the basin of the River Avia. At a height of 100 to 300 metres and with 3,000 hectares under vines, it produced nine million litres of wine in 1997-'98. It is subdivided into three districts: Ribeiro de Avia, the oldest and most traditional area, making excellent white wines from Gomariz and reds from Beade, Regada and Costeira; Ribeiro del Miño, also producing good red and white wines; and Ribeiro de Arnoia, with its light and fragrant growths. The best of the white grapes are the Treixadura, Torrontés, Godello, Macabeo, Albilla and Loureiro, the Godello in particular giving the wines a fresh and fragrant nose. The best and most perfumed of the red wines are made from the Sonsón. By far the largest producer in the region is the Bodega Cooperativa del RIBEIRO.

Of other concerns bottling their wines, the newest and most spectacular is Bodegas LAPATENA, opened in 1990 but non-DO, because it draws on fruit from outside the region, eg Ribeira Sacra.

Ribeiro, Bodega Cooperativa del
DO r p w pt ★→★★

Ribadavia (Orense). DO Ribeiro. Situated in Ribadavia at the confluence of the Miño and Sil rivers, this is by far the largest cooperative in Galicia, with some 800 members. It has modern equipment for vinifying, refrigerating and bottling the wine, and produces some six million litres annually with storage capacity for another four million.

The wines are sold under the PAZO label (meaning a baronial house). The white is flowery, dry and not too acidic, without much sparkle, and has won prizes in international exhibitions. The red is definitely *pétillant*, dry and astringent to a degree, and resembles the red *vinhos verdes* from over the border. The cooperative also bottles superior white Amadeus, made with 85 per cent Treixadura and 15 per cent Torrontés, and Viña Costeira with 60 per cent Palomino, 30 per cent Torrontés and 10 per cent Treixadura.

Rodrigón
A post, usually of chestnut, used for training the vines clear of the damp ground, especially in the more westerly districts of Galicia.

Rosal, O
DO (r) w dr pt ☆☆→☆☆☆☆ *DYA*

Small subzone of the DO RIAS BAIXAS to the extreme southwest of the province of Pontevedra, near the mouth of the River Miño.

The main grapes are the ALBARIÑO, Treixadura and Loureira Blanca. In the past the wines, made unscientifically by a host of small proprietors, have been variable in quality. New regulations require DO wines to be made from at least 70 per cent Albariño or 70 per cent Loureira (or a blend of both), and a new generation of small, modern *bodegas* is producing fresh, soft wines, often with a peachy flavour.

Salvatierra, Condado de
An alternative name for the Condado de TEA.

Santa María de los Remedios, Cooperativa
DO r w dr ★→★★

Larouco (Orense). DO Valdeorras. The cooperative bottles limited amounts of dry red and white VALDEORRAS, without *pétillance*, under the label Silviño and also a clean, fresh and fragrant Arame, made from 100 per cent Godello.

Santiago de Compostela
Santiago lies northeast of the VAL DO SALNES, less than an hour's drive from CAMBADOS. It is the only city in Galicia with direct flights from Madrid, Barcelona and abroad. It possesses an old university, but most importantly it is the shrine of St James the Apostle, the patron saint of Spain, whose remains are buried there, and from the 11th century onwards it has been the destination of pilgrims from all over Europe. Its cathedral is one of the most impressive in Spain.

Santiago Ruíz
DO w dr ★★★ *DYA*

San Miguel de Tabagón (Pontevedra). DO Rías Baixas. This *bodega*, which pioneered new techniques in O ROSAL, is still one of the best. It now belongs to the Riojan firm of LAN. Don Santiago makes and bottles a first-rate 100 per cent ALBARIÑO, also one containing 20 per cent Loureira and 10 per cent Treixadura.

Señorío, Bodegas SAT
DO w dr r ★→★★

Villamartín de Valdeorras (Orense). DO Valdeorras. The *bodega*'s wines include a soft and peachy 100 per cent Godello Valdesil and a lively young 100 per cent Valderroa Mencía.

Socalco
Name given to the steep hillside terraces in Galicia, sometimes so difficult to access that the peasants set up simple presses to vinify the wine *in situ*.

Tea, Condado de
DO w dr r ☆→☆☆☆ DYA

Also known as the Condado de Salvatierra, this small subzone of the DO RIAS BAIXAS lies in the south of the province of Pontevedra, flanking the River Miño. Principal grape varieties are the black Caiño, Brancellao, Espadeiro and Alicante; and white Treixadura and ALBARIÑO. The predominant wines are traditionally red and claret-like, but the new hi-tech *bodegas* make fresh and characterful Condado de Tea white from at least 70 per cent Albariño or 70 per cent Treixadura (or a blend of both).

Terras Gauda, Bodegas
DO w dr ☆☆☆ 97, 98

O Rosal (Pontevedra). DO Rías Baixas. The winery, renowned for the fragrance and elegance of its wines, has two large vineyards in the very south of the region, near the Miño, growing ALBARIÑO, Loureiro and Caiño. It makes three types of wine: Abadía de San Campio from 100 per cent Albariño; Terras Gauda from a blend of Albariño, Loureiro and Caiño; and Etiqueta Negra from a similar blend, but fermented in barrel.

Tutor
Another name for the RODRIGON, a wooden post used for supporting high-growing vines.

Val do Salnés
DO w dr ☆☆→☆☆☆☆

Now a subzone of the DO RIAS BAIXAS, the Val do Salnés, lying along the coast and *rías* north of Pontevedra, has always been the heartland of the famous ALBARIÑO grape. According to the new regulations, its DO wines must contain at least 75 per cent Albariño and are frequently made with 100 per cent. At their best, they are marvellously fresh and crisp with a long finish.

When in CAMBADOS, it is well worth visiting the historic *bodega* of the Marqués de Figueroa in the palace of Fefiñanes, but keep an eye on its opening hours.

Valdeorras
DO r w dr ☆→☆☆☆

The most easterly of the winemaking areas of ORENSE, Valdeorras lies in the mountainous valley of the River Sil and comprises three subregions, those of Rúa-Petín, Larouco and El Barco de Valdeorras, each of which possesses its own cooperative.

About 90 per cent of the white wine is made from the 'Xerez' (a variety of the Palomino) and 80 per cent of the red from the Garnacha de Alicante. The white wine is of 11 to 12 per cent alcohol, clean and a little drier than that from RIBEIRO; the red is cherry-coloured, fragrant and of 11 to 12 per cent.

By far the largest producer of bottled wine is the Bodega Cooperativa JESUS NAZARENO. Numbers of smaller concerns are, however, producing interesting wines from the traditional white Godello, whose popularity is now being revived, and red Mencia. At their best, the Godellos are now rated among the top white wines from Spain. *See especially* GUITAN GODELLO.

Verín
Wine town in the southeast of the province of Orense.

Vilariño-Cambados, Bodegas de
DO w dr ☆☆☆ *DYA*

Cambados (Pontevedra). DO Rías Baixas. New cooperative *bodega* with stainless steel and the latest equipment, founded in 1986. Its MARTIN CODAX is an excellent example of the new generation of clean, fruity and flowery ALBARIÑOS.

Viña Mein
DO w dr ☆☆☆

Leiro (Ourense). DO Ribeiro. Small, individual *bodega* with 12 hectares of vineyard, making perhaps the most sophisticated wine in Ribeiro, from a blend of white native grapes: Treixadura, Godello, Loureiro, ALBARIÑO, Torrontés and Albillo.

Vino de aguja
Term used to describe wines, like many from Galicia, with a slight *pétillance* derived from a secondary malolactic fermentation. These are also known in Spain as *vinos verdes* – to the annoyance of the Portuguese, who have registered the description *vinho verde* or 'green wine' with the OIV (Office International du Vin).

Virgen de las Viñas, Bodega Cooperativa
DO r w dr ☆

La Rua (Orense). DO Valdeorras. The cooperative sells most of its output in bulk, but bottles some red and white wine under the labels of Rua, Pingadelo, Amavia and Brisel-Godello.

WINE AND FOOD

Galicia is famous for its *mariscos* or shellfish – mussels, lobsters, scallops, prawns, scampi, clams, cockles, oysters, *percebes* (an edible barnacle) and *nécoras* (a species of spider crab). In seaside places you'll often find *marisquerías* which serve nothing else, pricing the portions by weight. There are strong affinities with the cooking of northern Portugal; in the soups, rich fish stews and highly spiced tripe – hearty fare suitable for the long, wet winters.

As regards wine to go with this rich and nourishing assortment of dishes, the Galicians by preference drink a white ALBARIÑO with shellfish, which is perfectly matched by the acidity of the wine. The astringency of the red wines is a good counter to the richness and full flavour of the more substantial dishes.

Caldeirada gallega Akin to the French *bouillabaisse*, this is served in two parts: first the broth, accompanied by slices of toast, and then the fish.

Caldo gallego A nourishing thick soup with shank or hock of ham and haricot beans.

Callos a la gallega Tripe with chickpeas, pigs' trotters, paprika, *chorizo* and hot seasoning.

Centollo relleno/Changurro relleno The spider crab is boiled and the meat removed, then added to a mixture of cooked hake, onion, parsley, garlic and lemon juice. This is filled back into the shell, topped with breadcrumbs and grated cheese and browned in the oven.

Empanada gallega Savoury tart containing a variety of meat or fish with tomatoes, onions, and *chorizo*. *Xouba*, for example, is filled with small sardine-like fish and *Raxo* with loin of pork.

Filloas Thick, fluffy pancakes, usually rolled and filled with jam.

Lacón con grelos Smoked shank of ham cooked with *chorizo* and sprouting turnip tops.

Lamprea a la gallega Lamprey prepared with shallots, garlic, olive oil, vinegar, sweet paprika, cinnamon and white wine.

Merluza al hinojo Hake cooked with fennel.

Pato al estilo de Ribadeo Duck cooked with turnips, orange segments, carrots, boiled chestnuts, pork, white wine, *anís* and a *bouquet garni*.

Pulpo a feira Stewed octopus with a sauce of olive oil, garlic and sweet red peppers.

Rape al queso Anglerfish baked with grated cheese.

Salsa salpicada Sauce made with hard-boiled eggs, onion, garlic, vinegar, olive oil and seasoning; served with fish and shellfish.

Santiaguiños Large crayfish appropriately marked with the cross of Santiago (Saint James).

Tarta de almendras Almond tart.

Tarta de Puentedeume A tart made with almonds, sugar and egg yolks.

Vieiras al Albariño Scallops marinated in ALBARIÑO wine, seasoned with parsley, garlic and nutmeg, sprinkled with breadcrumbs then browned in the oven or under the grill.

HOTELS

Bayona *Parador Conde de Gondomar* (on the coast south of Vigo. Luxurious *parador* with beaches and yacht basin; and conveniently situated for visits to winemaking areas).

Cambados *Parador del Albariño* (pleasantest of places to sample the ALBARIÑO wines and local shellfish).

Pontevedra *Parador Casa del Barón* (housed within an old baronial mansion).

Santiago de Compostela *Parador Reyes Católicos* (a 16th-century palace in the magnificent cathedral square): among the most memorable hotels in the country.

Tuy *Parador San Relmo* (on the Portuguese frontier and adjacent to O ROSAL and the CONDADO DE TEA).

Verín *Parador de Monterrei* (local wines and food).

RESTAURANTS

Cambados *O'Arco* (near the palace of Fefiñanes; shellfish plus regional dishes and ALBARIÑO wines).

La Coruña *Casa Pardo* (seafood, lobster salad); *A Penela* (local dishes, good wines and most reasonable prices).

Orense *San Miguel* (regional food, and Ribeiro and Condado de Tea wines); *Martin Fierro* (regional cooking).

Pontevedra *Doña Antonia* (scallops, braised anglerfish, roast lamb with honey); *Casa Solla* (seafood and Albariño wines).

Santiago de Compostela *Anexo Vilas* (regional cooking and wines); *Toñi Vicente* (scallop salad with truffles, braised sea bass).

Vigo *La Oca* (inventive and sophisticated); *Puesto Piloto Alcabre* (beach restaurant, fish and regional dishes, Albariño and Condado de Tea wines); *El Mosquito* (especially for fish and shellfish).

Villagarcía de Arosa *Lolina* (superb cooking of local ingredients in former customs house); *Chocolate* (celebrated Galician restaurant, specialising in grills – and the famous chocolate ice cream); *Paco Feixó* (try the medallions of anglerfish with sea urchins and algae sauce, and the chestnut cake with white chocolate).

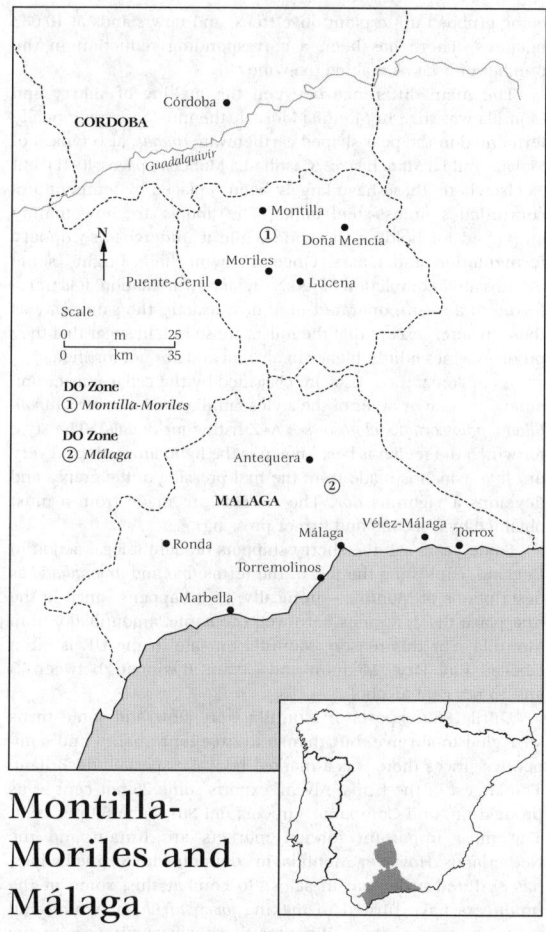

Montilla-Moriles and Málaga

Montilla-Moriles, one of the hottest and sunniest parts of Spain, lies in hilly country south of Córdoba. It makes wines of the sherry type matured in *solera* and, until it was demarcated in 1945, much of its wine was shipped to Jerez for blending. Sweet Pedro Ximénez wines are still, by special dispensation, supplied to sherry *bodegas* for making sweet *olorosos* and cream sherries.

The best of its soils is the chalky white *albero* resembling the *albariza* of Jerez; but by far the most predominant grape is not the Palomino, but the Pedro Ximénez, picked here when fully ripe but still waxy white, and fermented to completion without sunning. Other grapes are the white Airén, Baladí and Moscatel and the yield from the low-pruned vines is small. The area under cultivation has declined sharply in recent years, with vineyards being grubbed up to plant olive trees, and now stands at 10,082 hectares. There has been a corresponding reduction in the number of *bodegas* making the wine.

The main difference between the making of sherry and Montilla was that, in Montilla-Moriles, the must was traditionally fermented in the pear-shaped earthenware *tinajas*, also typical of Málaga and La Mancha (*see* 'Castilla-La Mancha', pages 40-41); but as elsewhere, these have largely been replaced by temperature-controlled stainless-steel tanks. The *tinajas* are now mainly employed for holding the wine while it undergoes secondary fermentation and clears. Once the wine 'falls bright', some months after completion of its secondary fermentation, it is transferred to a *solera*, operated in almost exactly the same way as those in Jerez, except that the musts are so rich in sugar that they produce wines a little higher in alcohol and are not fortified.

As in Jerez, the musts are classified by the cellar master and emerge as one or other of the styles familiar in Jerez: *fino*, *amontillado*, *palo cortado*, *oloroso* (*see* A-Z listing for details). The style for which the region is best known is the light, aromatic and very dry *fino*, which is made from the first pressing of the grapes and develops a vigorous *flor*. The *olorosos* are made from a must obtained by a second and firmer pressing.

Some years ago the sherry shippers brought a legal action in England, contesting the use of the terms *fino* and *amontillado* as descriptions of Montilla – ironically, as it happens, since in the first place the Jerezanos borrowed the name 'amontillado' from Montilla. For this reason, Montilla on sale in the UK is often labelled 'Fine Dry', 'Medium' and 'Cream'. It contains between 13 and 15 per cent alcohol.

Until 1980 exports of Montilla were slow and some firms struggled to survive, but thanks to excellent quality and competitive prices there was a marked revival, especially in Britain. The largest of the firms, Alvear, exports some 25 per cent of its production, and Compañía Vinicola del Sur some 50 per cent. The most important foreign markets are Britain and the Netherlands. However, Montilla, in common with fortified wines, has suffered a decline in sales. To combat this, some of the producers have turned to making *joven afrutado* (young and fruity) beverage wines. Whether these can compete with the white wines from the regions of the north remains to be seen.

Sweet wines from Málaga were famous in Roman times and reached their zenith during the 19th century, with the largest exports to North America. Like other sweet dessert wines their popularity has declined, and the tourist boom along the Costa del Sol has taken its toll of vineyards (now 987 hectares) and *bodegas*. In 1829 production was 17.5 million litres, whereas in 1997-'98, with the closure of the famous Scholtz Hermanos, only two large firms remain: López Hermanos and Larios. Nevertheless, Málaga at its best remains a glorious wine, and not all of it is sweet.

The grapes are grown in two areas of the surrounding hills, one to the north of the city and neighbouring the DO Montilla-Moriles, and the other to the east. In days past there was a profusion of vine varieties, but the *consejo regulador* now authorises only the Pedro Ximénez and Moscatel for new plantations.

Some of the different styles of Málaga are separately described in the A–Z listing. The most common is the *dulce color*, dark amber in colour, full-bodied and sweet (sometimes cloyingly so) through to the end; but there are others, more resembling tawny port, with a bitter-sweet flavour and dryish finish.

Albero

The best of the soils, containing 30 to 60 per cent chalk. It is most widespread in the *sierras* of Montilla and Alto Moriles, where most of the large *bodegas* have vineyard holdings. Production is higher in the lower-lying areas, but the wines are not of the same alcoholic degree or quality.

Alvear

Montilla (Córdoba). DO Montilla-Moriles. The largest firm in the region was founded by the Alvear family, which settled in Montilla in 1729, planting vineyards and establishing the original *bodega*. It was much expanded by Don Francisco de Alvear y Gómez de la Cortina, Conde de la Cortina, during the early years of the present century and now possesses 20,000 American-oak casks in its SOLERAS and has a storage capacity of five million litres.

Alvear makes Montilla in a dozen styles, including two excellent dry *finos*, the soft and delicate Fino Capatáz and Fino CB, named after a former head cellarman, Carlos Billanueva; Amontillado Carlos VII, fruity, fragrant and bone dry, more resembling a *fino* than an *amontillado* from Jerez; Oloroso Asunción; the bitter-sweet Oloroso Asman Abocado; a sweet Festival Cream; and a smooth, full-bodied Pedro Ximénez 1830 with a flavour of figs. Alvear also produces a light wine, the Marqués de la Sierra, and large amounts of brandy made from *holandas* (*see* 'Spirits, Aromatic Wines and Liqueurs', page 202).

Amontillado

The original style of Montilla, first made by a Conde de la Cortina in the 18th century, but without maturation in SOLERA. The Jerezanos later produced a wine with similar characteristics, but aged it in SOLERA; and the *bodegueros* from Montilla followed suit. *Amontillados* from Montilla are 16 to 22 per cent strength, amber-coloured, full on the palate and with a pungent, nutty nose.

Antequera

The old town of Antequera lies north of Málaga on the winding uphill road to Córdoba and Sevilla, and on the southern fringe of one of the two main vineyard areas of the DO MÁLAGA. This northern area, at a height of 500 metres, is a limestone region, and the predominant grape is the Pedro Ximénez.

Aragón y Cía

Lucena (Córdoba). DO Montilla-Moriles. Well-known firm whose wines include the *fino* Moriles 47; *amontillado* Pacorrito and

Boabdil (20° alcoholic strength); Moriles Palo Cortado; and the sweet Araceli and Pilycrim Pedro Ximénez.

Axarquia

The second and larger of the vineyard areas of the DO Málaga, to the east of the city and stretching back from Vélez-Málaga and Torrox near the coast into the mountains, which rise sharply to a height of 2,000 metres. The soils are a mixture of decomposed slate and a limestone clay, and its vineyards are planted with 90 per cent Moscatel.

Benavides

The vineyards here are among the best in the MORILES area; they supply wine only to TORO ALBALA.

Compañía Vinícola del Sur

Montilla (Córdoba). DO Montilla-Moriles. A large company, the Compañía Vinícola del Sur was formerly a part of the Rumasa group (see 'Sherry and Manzanilla', page 170), whose Monte Cristo wines are well-known in Britain. Dry, Medium, Pale Cream and Cream are also exported to the US.

Conde de la Cortina

Montilla (Córdoba). DO Montilla-Moriles. The company is controlled by ALVEAR, with which it shares premises. Its best-known brands are the well-made Cortina Pale Dry, Medium, Cream and Pale Cream.

Córdoba

A little to the north of the DO Montilla-Moriles, Córdoba was formerly the headquarters of a number of firms which maintained *bodegas* and SOLERAS in the city for maturing their wines.

For 300 years, until the Caliphate disintegrated in 1031, Córdoba was the capital of Moorish Spain; and the Great Mosque, now the cathedral, resembling nothing so much as a cool grove of palm trees with its myriad arches and columns, was the most important in western Islam and second only in size to that of Mecca. Other Moorish survivals are the 14th-century Alcázar or fortified palace, with its mosaics and gardens, and the Judería, or ancient Jewish quarter, a maze of narrow alleys, criss-crossing at random and providing shelter from the sun.

About half-an-hour's drive from MONTILLA, Córdoba, with its historic interest and restaurants, is the obvious base for a visit to the region.

Crismona

Doña Mencia (Córdoba). DO Montilla-Moriles. Maker of the good Los Cobales *fino*.

Cruz Conde, Bodegas

Montilla (Córdoba). DO Montilla-Moriles. Well-known for attractive Cruz Conde *fino* and Pedro Ximénez; also makes a light white wine.

Doña Mencía

Village to the southeast of MONTILLA with three concerns making DO wines: Bodegas CRISMONA, Bodegas (Miguel Fernández Gan) Lama, and Bodegas Luque.

Dulce color

The most familiar style of Málaga wine, sweetened with ARROPE – to which it owes its dark amber colour, as well as the hint of treacle in the nose and the high 8° to 12° *baumé*. The alcohol content ranges from 14 to 23 per cent.

El Naranjo

Another favoured vineyard area near MORILES.

Fino

Pale, dry with a greenish tint, slightly bitter, and light and fragrant on the palate, the unfortified *fino*, containing 14 to 17.5 per cent alcohol, is the best known of the various styles of Montilla.

Gracia Hermanos

Montilla (Córdoba). DO Montilla-Moriles. Firm within the same group as PEREZ BARQUERO and COMPAÑIA VINICOLA DEL SUR making traditional, good-quality Montillas. Labels include María del Valle *fino*, Montearruit *amontillado*, Cream *oloroso* and PX Dulce Viejo.

Jesús Nazareno, S Coop Vitivinicola

Baena (Córdoba). DO Montilla-Moriles. Large co-op making light white Don Bueno; Baena and Cancionero *finos*; Minguillar *oloroso*.

Lágrima

The word means 'tear' and is used to describe the choicest and most luscious of the wines, made with the juice which emerges from the grapes without the use of mechanical means and simply as a result of the pressure from the grapes at the top of the load. It therefore comes from the pulp nearest the skins of the ripest grapes, and is vinified separately from the *yema* (or 'yolk') which is obtained by further light pressing.

The wine is old-gold in colour, very full bodied, with an aromatic *oloroso* nose and long sweet finish. It has 6° to 10° *baumé* and 14 to 23 per cent alcohol.

Larios

Málaga. DO Málaga. Known for its gin, Larios also makes good Málagas, especially the 100 per cent Pedro Ximénez Benefique *oloroso* and the *dulce* (sweet) Málaga Larios. *See also* 'Spirits, Aromatic Wines and Liqueurs', page 204.

López Hermanos

Málaga. DO Málaga. Founded in 1885 and run by the third generation of the López family, the *bodega* owns 500 hectares of vineyards in the Mollina area and makes some of the most popular Málagas in Spain, including the dry Trajinero, made from

95 per cent Pedro Ximénez; the sweet dessert Málaga Virgen, containing 60 per cent Pedro Ximénez and 40 per cent Moscatel; and the luscious Moscatel Cartojal.

Lucena
Pleasant little town southeast of Montilla and halfway between CÓRDOBA and Antequera (see page 105). Apart from wine it produces olive oil and is known for its decorative metalwork.

Málaga
The city of Málaga lies on the coast at some distance from the vineyards in the hills behind it, but to qualify for the DO the musts have either to be vinified in one of its *bodegas* or, as is more usual, brought there for blending and maturation.

The inexorable pressure of tourism has ringed it with high-rise apartments but the port remains and, behind it, a network of narrow streets clustering around the market, some of which have restaurant tables on the pavement and cavernous bars where one can settle down to tasting such Málagas as remain.

Mollina
The most important of the vineyards in the region's northern zone, beyond ANTEQUERA.

Monte Cristo
Well-known MONTILLAS from COMPAÑIA VINICOLA DEL SUR.

Montilla
With the nearby village of MORILES, this quiet hill town, the *Munda Betica* of the ancients and birthplace of Gonzalo de Córdoba, the Gran Capitán, boasts the early 18th-century house of the ALVEAR family, with its splendid arcaded patio. The wine centre of the region, Montilla possesses a number of *bodegas* making DO wines.

Montisierra
Exporters' association, comprising ALVEAR, COMPAÑIA VINICOLA DEL SUR, GRACIA HERMANOS and PEREZ BARQUERO.

Montulia, Bodegas
Montilla (Córdoba). DO Montilla-Moriles. Established, well-known firm, now part of the NAVISA group, and maker of some dozen styles of Montilla, including JR *fino*, *amontillado*, Fabiola, Pedro Ximénez and an excellent *palo cortado*. Also makes brandy and *anís*.

Moriles
Although famous for its wines, and lying at the centre of some of the best vineyards in the area, Moriles remains only a tiny village on a by-road 20 kilometres south of MONTILLA.

Moscatel
As the name implies, a style of Málaga made solely with Moscatel grapes, from AXARQUIA, the larger of the vineyard areas of the DO

Málaga. The colour varies according to age from golden yellow to light golden brown, and the wine is soft and sweet, with a deep and fruity Moscatel nose. It varies from 6° to 13° *baumé* with an alcohol content of 15 to 20 per cent.

'Mountain Wine'

Soubriquet for Málaga in its Victorian heyday. You can still occasionally find silver wine labels with this name in English antique shops.

Navarro, Bodegas

Montilla (Córdoba). DO Montilla-Moriles. A sizeable exporter, established in 1830 and belonging to NAVISA. Its range of wines includes Andalucía, Montilla and La Aurora *finos*; NR *oloroso*; and a sweet Pedro Ximénez.

Navisa Industrial Vinícola Española

DO Montilla (Córdoba). This group controls Bodegas MONTULIA, Bodegas Velasco Charcón and Bodegas Cobos. The family-owned Cobos was formerly a household name and one of the largest and most important *bodegas* in Montilla. Navisa makes Cobos and Pompeyo *finos* and an excellent Tres Pasas Cream, together with Viña Carrerón, a refreshing light wine of 11° strength, made from a blend of Pedro Ximénez, Airén and Baladi.

Oloroso

Style of wine resembling its counterpart from Jerez (*see* page 167), with 16 to 18 per cent alcohol, rising to 20 per cent when very old. Mahogany-coloured, full-bodied, soft and highly aromatic, it can either be dry or with a hint of sweetness.

Palo cortado

With 16 to 18 per cent alcohol, this is a style combining the nutty bouquet of *amontillado* with the flavour of *oloroso*.

Pedro Ximénez

1. A sweet Montilla with a high alcoholic degree, which takes its name from the PX grape variety. Made in part with sunned grapes, it is a dark, ruby colour and contains at least a massive 272 grams per litre of sugar.
2. A style of Málaga made solely with Pedro Ximénez grapes from the northern zone. When fully mature it is a dark, treacley colour with a yellow rim and an intense *oloroso* nose, and is full-bodied and very soft, with a bitter-sweet finish. It varies from 6° to 13° *baumé* with an alcohol content of 16 to 20 per cent.

Pérez Barquero

Montilla (Córdoba). DO Montilla-Moriles. Another company, formed at the turn of the century, that was formerly part of Rumasa (*see* page 170). Among its labels are Diogenes and Viña Amalia light white wines and Gran Barquero *fino*, *amontillado* and *oloroso*, all of outstanding quality.

Puente-Genil
Small town southwest of MONTILLA. As well as its wines it is famous as the chief producer of *membrillo*, the quince paste so popular in Spain. It is also the headquarters of Cooperativa Vitivinícola de la Purísima, and Delgado Hermanos.

Raya
A Montilla similar to OLOROSO, but with less flavour and bouquet.

Ruedo
Not a Montilla proper, but a dry, pale, light white wine containing about 14 per cent alcohol and made without any time in SOLERA.

Ruedos de Montilla, Los
The area's grapes are among the best from the Sierra de Montilla.

Scholtz Hermanos
Málaga. DO Málaga. One of the best and most famous *bodegas*, the firm was founded in 1807, passed into German control in 1885 and reverted back to Spanish after World War I. It recently closed. Of its 18 or so styles of wine, the best known was the Solera 1885.

Solera
An assembly of 500-litre butts used for maturing the wine. As in Jerez (*see* page 165), the butts are loosely stoppered and arranged in 'scales' containing progressively older wine, and when wine is drawn off for shipment or bottling, the final 'scale' is 'refreshed' with younger wine. A Montilla *solera* usually contains five 'scales' for the *finos* and four for the *olorosos*. The *soleras* operate almost exactly as those in Jerez, except that the musts are brandied only in occasional years, when they are low in alcohol.

Tercia, La
Well-known vineyard area near MORILES.

Tinajas
Large, pear-shaped earthenware vessels traditionally used for fermenting the wine. The tops are left open during the first stages of fermentation and later covered with wooden lids. Once the wine clears after completion of the secondary fermentation, it is racked and transferred to a SOLERA for maturation. In the large modern *bodegas tinajas* are being replaced with stainless-steel tanks, and are used only to allow the wine to settle and clarify. *See also* 'Castilla-La Mancha', pages 40-1.

Tomás García
Montilla (Córdoba). DO Montilla-Moriles. Belongs to the same group as Carbonell, one of Spain's largest olive oil producers and, until recently, a maker of Montilla which it matured in cellars in Córdoba. It makes a fresh Verbenera *fino*, a fragrant, intense Flor de Montilla *amontillado*, a complex, well-constructed nectar TG *oloroso* and a sweet 100 per cent Pedro Ximénez TG.

Toro Albala
Aguilar de la Frontera (Córdoba). DO Montilla-Moriles. One of the oldest MONTILLA firms, founded on the site of a power station – hence the name of its excellent Eléctrico wines. Makes a beautiful, light Amontillado Viejisimo 1922; a delicious Don PX (on sale in the UK); and a superb Bacchus dessert wine (at over £100 a bottle).

Vitivinícola Local SCA, Cooperativa
Aguilar de la Frontera (Córdoba). DO Montilla-Moriles. One of the largest and best-run cooperatives in the region, making its own Ipagro *generosos* and selling wine to many of the private firms.

Zona del Albero
Name given to the area around MORILES, where the soils are particularly rich in the chalky ALBERO.

WINE AND FOOD
On gastronomic maps of Spain, Andalucía is often labelled the *zona de los fritos* or 'region of fried food'. High on the list of such dishes must come the fries of mixed fish, equally good around Málaga or in Cádiz and the sherry region.

The shellfish on offer is varied and abundant; another speciality are the *gazpachos* or cold soups, always containing garlic and a little olive oil and vinegar, but made with a variety of vegetables, chopped or puréed.

Málaga is not for drinking with a meal, but afterwards. It is the custom in these parts to begin with a glass of chilled *fino* Montilla, often served with *aceitunas alinados* (marinated king-sized olives) and to continue drinking it throughout the meal.

MONTILLA-MORILES
Brazo de gitano Popular sweet made with eggs, flour and jam, and resembling a Swiss roll.
Callos a la andaluza Tripe stewed with calves' feet and chickpeas.
Caracoles a la andaluza Snails cooked with garlic and toasted almonds, paprika, tomatoes, onions, white pepper and lemon.
Huevos a la flamenca Eggs cooked in an earthenware dish with onions, ham and fresh tomatoes, and decorated with prawns, slices of *chorizo*, asparagus tips and red pepper.
Membrillo A sweet quince paste, served on its own as a dessert or with cheese.
Perdices a la torera 'Bullfighters' partridge', garnished with ham, anchovies, green peppers and tomatoes.
Polvorones A dry, powdery sweetmeat, a speciality of Estepa, just west of Montilla-Moriles, made with flour, pork fat, sugar and cinnamon; often served with sherry or Montilla.
Rabo de toro Popular Córdoban stew of oxtail with vegetables.
Revuelto de aspárragos trigueros Scrambled eggs with young asparagus.
Salmorejo A thick variation of *gazpacho*, made with garlic, olive oil and breadcrumbs, but without peppers or tomatoes.
Salsa de patatas A sauce originating from the Sierra Morena,

north of Córdoba. Its base is made with fried puréed potatoes, it contains peppers, a bay leaf, cumin, olive oil and seasoning, and is served with fish.

Ternera con alcachofas a la cordobesa Veal, served with artichokes and cooked with Montilla and seasoning.

Tocino de cielo A sweet popular throughout Andalucía, made with egg yolks and sugar flavoured with vanilla.

MALAGA

Ajo blanco con uvas de Málaga A cold soup prepared with almonds, garlic, vinegar and olive oil, together with white grapes, skinned and without pips.

Chanquetes A minute fish (*Aphia minuta*) which is fried crisp like whitebait.

Dulce malagueño A sweet made with semolina, egg yolks, sugar, raisins and *membrillo*, a quince paste.

Frito de pescados a la andaluza A mixed fry of small fish, sometimes dipped in seasoned flour or maybe dredged in egg and breadcrumbs, and fried in hot olive oil. Fish such as *chanquetes*, *boquerones* (fresh anchovies) or squid cut into rings are also fried and served by themselves.

Moraga de sardines Motril Fresh sardines marinated with salt, olive oil, white wine, lemon juice, parsley and garlic.

Raya en pimentón Skate cooked with sweet paprika.

Salsa andaluza Sauce made with pumpkins, tomatoes, pepper and garlic.

Sopa al cuarto de hora A soup so called because of the cooking time of 15 minutes, and containing chopped ham and clams, hard-boiled eggs, onion, parsley, garlic and bread.

Sopa de almendras de Ronda A sweet soup containing pounded almonds, sugar, a stick of cinnamon and grated lemon peel, with thin slices of bread.

Tarta helada Sweet made with alternate layers of sponge cake and ice cream.

Tortilla al Sacramonte Omelette originating from the gypsy quarter of Granada and containing lambs' brains, sweetbreads, fresh peppers, potatoes and toasted breadcrumbs.

HOTELS

Antequera The *Parador de Antequera* is a pleasant place to spend a night in the area, and the cooking in its restaurant using local ingredients is inventive.

Córdoba About half-an-hour's drive from Montilla, Córdoba has a number of good hotels: the five-star *Amistad Córdoba* and *Meliá Córdoba*, the four-star *Tryp Gran Capitán* and the three-star *Maimónides* opposite the mosque. Perhaps the quietest, most relaxing place is the spacious, comfortable, modern *Parador de la Arruzafa*, which looks down on the city from the north.

Málaga Since the demise of the splendid *Miramar* the quietest place to stay is at the *Parador Nacional de Gibralfaro*, set on a hill above the centre.

RESTAURANTS
Antequera *Parador Nacional* (inventive Andalucían food).
Córdoba *El Caballo Rojo* (facing the Mosque, serving sophisticated Andalucían cooking); *Almudaina* (Córdoban cooking in atmospheric surroundings); *El Churrasco* (pleasant patio and bar, Córdoban dishes).
Málaga *Café de Paris* (sophisticated cuisine with local ingredients); *Casa Pedro* (on the shore and vastly popular; mixed fried fish and first-rate shellfish).
Montilla *Las Carmachas* (formerly owned by the Cobos family and known for its regional cooking).

There are also scores of good restaurants, some outstanding, such as *La Meridiana* and *La Hacienda* in Marbella and in the other Costa del Sol resorts.

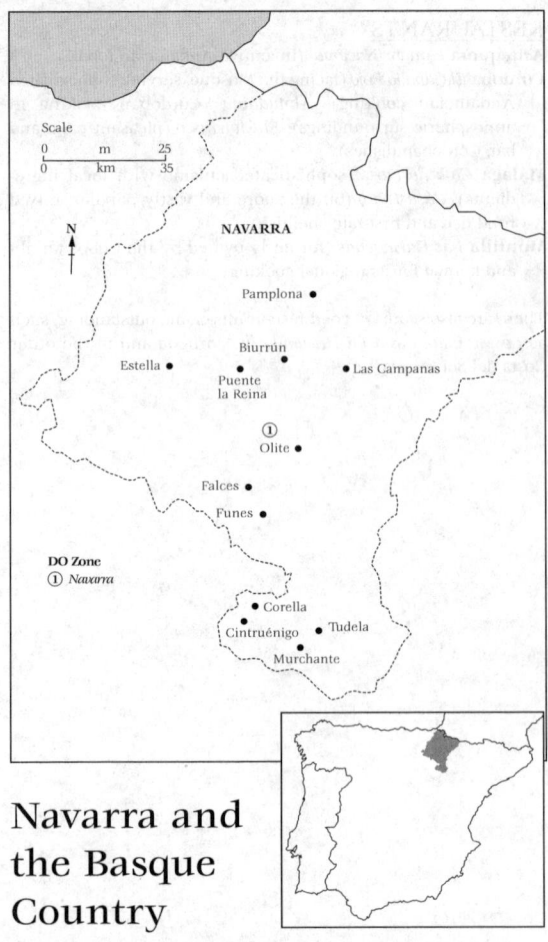

Navarra and the Basque Country

Navarra, to the west of Cataluña and extending from the Pyrenees to the Ebro basin, was a kingdom in its own right until it fell to Ferdinand the Catholic in 1512. At one time it extended over the Pyrenees, hence the alternative spelling of 'Navarre' for the portion now lying in France. It is an autonomy with wide variations in climate, between the subhumid conditions of the mountainous north and the dry, Mediterranean-like climate of central and southern Spain which is felt in the Ebro in southern Navarra. The soils are in general chalky, with deposits of silt and gravel along the river valleys, and are well-suited to viticulture.

The vine-growing districts extend south from the provincial capital, Pamplona, and were demarcated in 1967. The DO Navarra is further subdivided into the five *comarcas* of Baja Montaña,

Valdizarbe, Tierra de Estella, Ribera Alta and Ribera Baja, with a combined area of 13,945 hectares under vines and an output in '97/'98 of 52.3 million litres. The small area of the Rioja Baja, spilling into the province of Navarra and including the town of San Adrián, is separately described (*see* 'Rioja', page 146-7). Lying to the west of Navarra, the Basque Country (País Vasco) and autonomy of Cantabria drink considerably more wine than they produce.

The predominant grape – until recently to the extent of some 70 per cent – is the red Garnacha Tinta, but producers are being encouraged by the government research station EVENA to plant Tempranillo to make longer-lived red wines more suited to oak-ageing. Some 26 per cent has been planted; there are smaller plantations of red Graciano and Mazuelo, and of the white Viura, Malvasía and Garnacha Blanca. Cabernet Sauvignon, Merlot and Chardonnay are also being grown here in sizeable amounts.

Navarra was once a prolific producer of sturdy red wines and fresh rosés, said to have been a favourite of Catherine the Great of Russia in the early 18th century. More recently it has been the rosés – among the best in Spain – the region has been known for and for which Garnacha is well suited, but now the thrust is towards quality red wines. Bodegas Ochoa has produced a delicious 100 per cent Tempranillo, but in general EVENA is working towards red wines made with 50 per cent Tempranillo, 30 per cent Garnacha and 20 per cent Cabernet Sauvignon. The Garnacha is also ideal for making fresh young *vinos jóvenes* in the style of Beaujolais Nouveau, by carbonic maceration.

Thanks to the innovative ideas of EVENA and the re-equipment of the cooperatives, Navarra is making great strides and is a region to watch. Like Aragón, the district may be visited en route to Rioja from Barcelona via the A2 and A68 *autopistas*; and the A15 to Pamplona, branching off the road to Logroño beyond Tudela, will take you through the heart of the vine-growing areas.

Vintages

'78	very good	'88	very good
'79	fair	'89	very good
'80	fair	'90	good
'81	excellent	'91	good
'82	excellent	'92	good
'83	excellent	'93	good
'84	red, good; white and rosé, very good	'94	good
		'95	excellent
'85	red, excellent; white, very good	'96	very good
		'97	good
'86	good	'98	very good
'87	good		

Agramont
DO r p dr ★★

One of the labels used by the large Navarra concern of Bodegas PRINCIPE DE VIANA for its well-made wines.

Ambrosio Velasco See PALACIO DE LA VEGA

Baja Montaña
DO p ☆→☆☆

Subdivision of the DO Navarra, to the region's east on the borders of Aragón. It is the highest and wettest of the vine-growing areas and produces some of the best rosés, of 12 to 15 per cent strength.

Baso
DO r ★★

Brand name of very drinkable red Garnacha made by gifted young oenologist Telmo Rodríguez, of La Granja Remelluri in Rioja.

Las Campanas
Village south of Pamplona and headquarters of the well-known VINICOLA NAVARRA, which uses the name for some of its wines.

Cantabria
Autonomy in the north and one of the wettest parts of Spain, bounded by the Bay of Biscay and to the south by the Cantabrian mountains. It produces only the *pétillant* and astringent CHACOLI.

Carricas, Bodegas
DO r p w dr ☆☆

Olite (Navarra). DO Navarra. Old-established firm with bodegas in the subterranean passages of the 15th-century castle of OLITE. The innovative Carricas brothers label their wines as Mont-Plané: they include a 100 per cent Garnacha rosé and reds made from 100 per cent Garnacha, 100 per cent Tempranillo or a blend of both.

Castillo de Monjardín
DO w dr r (p) ☆☆→☆☆☆ **93, 94, 95, 96, 98**

Villamayor (Navarra). DO Navarra. Founded in 1988, this small family concern makes an excellent barrel-fermented Chardonnay ('96), a fruity 100 per cent Pinot Noir and good but less impressive reds from Cabernet Sauvignon, Tempranillo and Merlot.

Cenalsa, Bodegas See Bodegas PRINCIPE DE VIANA

Chacolí (Txacoli)
DO (r) w ☆→☆☆ *DYA*

A 'green', *pétillant* wine from the Basque Country (País Vasco), containing only 9 to 11.5 per cent alcohol. The vines are ungrafted because the flooding of the vineyards in winter kills the phylloxera bug. There are two types of wine: white Txakoliñ Gorri, from the white Ondarrubi Zuri (akin to the Courbut Blanc), and the red Txakoliñ Zuri from the Ondarrubi Beltza.

When the area around Guetería in Guipúzcoa was first demarcated in 1990 it ran to only 47 hectares. Currently with 89 hectares this is now known as the DO Chacolí de Guetaría-Getariako Txakolina and still produces the best Chacolí. However, the growers in the neighbouring province of Vizcaya to the east have lobbied for their 120 hectares to be demarcated, with the result that a DO Chacolí de Vizcaya Bizkaiko Txakolina has recently been established.

The white and red wines are thin, astringent and rather acidic, although the nose of the white is fragrant enough. The Basques enjoy them in mouthfuls with the excellent local shellfish.

Chivite, Bodegas Julián
DO r p w dr res ★★→★★★ *89, 90, 92, 94, 95, 96, 98*
Cintruénigo (Navarra). DO Navarra. Founded in 1860, this family firm is the largest private wine concern in Navarra, with a total capacity of 18.75 million litres, and vineyards and *bodegas* in other districts of Navarra and in the provinces of La Rioja and Aragón. Its well-made wines range from fresh and fruity young whites, such as the outstanding barrel-fermented Colección 125 Chardonnay ('97) and a good '98 rosé, to the attractive young red Viña Marcos, soft and plummy GRAN FEUDO *crianza*, the rich and oaky Gran Feudo *reservas* and superb Vendimia Tarde Moscatel, the best from Spain ('98).

Cintruénigo
Wine town just to the south of the Ebro in the RIBERA BAJA.

Corella
w sw ☆→☆☆
This village, near CINTRUENIGO, makes a little luscious Moscatel.

Ebro, River
After crossing the Rioja, the Ebro skirts the far south of Navarra, flowing through the RIBERA BAJA. The northerly wine districts lie in the basins of its tributaries, the Ega, Arga, Cidacos and Aragón.

Etxaniz Txakolina
DO w dr ☆☆ *DYA*
Guetería (Guipúzcoa). DO Chacolí de Guetería. Largest and best producer of Chacolí; owner Iñaki Chueca has done much to revive interest in the wines. White Txakolí Txomin Etxaniz is freshly floral.

EVENA
The government-funded *Estacion de Viticultura y Enología de Navarra*. Founded in 1981 and formerly headed by Don Javier Ochoa, it is one of the most forward-looking and up-to-date establishments of its kind in the country. The *estacion* maintains elaborately equipped laboratories at OLITE and its advice is available not only to the cooperatives and large concerns, but also to the humblest smallholder.

Ezcaba, Chacolí Tinto de
r w dr pt ☆
One of the few wines to be made in the mountainous north of Navarra; astringent and *pétillant*, the wines resemble the better-known *chacolís* from Guipúzcoa.

Falces
r p ☆→☆☆

Vine-growing area in the south of RIBERA ALTA, making good red and rosé wines. It also has one of the few monasterial *bodegas* to survive in Europe, that of Nuestra Señora de la Oliva.

Funes

This village between FALCES and Calahorra is the site of a well-preserved Roman winery from the first century AD. With cement paving and chambers for making and storing the wine, its capacity was of the order of 75,000 litres.

Gran Feudo
DO r p w dr ★★→★★★ 91, 92, 93, 94, 95, 96

Well-made and affordable range of red, white and rosé wines from Bodegas Julián CHIVITE.

Guelbenzu, Bodegas
DO r res ★★→☆☆☆ 92, 93, 94, 95, 96, 97

Cascante (Navarra). DO Ribera del Duero. Family firm which has revived estate-bottled red wines from its 40 hectares of vineyards, with excellent results. The wines are a blend of Cabernet Sauvignon and Tempranillo, sometimes with a touch of Merlot. They are concentrated and meaty, and repay opening an hour or two before drinking. The '94 was outstanding.

Gurpegui Muga, Luís
DO w dr p r ☆☆

Vilafranca (Navarra). DO Navarra. Decent Monte Ory wines produced by the firm that owns Bodegas Berceo in Rioja.

Irache, Bodegas
DO r p w dr res ☆☆ 94, 95, 96

Estella (Navarra). DO Navarra. Well-known and old-established firm, whose *bodega* is next to the beautiful monastery of Irache near Estella. A plum-coloured and full-bodied young Irache has been shipped to the UK. Older wines, matured in its 2,000 American-oak *barricas*, include red Castillo Irache, Gran Irache and Real Irache, *reserva* Castillo Irache and *gran reserva* Real Irache ('83); all made with a sizeable proportion of Tempranillo.

Magaña, Bodegas
DO r res ☆☆→☆☆☆ 85, 87, 91, 95, 97

Barillas (Navarra). DO Navarra. Small *bodega*, a pioneer grower of French grape varieties in Navarra. It makes distinguished reds from 100 per cent Merlot or a blend of Merlot and Cabernet Sauvignon, from its own 120 hectares of vineyards.

Malumbres, Bodegas Vicente
DO r p w dr ☆☆ 95

Corella (Navarra). DO Navarra. A sizeable concern with 60 hectares of vineyards. The wines are labelled as Malumbres and

Ontinar: the best include the fresh and fruity '98 Garnacha rosé and the meaty '98 red, both from Garnacha with Tempranillo.

Nekeas, Bodegas
DO r p w dr ★★→★★★

Añorbe (Navarra). DO Navarra. This young co-op, with 220 hectares planted with both native and foreign grape varieties, is justly known for the care with which it makes its wines. These include a 100 per cent Chardonnay fermented in barrel, a 100 per cent Cabernet Sauvignon rosé, and fruity reds made either from Tempranillo and Merlot or Cabernet Sauvignon and Tempranillo.

Nuestra Señora del Romero, Cooperativa
DO r p w dr res ★★ 88, 89, 90, 91, 94, 96

Cascante (Navarra). DO Navarra. This is one of Spain's largest cooperatives, with 1,200 hectares of vines. Although situated in an area best known for its robust Garnacha wine, by modern methods it has succeeded in making wines such as the magnificently light, fresh and fruity Málon de Echaide rosé, an attractive young Nuevo Vino in the style of Beaujolais Nouveau, and good Señor de Cascante *gran reservas* which include 80 per cent Tempranillo.

Ochoa, Bodegas
DO r p w dr res ★★→★★★ 91, 92, 93, 94, 95, 96, 97

Olite (Navarra). DO Navarra. This small firm, which owns vineyards near OLITE, has been in family hands since 1845. Its respected oenologist, Don Javier Ochoa, is one of the most expert in the region.

All of its wines are well made by modern methods and among the best from Navarra. They include a 100 per cent Viura white, a recently introduced and first-rate sweet Moscatel ('98), a 100 per cent Garnacha rosé, and intensely fruity red *crianzas* and *reservas* made from 100 per cent Tempranillo, 100 per cent Cabernet Sauvignon or a blend of both.

Olite
Olite, south of Pamplona in one of the best winemaking areas of RIBERA ALTA, is the site of a fortified palace, once the favourite residence of the Kings of Navarra. Begun by Charles III ('The Noble') in 1403, in its finished form it was the largest palace in Spain.

Palacio de la Vega
DO w dr p r res ☆☆→☆☆☆ 91, 92, 93, 94, 95, 96

Dicastillo (Navarra). DO Navarra. Wines from the young (1991) and promising *bodega* of Ambrosio VELASCO: good, juicy reds, including 100 per cent Tempranillo, 100 per cent Merlot, 100 per cent Cabernet Sauvignon, as well as 100 per cent Chardonnay.

Pamplona
Pamplona, capital of Navarra, dear to Hemingway and famous for the bull-running through its streets during the Festival of San

Fermín in early July, is also a good centre for visiting the more northerly wine areas. An elegant city with a fine cathedral and a spacious central square, it possesses numerous good restaurants.

Piedmonte, Bodegas
DO p r ★★→★★★ *93, 94, 95, 96, 98*

Olite (Navarra). DO Navarra. Produces 100 per cent barrel-fermented Chardonnay, good reds made from 100 per cent Cabernet Sauvignon and blends with Tempranillo and Merlot.

Príncipe de Viana, Bodegas
DO r p w dr sw ★★→★★★ *91, 93, 94, 95, 96, 97*

Murchante (Navarra). DO Navarra. This large firm, founded in 1982 as Cenalsa, has done much to improve winemaking standards in Navarra. It makes wine either by blending and maturing musts bought from the co-ops or by buying in and vinifying grapes. Labels include Agramont and Príncipe de Viana. Red wines are made from 100 per cent Tempranillo, Merlot and Cabernet Sauvignon; and from blends of these grapes. There is also a concentrated and vibrant 100 per cent red Garnacha from century-old vines.

Puente la Reina
Small town southwest of Pamplona and a few kilometres from one of Navarra's most famous *bodegas*, the Señorío de SARRIA. Puente la Reina was one of the staging posts on the medieval pilgrim route from France to Santiago de Compostela (*see* page 98), its bridge joining the two main roads over the Pyrenees. Visit the great stone bridge across the River Arga and the honey-coloured churches, especially those of the Crucifix (Crucifijo) and of St James (Santiago), decorated with the scallop shells of the pilgrims.

Ribera Alta
DO r p (w dr) ☆→☆☆☆

Lying centrally between VALDIZARBE and BAJA MONTAÑA to the north and RIBERA BAJA to the south, this is the largest of the subregions, with 30 per cent of the province's vineyards. The best of its wines are the soft, fruity reds and rosés from around OLITE, containing some 11.5 to 15 per cent of alcohol.

Ribera Baja
DO r (w dr) ☆→☆☆

The Ribera Baja centres on the Ebro basin in the extreme south of the province. The climate is hot – much drier than in more northerly *comarcas* – and the soils contain large amounts of alluvial silt, conditions producing grapes high in sugar. Cascante and CINTRUENIGO make sturdy, full-bodied wines of up to 16 per cent strength.

Sanguesa
(r w) p

Area in the hilly BAJA MONTAÑA centred on the basin of the River Aragón. Its soils are a mixture of gravels and chalk, and the best of its wines are the fresh and drinkable rosés.

Sarría, Bodega de
DO r (p w dr) res ☆☆→☆☆☆☆ *87, 90, 91, 92, 94, 95, 96*

Puente la Reina (Navarra). DO Navarra. The Señorío de Sarría has made wines since medieval times, and they have been among Navarra's best. The vineyards and winery, owned by a local bank, were the brainchild of a Señor Huarte of the large Spanish construction company, who bought the abandoned estate in 1952. Its 1,200 hectares embrace a large French-style château, orchards, farms, 60 kilometres of cypress-lined private roads and 160 hectares of vineyards, planted with Tempranillo, Garnacha, Mazuelo, Graciano and Cabernet Sauvignon for red wines, plus Malvasía, Viura and Garnacha Blanca for whites.

Since the departure of the Huartes and the death of oenologist Francisco Morriones the model village is deserted, and the estate's international reputation dimmed. Made in Rioja style, the wines mature in the *bodega*'s 8,900 *barricas*, 70 per cent of Armagnac oak and the rest American or Yugoslavian. All labelled Señorío de Sarría, they include dry and semi-sweet whites; a 100 per cent Garnacha rosé; *crianzas* and *reservas* from 100 per cent Cabernet Sauvignon or 100 per cent Merlot; and blends of Cabernet Sauvignon with Tempranillo, Garnacha, Mazuelo and Graciano.

Tierra de Estella
DO r p ☆☆→☆☆

Subdivision of the DO Navarra, lying to the northeast of Rioja Alavesa and centred on Estella, a town of Romanesque churches and balconied houses, and once the court of the kings of Navarra. Its wines are very similar in character to those of VALDIZARBE further east, some full-bodied and robust reds and finer *reservas*.

Valdizarbe
DO r p ☆→☆☆☆

A subdivision of the DO Navarra, just south of PAMPLONA in the River Arga basin. Because of its chalky soils and more temperate climate it produces perhaps the best wines of the region, including those of the Señorío de SARRIA and the VINICOLA NAVARRA.

Vinícola Navarra
DO r (p w dr) res ★★ *91, 94, 95, 96, 98*

Campanas (Navarra). DO Navarra. Controlled by Bodegas y Bebidas (formerly Savín, *see* page 132), this traditional *bodega* was built in 1880 against an abbey on the pilgrim route. Until recently it began maturation of some wines in large oak vats inherited from an earlier French firm. The dry white Las Campanas (100 per cent Chardonnay) is clean, fruity and fresh. The red Las Campanas and Castillo de Tiebas *crianzas* and *reservas* (a blend of Cabernet and native grapes) are full and fruity, and proof of good traditional winemaking.

WINE AND FOOD

Cooking in Navarra has similarities with that of Aragón to the east and the Basque Country to the north. The mountain region in the north is famous for its lamb, served stewed with tomatoes (*espárragos mantañeses*), as a fricassée (*cochifrito*) or in a spicy *chilindrón* sauce. Another speciality is trout, sometimes served with ham. Local wines are varied enough to accompany these dishes. Vegetable dishes and fish call for a white wine; try a rosé with the snails and a good red with the lamb.

Alcachofas con almejas Artichokes with clams.
Caracoles a la corellana Snails cooked with garlic, and parsley, cloves, bay leaves, thyme and lemon juice.
Caracolillas de Navarra Small snails cooked in earthenware dishes with olive oil, tomatoes, green peppers, chillis, breadcrumbs and seasoning.
Cardo a la Navarra Boiled cardoon (a vegetable that resembles celery) accompanied by a white sauce with ham.
Ensalada de pimientos piquillo Fish salad with langoustines, monkfish, fennel, garlic, olive oil and sherry vinegar.
Huevos revueltos con ajos tiernos Eggs scrambled with young garlic shoots.
Menestra de habas de Tudela Fresh broad beans cooked with garlic, mint, saffron, almonds, artichoke hearts, boiled eggs, white wine, thyme and seasoning.
Remojón Orange and cod salad.
Ternasco asado Roast leg of lamb basted with lemon juice and white wine.
Tortilla de Tudela Omelette made with the excellent locally grown asparagus.
Truchas a la Navarra The trout is first marinated and then cooked in an earthenware dish with onions, red wine, pepper, mint, thyme and bay leaves.
Truchas con jamón Fried trout served on top of (or stuffed with) slices of fried ham.

HOTELS
Olite *The Parador Príncipe de Viana* lies more or less centrally in the wine area – ideal for visiting vineyards and *bodegas*.
Pamplona Has several extremely comfortable hotels, including: *Iruña Palace Tres Reyes*, *Iruña Park* and *Blanca de Navarra*.

RESTAURANTS
Olite *Parador Príncipe de Viana* (regional dishes and a good list of local wines).
Pamplona *Hartza* (hake with scallop sauce; *menestra*), *Josetxo* (particularly recommended for its game and *foie gras* with grapes; good wine list); *Rodero* (sophisticated French and local cuisine); *Europa* (stewed ox-tongue in Cabernet Sauvignon, salad of prawns and duck's sweetbreads); *Alhambra*.
Puente la Reina *Mesón del Peregrino* (pleasant country style).
Tafalla *Tubal* (crêpes with borage and clam sauce; pheasant breasts with onions).
Tudela *El Choko* (good hearty local dishes and pleasant red house wine); *Mesón Julián*.

Rioja

Apart from sherry, Rioja is the best known of Spanish wines and, thanks to good quality and reasonable prices, foreign sales have leapfrogged in recent years: in Britain alone, they increased from 180,000 litres in 1970 to some 13 million litres today, with correspondingly huge increases in sales to Denmark, Germany, Switzerland and the US. The bulk of its wines are red and have traditionally been characterised by the long periods they spend in cask, and by their oaky nose and flavour. In recent years, however, the reds have spent less time in wood and more in bottle, and Rioja has also been making a new style of white wine: light, fresh and fruity, without age in wood.

Rioja was the first Spanish region to be demarcated, when a *consejo regulador* was set up in 1926 to control production and quality, and in 1991 it became the first to achieve the status of *denominación de origen calificada*, or DOCa, reserved for wines of the highest quality. It now comprises 53,238 hectares of vineyards within the provinces of La Rioja (formerly known as Logroño), Alava and Navarra, with an average production over the last five years of 197 million litres of wine. The vineyards extend for 120 kilometres on both sides of the River Ebro, which flows from the rocky Conchas de Haro in the hilly west of the region to Alfaro in the east. The valley is bounded by mountains on either side and is a maximum width of 40 kilometres. The soils are a mixture of calcareous clay, ferruginous clay and alluvial silt, with a predominance of calcareous clay in Rioja Alavesa (one of the three subregions) to the north of the river.

In the west of the area the climate is temperate and fairly predictable, with mild, wet springs, short, hot summers, long, warm autumns and a little snow and frost in winter. The hotter and more Mediterranean-like Rioja Baja in the east is classified as semi-arid.

The Rioja DOCa is divided into the three subregions of Rioja Alta, Rioja Alavesa and Rioja Baja, of which the first two produce the more delicate wines. In this chapter the subregion, not the province or DO zone, is given in parentheses.

Wine was being made in Rioja long before the Roman occupation of the area: the traditional method, which is still practised in the *bodegas* of smallholders, was to tip the bunches of grapes, stalks and all, into open stone troughs, or *lagos*. Fermentation then proceeded in stages, with progressively firmer crushing of the grapes.

Production of Rioja in its present style began after the double disasters of oidium and phylloxera in France in the late 1800s, when French *négociants* moved into the district and introduced the methods employed in Bordeaux, notably the destalking of the grapes and the ageing of the wines in 225-litre oak casks. Long after the French reduced the period in wood, the Riojans continued to age the wines, both red and white, for long years in oak – hence the characteristically vanilla-like bouquet and flavour – and it is only recently that more attention has been given to

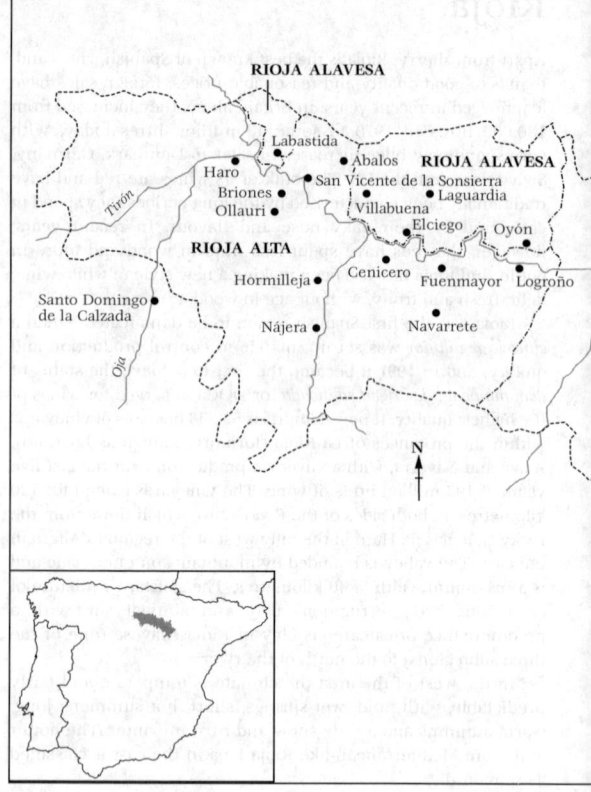

bottle-age. With the widespread production of cold-fermented white wines without maturation in cask, matters have turned full circle, and now a new generation of cask-aged whites has appeared – albeit less fiercely oaky than their predecessors.

The first great Rioja boom took place during the latter decades of the 19th century; and the *bodegas* constructed during that period – Riscal, Murrieta, López de Heredia, CVNE, La Rioja Alta and the rest – are still among those producing the best wines. Another phase of expansion – financed by banks, sherry firms, Spanish industrialists and foreign wine concerns – took place in the 1970s. These *bodegas* are characterised by their size and the modernity of their equipment, but all of them – in conformity with the regulations laid down by the *consejo regulador* – mature their better red wines in the traditional 225-litre oak *barricas*. More recently, a new generation of small *bodegas* has sprung up, often based in old houses or castles and relying entirely on grapes grown in their own vineyards.

Present practice in the newer *bodegas* is to macerate the red

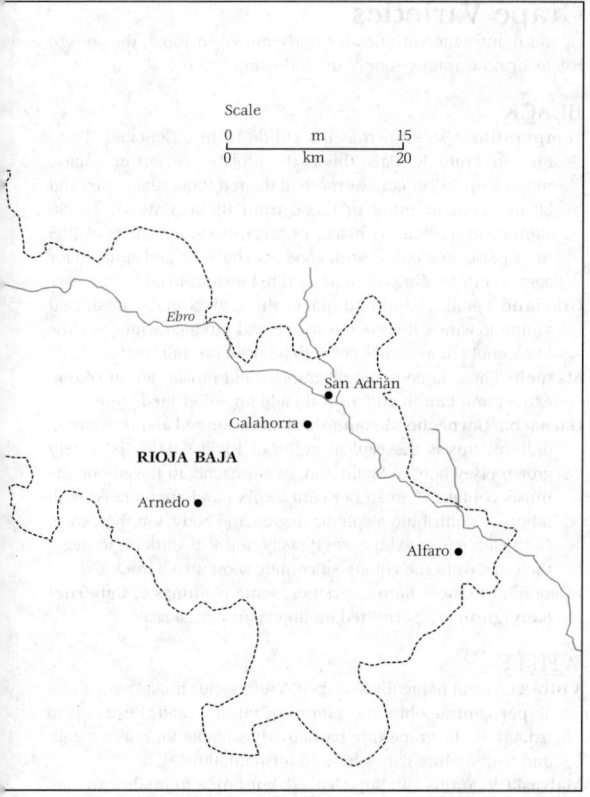

wines, to ferment at controlled temperatures in stainless steel, to avoid prolonged ageing in wood and to give them more time in bottle. This results in more immediately juicy and fruity wines, which do not always last as long as they used to (*see* 'Keeping Riojas', page 128).

Although most of the large *bodegas* own sizeable vineyards of their own, and some of the newer ones, such as Domecq, have embarked on extensive new plantations, traditional patterns of agriculture persist, with most of the grapes being grown by smallholders on plots interspersed by wheat, potatoes and other vegetables. All the large concerns buy substantial amounts of fruit from the independent farmers, and some also make use of wine made in the cooperatives, of which there are 30 in the area.

In contrast to Bordeaux, the vines are normally grown low, without supporting stakes and wires, and pruned *en vaso* ('goblet-shaped'), with three *brazos* or main stems, each of which bears two *sarmientos* or grafted shoots, bearing two bunches of grapes, so there are 12 bunches in all.

Grape Varieties

Of the many vine varieties formerly grown in Rioja, the *consejo regulador* now approves only the following seven:

BLACK

Tempranillo Also known as the Ull de Llebre, Cencibel, Tinto Fino or Tinto del País, this is the Rioja grape *par excellence*, making up 50 per cent or more of the red Rioja Alta wines and 80 per cent or more of those from Rioja Alavesa. Thick-skinned and intensely black, its grapes produce wines of 10.5 to 13 per cent alcohol, with good acid balance and suitable for ageing, but tending on their own to be short-lived.

Graciano Small, round and black, the grapes make fresh and aromatic wines, but are too scarce and produce wines too low in alcohol (10 to 12 per cent) to be used on their own.

Mazuelo These large 'pointed' grapes yield musts rich in colour, extract and tannin and are valuable for wood-aged wines.

Garnacha/Garnacho Medium-sized, thin-skinned and resistant to oidium, this is the typical grape of Rioja Baja. It is widely grown elsewhere in Spain and, as Grenache, in the Rhône. Its musts contain 15 to 16 per cent alcohol and are blended with others to contribute alcoholic degree and body. On their own, Garnacha wines oxidise very easily and it is difficult to judge their age from the colour, since they soon turn a brick red.

In addition to these native varieties, some plantings of **Cabernet Sauvignon** are permitted on an experimental scale.

WHITE

Viura The local name for Macabeo, Viura yields musts with about 11 per cent alcohol and plenty of tartaric acid. Resistant to oxidation, the grapes are particularly suitable for making light and fruity white wines by cold fermentation.

Malvasía Vigorous and large-leaved, but prone to mildew. White-tinted with red when fully mature, these produce fresh wines of about 11 per cent, often made in an admixture with Viura.

Garnacha Blanca Not so much used in the Rioja as the other two varieties, these grapes produce pleasant white wines, but higher in alcohol and with less acidity.

There was a popular superstition that red Riojas are made in *solera* (see 'Sherry', pages 171-2), but this is entirely untrue. They were traditionally made by blending wines from different grape varieties, often grown in separate areas of the region. Varietal wines, often containing 100 per cent Tempranillo, are increasingly produced.

There is sometimes a limited admixture of wines of different vintage, but the bottle must contain not less than 85 per cent of the vintage stated on the label. It was usual in the past – and the custom lingers in other parts of Spain – to label them with a description such as 3° *año* or 5° *año*, meaning the wine was bottled during the third or fifth year after harvest. Without knowing how long the wine had been in bottle it was impossible to gauge when it had been made. All exported wines are now labelled with a vintage.

Vintages

Because of the more predictable climate and the former practice of blending a proportion of better wine with the poorer growths, in the past vintage years were not as variable as those in Bordeaux. They are now important – increasingly so as the *consejo regulador* tightens the regulations. Outstanding among earlier years were:

1915	'31	'49	'68
'20	'34	'52	'70
'22	'42	'55	'73
'24	'47	'58	
'25	'48	'64	

Official ratings for more recent years follow, with a personal assessment (in parentheses) of the current status of the wines since the 1982 vintage. Of course producers vary, and there are significant exceptions.

Year	Yield (millions of litres)	Rating
'76	93	good
'77	65	very bad
'78	81	excellent
'79	140	average
'80	125	good
'81	130	very good
'82	113	excellent (although rated above '81, it has not lasted as well)
'83	106	good (now thin and watery, avoid)
'84	130	average (as above, avoid)
'85	176	good (fair intensity, peaked or peaking)
'86	120	good (good but lean, now drying out)
'87	133	very good (unduly praised in Spain)
'88	132	good (thin and mean, avoid)
'89	160	very good (middle weight, a few hanging on)
'90	166	very good (light, beyond its best)
'91	146	very good (medium intensity, drink now or will keep for a while)
'92	150	good (soft and immediate, drink now)
'93	175	good (looking a bit thin and immediate)
'94	169	excellent (but maturing sooner than expected)
'95	218	very good (good, and currently drinking well)
'96	244	very good (lighter, drink now)
'97	253	good (but somewhat lacking structure and concentration)
'98	273	very good (record vintage, but rain and lack of sunshine do not augur well)

NB: Keeping Riojas

An extended range of vintages is printed for a number of Rioja *bodegas*. However, the quality of the older *reservas* and *gran reservas* is dependent on proper cellarage. Old wines kept for any period in the racks of a warm restaurant will soon deteriorate. My own experience is that red Riojas do not now last as long as their oakier predecessors. For example, some of the '85s '86s '87s, '89s and '90s are already drying out – although, depending upon the *bodega*, an older vintage may well be delightful. Currently, the '94, '95 and '96 vintages are the safest choice.

As when visiting most wine areas, it is a great advantage to have a car, though, once in Logroño there is a charming local train which wends its leisurely way by Fuenmayor, Cenicero and Briones to Haro, depositing you on the doorstep of many of the *bodegas* and affording better views of the Ebro and the vineyards than those from the main road.

The quickest approach to the region is to fly to Bilbao, hire a car and drive to Haro or Logroño, one and a half to two hours away off the A68 *autopista*. Alternatively, drive from Barcelona by way of Zaragoza and the A2. This route will take you through the heart of the Rioja Baja. It is easy enough to make a leisurely circuit of the Rioja Alta and Rioja Alavesa in a day by driving from Logroño to Haro on the N232 by way of Fuenmayor, Cenicero and Briones, and returning by the road north of the Ebro, also labelled the N232, through Labastida, Abalos and Laguardia. It is especially worthwhile to visit Briones and Laguardia, just off the road, two of the most picturesque hilltop towns of the Rioja.

Stay in Logroño, Haro or Santo Domingo de la Calzada for Rioja Alta and Rioja Alavesa; Calahorra for Rioja Baja. Numerous restaurants serve good regional food and wines in towns and villages up and down the region (*see* pages 150-2).

Abalos

This picturesque village east of Haro is set in a small enclave of RIOJA ALTA to the north of the Ebro. Dominated by the mountains of the Sierra Cantábrica and surrounded by vineyards, it possesses an old palace and impressive 15th-century church and is the headquarters of Bodegas REAL DIVISA.

AGE, Bodegas Unidas
r (p) w dr res ☆☆

Fuenmayor (Rioja Alta). This large *bodega*, formed in 1964 by the union of three much older concerns, Azpilicueta, Cruz García and Entrena, is now owned by the BODEGAS Y BEBIDAS group. Its labels are Azpilicueta, Marqués de Roméral and Siglo, and the wines are reliable if unspectacular.

Ageing

Riojas, both red and white, have traditionally been aged in cask for much longer than Bordeaux or Burgundy wines, and they have from time to time been criticised for a pronounced oaky nose and flavour (see OAK). The present trend is to cut down on the period in cask and to give the better red wines at least a year or two in bottle. *See also* CRIANZA. Significant amounts of wine are also being made by *maceration carbonique* and sold without ageing in wood as *vinos jóvenes*.

Alambrado

A fine wire mesh sometimes used around bottles of *reservas*, now decorative but originally to prevent tampering.

Alavesas, Bodegas

r (p) w dr res ✩✩ 89, 94

Laguardia (Rioja Alavesa). This large concern, with 84 hectares of vineyards, has a capacity of 18 million litres and matures its wine in 5,500 oak BARRICAS.

The best known of its wines, made from 100 per cent Tempranillo, are labelled Solar de Samaniego, after a local poet and composer of fables. Once light and thoroughly typical of RIOJA ALAVESA, they are now fuller-bodied in style. To be recommended is the fruity unoaked Vino Joven.

Albor

r ★→★★

This moderately priced and huge-selling middle-of-the-road wine is no longer a Rioja, but is made in Valdepeñas with Tempranillo from Manchuela.

Aldeanueva, Viñedos de

r ★★ 94, 95, 96, 98

Aldeanueva de Ebro (Rioja Baga). Huge co-op, with 2,600 hectares of vineyard and 6,000 oak BARRICAS. Good red Azabache wines.

Alfaro

This small town at the eastern extreme of RIOJA BAJA is the home of two *bodegas*. Its name is derived from El Faro (meaning 'the lighthouse'), and it was the furthest point on the Ebro reached by the Phoenicians in their shallow draught boats. It is an attractive little place with some fine baronial houses and a beautiful 17th-century church.

Allende, Finca

r ✩✩✩→✩✩✩✩✩ 96, 97

Briones (Rioja Alta). Miguel Angel Gregorio opened a small *bodega* in his native Briones only a few years ago and already his wines have been acclaimed by Robert Parker and others as some of the best from Spain. Best (and vastly expensive) is the dark, concentrated and intensely fruity Aurus '96, made from 85 per cent Tempranillo and 15 per cent Graciano.

Amézola de la Mora, Bodegas

r res ✩✩→✩✩✩ 90, 91, 94

Torremontalbo (Rioja Alta). Winemaking at Torremontalbo, an

historic castle between Logroño and Haro, was revived in 1986, when the 130-year-old cellars were completely re-equipped. The estate-grown Viña Amézola and Señorío Amézola, both made from 90 per cent Tempranillo and 10 per cent Mazuelo, are attractive and well-made reds.

ARCO-Bodegas Unidas
Newly formed group comprising BERBERANA, MARQUES DE MONISTROL, MARQUES DE GRIÑON, AGE and LAGUNILLA.

Arnedo
Picturesquely situated in the gorge of the River Cidacos with its red sandstone cliffs, Arnedo is one of the most pleasant of the RIOJA BAJA towns.

Artadi
w dr p r res ★★ →☆☆☆☆ *92, 93, 94, 95, 96, 98*
Label used by COSECHEROS ALAVESES for its well-made wines.

Banda Azul
r ☆
Big-selling but undistinguished red Rioja from Federico PATERNINA.

Barón de Chirel
res ☆☆☆☆ *88, 91, 94, 95*
Premium wine from MARQUES DE RISCAL; concentrated, fruity and one of the very best from Rioja.

Barón de Ley
r res ☆☆☆ *91, 94, 95, 96*
Mendavia (Rioja Baja). The Barón de Ley was established in the late 1980s by the owners of Bodegas EL COTO. Its headquarters are in a meticulously restored hunting lodge, situated in 90 hectares of vineyards. The wines, made from 100 per cent Tempranillo, are savoury and well-balanced with overtones of oak.

Barón de Oña
DO r res ☆☆☆
Excellent red *reserva* from BODEGA TORRE DE OÑA SA.

Barrica
The 225-litre oak cask in which all the CRIANZA and *reserva* wines must statutorily be matured is a legacy of the *vignerons* from Bordeaux, who settled in Rioja during the phylloxera epidemic of the late 19th century.

Berberana, Bodegas
r (w dr) res ★★→★★★ *87, 89, 90, 92, 94, 95, 96*
Cenicero (Rioja Alta). The company, now one of the largest in Rioja and part of the ARCO-BODEGAS UNIDAS group, was founded in 1877 by the Berberana family in Ollauri, where it still maintains cellars for ageing the wines in bottle. It underwent a

major expansion in 1972 and belonged for a period to RUMASA, after which it was temporarily nationalised and then sold to various shareholders in 1985.

The vinification plant in CENICERO incorporates modern stainless-steel fermentation tanks and a huge ageing floor accommodating 40,500 oak BARRICAS. Berberana embarked on ambitious new plantations of some 900 hectares at Monte Yerga near Aldeanueva del Ebro in the RIOJA BAJA, growing a high proportion of Tempranillo and Viura in addition to the Garnacha typical of the area, but these are now owned by a separate company. The fruity red CARTA DE PLATA is one of the biggest-selling CRIANZAS, and there are full-bodied and velvety older wines, such as CARTA DE ORO, Berberana Reservas and Gran Reservas. Berberana is increasingly selling its best wines under the MARQUES DE GRIÑON label.

Berceo, Bodegas
r w dr p res ☆☆→☆☆☆☆ 92, 94, 95, 96

Haro (Rioja Alta). The sister ship of Bodegas GURPEGUI MUGA, making worthwhile red Viña Berceo and Gonzalo de Berceo.

Beronia, Bodegas
r w dr res ☆☆→☆☆☆☆ 87, 89, 92, 93, 94, 95

Ollauri (Rioja Alta). The firm, with seven hectares of vineyards in one of the best areas of the RIOJA ALTA, began operations in 1970, working from a small *bodega* in the village of Ollauri. Later it moved to an elegant new winery in the midst of the vineyards, and it was the intention of Don Javier Bilbao Iturbe to make wines by traditional methods on a limited scale, but also to take advantage of modern technology. Such was the success among the cognoscenti of the dry, fruity and well-balanced red Berón and the Beronia *reservas* which are made with a high percentage of Tempranillo, that in 1982 the *bodega* was taken over by the sherry firm of González-Byass, which has since more than tripled production, buying in fruit and sometimes wines to do so. The red wines, including a 100 per cent Mazuelo, maintain high standards and are generally more interesting than the white.

Bilbaínas, Bodegas
r (p) w dr sw sp res ☆☆→☆☆☆☆ 89, 90, 91, 92, 94, 95

Haro (Rioja Alta). Bilbaínas, founded in 1901, was one of the first firms to build a *bodega* adjacent to the newly opened railhead from Bilbao, and its wines have long been known in the UK, where at one time it maintained its own cellars and office. It owns 266 hectares of vineyards, mostly around Haro, with a smaller holding at Leza in the RIOJA ALAVESA.

The *bodega's* wines include the dry white Viña Paceta; a young red Ederra; a light and first-rate Viña Zaco; the more fully bodied red VIÑA POMAL, made basically with grapes from Leza; and good La Vicalanda *reservas*. The firm, which has recently been taken over by CODORNIU, also makes wines by the Champagne method (*see* 'Sparkling Wines', page 189).

Bodegas y Bebidas

Formerly called Savín, this is one of the largest Spanish wine companies, specialising in inexpensive branded wine made to good standards, but also making prestige wines such as the CAMPO VIEJO *reservas*.

The company possesses wineries up and down Spain, such as the CASA DE LA VIÑA in Valdepeñas and the VINICOLA NAVARRA; in the Rioja it operates a *bodega* at Aldeanueva del Ebro in the RIOJA BAJA and also controls CAMPO VIEJO in Logroño, Bodegas AGE and the MARQUES DEL PUERTO in FUENMAYOR.

Bordelesa

An alternative name, reflecting its Bordeaux origins, for the 225-litre oak BARRICA.

Bretón y Cía, Bodegas

w dr p r ☆☆→☆☆☆ *90, 91, 94, 95, 96*

Logroño (Rioja Alta). Founded in 1985, the *bodega* is making a name for itself with its modern-style Loriñon wines, and the '95 Dominio de Conte and Alba de Bretón *reservas* are outstanding.

Briones

A little east of Haro, the small hilltop town of Briones, with its stone-built baronial houses, statuesque church and long views over the Ebro, is one of the most attractive in RIOJA ALTA and is home to the small but sophisticated *bodegas* of FINCA ALLENDE and MIGUEL MERINO.

Calahorra

The largest town in RIOJA BAJA, the birthplace of Quintilian and famous for its protracted siege by Pompey in the first century BC, Calahorra is a convenient stopping place en route to Logroño from Zaragoza and a good base for visiting the subregion. There is a comfortable *parador*, the Marco Fabio Quintiliano.

Campeador

r res ☆☆→☆☆☆ *85, 89*

Label for oaky old *reservas* and *gran reservas* from MARTINEZ LACUESTA.

Campillo, Bodegas

r res ☆☆☆ *89, 91, 92, 94, 95*

Laguardia (Alava). Opened in 1990 by the group owning FAUSTINO MARTINEZ, its first vintages were made with Faustino's grapes. It has an elegant new winery and 50 hectares of vineyards, and makes lightish, high-quality reds from 100 per cent Tempranillo.

Campo Viejo, Bodegas

r (p w dr) res ★→★★★ *82, 85, 89, 90, 91, 92, 94, 95, 96, 97*

Logroño (Rioja Alta). Owned by the ubiquitous firm of BODEGAS Y BEBIDAS and situated in Logroño itself, Campo Viejo is the largest firm in Rioja, with 80,000 barrels. Its widely advertised

San Asensio is among the biggest selling of young *sin crianza* Riojas, and the *bodega* also produces some big red *reservas*, including the first-rate Marqués de Villamagna, Viña Montalvó and good 100 per cent Tempranillo Alcorta. The inexpensive red Albor, made by carbonic maceration, is no longer produced in Rioja. Campo Viejo is soon to move to a huge new *bodega* in Fuenmayor, the largest in Spain.

Cañas, Bodegas Luís
r res (w dr p) ★★→☆☆☆☆ 89, 92, 94, 95, 96

Villabuena (Rioja Alavesa). This small *bodega* makes a fresh and fruity Recien ('98) with 95 per cent Tempranillo and 5 per cent Viura and good CRIANZAS and *reservas*. The Reserva Amaren '96, made mainly from Tempranillo, was outstanding.

Carlos Serres, Bodegas
r (p w sw) res ☆→☆☆☆ 89, 92, 93, 94, 95, 96, 98

Haro (Rioja Alta). Well-known Haro firm, whose younger wines are labelled as Carlos Serres. Its best wines are the red Carlos Serres and Onomástica *reservas* and *gran reservas*.

Carta de Oro
r ★★

Fruity red and white CRIANZA wines from BERBERANA.

Carta de Plata
r ☆

Inexpensive young unoaked white and rosé wines from BERBERANA and a pleasant non-vintage red.

Casa del Vino *See* LAGUARDIA.

Castillo de Cuzcurrita
r res dr ☆☆→☆☆☆

Río Tirón (Rioja Alta). Small *bodega* in a 14th-century castle. It makes good but somewhat astringent red wines from grapes grown in its own vineyards. The wines are labelled as Señorío de Cuzcurrita, Castillo Cuzcurrita and Reserva Conde de Alacha.

Castillo Ygay
res ☆☆☆☆ 25, 34, 42, 52, 59, 64, 68, 70, 75, 78, 82, 85, 87, 89

Gran reserva from the MARQUES DE MURRIETA, made only in exceptional years. The '34 was one of the most complete and beautiful Riojas I have ever tasted. There are also excellent and very expensive white Ygays.

Cenicero

Town on the Ebro west of Logroño in RIOJA ALTA, and the headquarters of important *bodegas*. It was the burial place of the Roman legions stationed in the area, hence the name, which in Spanish means 'ashtray'. Cenicero stages an interesting wine festival in September, held in its large, covered *pelota* court.

Compañía Vinícola del Norte de España (CVNE)
r (p) w dr sw res ★★→★★★ 89, 90, 91, 92, 93, 94, 95

Haro (Rioja Alta). CVNE was founded in 1879 in the full flush of the 19th-century Rioja boom, and has been making excellent wines ever since. At one time it included sparkling wine made by the Champagne method and a brandy.

The *crianza* Cune is a reliable young red Rioja; the Imperial and VIÑA REAL *reservas*, the latter a full-bodied and aromatic Alavesa made in Elciego, are superb, as is the newly-introduced Real de Asua ('94). CVNE makes a new-style white Rioja without maturation in wood: the oaky Monopole is a traditional white Rioja; and the superior single-vineyard red, CONTINO, made by a subsidiary, is grown in vineyards at La Serna in RIOJA ALAVESA, west of Oyón. These big, mellow, full-bodied wines with blackberry flavour and a long finish are among the best in Rioja.

Conde de los Andes
res ☆☆☆ 78, 89

Gran reserva from Federico PATERNINA, named after the Madrid gastronome. The much-lauded '78 is strictly for fans of vegetal oak and volatile acidity.

Conde de Valdemar
res ☆☆☆ 89, 90, 92, 93, 94, 95, 96

Excellent red *reservas* made by MARTINEZ BUJANDA.

Contino
res ☆☆☆☆ 89, 91, 92, 94, 95, 96, 97

Superior single-vineyard red *reserva* made by Viñedos de Contino in RIOJA ALAVESA, owned by COMPAÑIA VINICOLA DEL NORTE DE ESPAÑA. The first vintage, made in '74, is fragile but still beautiful, and a new introduction, Viña del Olivo ('96), is outstanding. The *bodega* also makes a rare and excellent 100 per cent Graciano ('96).

Corral, Bodegas
r (p w dr) ☆☆

Navarrete (Rioja Alta). The *bodega* stands by the Pilgrim Way to Santiago and is best known for its Don Jacobo wines.

Cosecheros Alaveses
r w dr res ★★→☆☆☆ 90, 91, 92, 94, 95, 96

Laguardia (Rioja Alavesa). Innovative firm, formerly a cooperative, best known for its unoaked, well-balanced and fruity red Artadi, but now making excellent 100 per cent Tempranillo Viñas de Gain and Pagos Viejos CRIANZA and *reserva* wines. Also home to an outstanding Viña el Pisón *reserva* from 70-year-old single vineyard grapes.

Crianza
Literally 'nursing'; in terms of wines the word refers to their maturation in oak cask. The regulations of the *consejo regulador* are strict: to be labelled *con crianza*, a Rioja, red or white, must be

matured for two years with a minimum of one in a 225-litre oak BARRICA and not released before the third year. For the *reservas* and *gran reservas*, *see* 'Glossary', pages 14–17. Riojas need not, however, be aged in oak to qualify for *denominación de origen*. There are no rules as regards the ageing of wines *sin* CRIANZA ('without ageing'), which may nevertheless spend a few months in cask. These are now known as *vinos jóvenes*.

Cumbrero
r w dr ☆☆

Label used by Bodegas MONTECILLO for its pleasant, young red and white Riojas.

CVNE

Abbreviations of COMPAÑIA VINICOLA DEL NORTE DE ESPAÑA, whose wines are known colloquially in Spain as 'Cune' (*see* previous page).

Domecq, Bodegas
r (p) w dr ★★→☆☆☆ 85, 87, 90, 92, 94, 95, 96

Elciego (Rioja Alavesa). The origins of the company date from the early 1970s, when the sherry concern of Pedro Domecq and the Canadian firm of Seagram joined forces to take over Bodegas PALACIO. The partners later parted ways, and in due course Pedro Domecq constructed its own *bodega*, with modern stainless-steel fermentation tanks and a capacity of some 21,000 oak BARRICAS for maturing the wines. Bodegas Domecq has also planted 571 hectares of new vineyards in one of the best parts of RIOJA ALAVESA, a venture notable among other aspects for training the vines in Bordeaux style, rather than pruning them low in traditional Riojan fashion. The younger wines, always sound and drinkable, are labelled Viña Eguia. The MARQUES DE ARIENZO *reservas* and *gran reservas* are fruity, complex and have a long finish.

Don Darius/Don Hugo
r w dr ☆

Huge-selling, modestly-priced, sound-quality Rioja lookalikes from the undenominated Bodegas Vitorianas, in the Alto Ebro.

Ebro, River

The Ebro flows through Rioja from west to east, entering through the rocky gorge of the Conchas de Haro and leaving near Alfaro in Rioja Baja. Vineyards extend upwards from both sides of the river or lie in the valleys of its seven tributaries, the Tirón, Oja, Najerilla, Iregua, Leza, Cidacos and Alama.

El Coto de Rioja
r w dr res 91, 94, 95, 96

Oyón (Rioja Alavesa). Large *bodega* founded in 1973, later acquired by Alexis Lichine and then by owners of the new BARON DE LEY, it owns 100 hectares of vineyards and 45,000 oak BARRICAS. Red *reservas* and *gran reservas* (100 per cent Tempranillo from the RIOJA ALAVESA), are labelled Coto de Imaz. Among the best were the light, well-balanced '78 and '82, with a deep, raspberry flavour, but recent vintages have been lighter without the same intensity of flavour.

Elciego

Hill village in RIOJA ALAVESA over the Ebro from CENICERO. With steep, narrow streets, and a church dominating the surrounding vineyards, it is famous as the home of the *bodegas* of the MARQUES DE RISCAL.

Estación de Viticultura y Enología

Government laboratory in HARO, working in conjunction with the *consejo regulador*. Its main job is to ensure that wines conform to the standards of the *reglamento*, but it also conducts research into the production of Rioja wines. It has an excellent wine museum.

Faustino, Bodegas

r (p) w dr res ★★→☆☆☆ 89, 90, 91, 93, 94, 95

Oyón (Rioja Alavesa). The Martínez family has been making good wines in Oyón since before 1860, and began bottling them in 1931. Still a family firm, it owns 700 hectares of vineyards in one of the best areas of RIOJA ALAVESA. It does not age its wines overlong in oak, and its excellent *gran reserva*, Faustino I, spends only two years there, followed by more in bottle. There is a light, well-balanced 100 per cent Viura white and the *bodega* markets a *vino joven* (young) red, made in traditional fashion by carbonic maceration: it is a dark, plum colour, with a yeasty nose and a good blackberry flavour reminiscent of Beaujolais Nouveau.

Franco-Españolas, Bodegas

r (p) w dr sw res ☆→☆☆

Logroño (Rioja Alta). Large, established firm with *bodegas* in the heart of Logroño, just across the bridge over the EBRO. It was taken over by RUMASA in 1973 and later resold to entrepreneur Marcos Equizábal. It makes a sweet white Diamante and red Bordón, but the wines are not up to pre-takeover standards.

Fuenmayor

On the main road from LOGROÑO to HARO and close to the Ebro, Fuenmayor, together with CENICERO, is next in importance to HARO among Riojan wine towns.

Gurpegui Muga, Bodegas Luís

r p w dr ★→★★

San Adrián (Rioja Baja). Large family firm founded in 1921 and owning 250 hectares of vineyards in the vicinity of San Adrián. A large supplier of bulk wine, its inexpensive bottled wine is sold under the labels Viñadrián and Gurpegui. The rosé has always been particularly fresh and good. *See also* BODEGAS BERCEO.

Haro

Near the western tip of the region, Haro, a busy little town with a population of 9,000, is the wine capital of RIOJA ALTA and the home of more than a dozen *bodegas*. Built uphill and downhill above the

EBRO, it is a place of narrow streets and stylish old houses, with a wide central square. Points of interest inlcude the wine shops of Juan González Muga, specialising in old and rare vintages and special offers of Riojas from the local *bodegas*. Haro is the headquarters of a government wine laboratory, the ESTACION DE VITICULTURA Y ENOLOGIA. At Briñas, on the road north to Vitoria facing the rocky Conchas de Haro, there is a wine museum displaying bottles from most of the *bodegas* in Rioja and where the wines may also be tasted.

Hormilleja

Village near Nájera in the centre of vineyards producing most of the Garnacha grown in RIOJA ALTA.

Ijalba, Viña

r res w dr p ★★→☆☆☆ *93, 94, 95, 96, 97, 98*

Logroño (Rioja Alta). Founded in 1990, the firm has already established a reputation for the quality of its young wines, like the 100 per cent Tempranillo Solferino made by carbonic maceration. It makes that rarity, a 100 per cent Graciano, and its attractive CRIANZA is the house wine at the Hotel Los Agustinos in Haro.

Labastida

Village in the RIOJA ALAVESA northeast of HARO, and home of one of the best cooperatives in the region.

Labastida, Unión de Cosecheros de

r (p) w dr res ★★→★★★ *89, 91, 94, 95, 96, 98*

Labastida (Rioja Alavesa). The cooperative, founded in 1956 and enlarged in 1965, has some 160 *socios* (members) growing grapes in three of the best areas of the region (Labastida, Samaniego and Villalba). With a total capacity of three million litres, it is one of the few cooperatives in Rioja to possess oak BARRICAS and to bottle its wines. These are sold under the labels Solagüen, Manuel Quintana and Montebuena and are very reasonably priced – and of excellent quality.

Laguardia

This old walled town crowns a hill in the heart of RIOJA ALAVESA, and is a landmark for miles around. Its narrow streets and old, dark houses are honeycombed with small peasant *bodegas*, now mostly disused, and there are large modern wineries on the outskirts. Although it is quiet enough on weekdays, at weekends and on holidays it is a target for visitors from Bilbao and San Sebastián, who come to picnic and to fill their carafes with local wine.

The old baronial house of the Fabulista Samaniego, the 18th-century author of some rather pointless fables, formerly housed a pleasant hotel, but has been converted into a centre for the study of Alavesa wines: the Casa del Vino. Apart from its interesting exhibits on local history as well as viticulture and oenology, it possesses modern laboratories and advises the smaller producers, or *cosecheros*, of the region.

Lagunilla, Bodegas
r (p) w dr res ☆☆

Formerly known for its Viña Herminia *reservas* (now made by Bodegas Viña Herminia in Rioja Baja), the *bodega* was recently bought by Bodegas BERBERANA and is used for making 'country wine' without DO.

LAN, Bodegas
r (p) w dr res ☆☆→☆☆☆ 91, 94, 95, 96

Fuenmayor (Rioja Alta). Large *bodega* founded in 1969, taken over by RUMASA and since resold. The wines have been uneven in quality over recent years, but are much improved, thanks to large investment and modernisation of the *bodega*. They include a fresh white Lan not matured in oak, and good red Lan CRIANZAS and *reservas*. Best are the Lanciano *reservas* made from 85 per cent Tempranillo and 15 per cent Mazuelo.

Líbano, Señorío de
r res ☆☆☆ 89, 91, 92, 94, 95

Sajazarra (Rioja Alta). Small *bodega* making Castillo de Sajazarra *reservas* from grapes grown on its 25 hectares of vineyards. Very oaky, they contain a proportion of Graciano.

Logroño
Capital of the province of La Rioja, Logroño – with a population of 128,000 – is the only large town in the Rioja and the commercial centre of its wine industry. A handsome city positioned by the Ebro, its spacious tree-lined square, the Espolón, is the focus of the Fiesta de SAN MATEO, which is held from September 21 to mark the beginning of the grape-picking season. Logroño is also the headquarters of the *consejo regulador*, of the Grupo de Exportadores and of three of the largest Rioja *bodegas*, FRANCO-ESPAÑOLAS, CAMPO VIEJO and OLARRA. It also possesses numerous good restaurants and hotels.

López Agos, Bodegas *See* Bodegas MARQUES DEL PUERTO

López de Heredia, R Viña Tondonia
r (p) w dr sw res ☆☆→☆☆☆☆☆ 54, 57, 61, 64, 68, 70, 73, 76, 78, 80, 81, 82, 83, 84, 85, 86, 87, 89, 90, 91, 92, 93

Haro (Rioja Alta). Founded in 1877 at the height of the phylloxera epidemic in France, López de Heredia is one of the most traditional of *bodegas*. All its buildings are made from quarried stone, the vessels for making and maturing the wine are mostly cut from American oak, and the cellars, like the famous El Calado, are tunnelled out of the sandstone 17 metres below ground, so that the temperature remains an even 12°C with a relative humidity of 80 per cent all year round.

The wines, made to last with no concessions to modernity, start rather tannic, but age gloriously after long periods in oak. The old white Tondonias, with a subtle blend of oak and fruit, are a revelation to people who think white wines of this age must be flat and oxidised – the '64 is at its peak. The youngest red is the stylish young Cubillo; older reds include Tondonia and Bosconia *reservas*, the latter rather softer and fuller-bodied. Some *reservas* can be described only as classics.

Luberri
r ☆☆→☆☆☆ 94, 95, 96, 98

Elciego (Rioja Alavesa). Small, modern *bodega* with 52 hectares of vineyard, making an excellent young red and CRIANZA.

Marqués de Arienzo
r res ☆☆→☆☆☆ 85, 87, 90, 91, 92, 94, 95

The label used by Bodegas DOMECQ for its excellent wines, both red and white.

Marqués de Cáceres, Union Vitivinícola
r (p) w dr res ★★★ 89, 92, 94, 95

Cenicero (Rioja Alta). The *bodega* was founded in 1970 by Don Enrique Forner, who, with his brother, owns châteaux in the Haut-Médoc. Its methods are more similar to those of Bordeaux than to most of the concerns in the Rioja, since it was planned with advice from Professor Peynaud of Bordeaux University. It describes itself as a *unión vitivinícola*, grapes being supplied by a group of substantial local producers.

The wines are fruity, well-balanced and less oaky than the traditional red Riojas, with a blackberry flavour and long finish. The firm was the first to introduce a new-style white Rioja made by cold fermentation and unaged in cask. Exceptionally light, fresh and fruity, it is still one of the best wines of its type. The *bodega* has now added two CRIANZA whites: 100 per cent Viura, and Antea, which is 90 per cent Viura and 10 per cent Malvasía. Both are attractively clean, fresh and fruity, and have a touch of oak and a long finish. The newly-introduced Gaudium *reserva* ('94), made from Garnacha, Tempranillo and Graciano, is a superb wine.

Marqués de Griñón
r res ☆☆→☆☆☆ 89, 90, 91, 92, 94, 95, 96, 97

Good, fruity 100 per cent Tempranillo wines with vanilla oak, made for the Marqués by Bodegas BERBERANA.

Marqués de Murrieta, Bodegas
r (p) w dr ☆☆→☆☆☆☆☆ 34, 42, 52, 59, 62, 64, 68, 70, 78, 83, 85, 87, 89, 90, 91, 92, 93, 96

Ygay (Rioja Alta). Second only in seniority to the MARQUES DE RISCAL, the *bodega* was founded by the Marqués de Murrieta in Ygay, a village just east of Logroño, in 1872. It remained in the family until some years ago when it was bought by the late Vicente Cebrián, Conde de Creixel.

With Riscal, it has been regarded as the aristocrat of Riojas, and the tradition has been to age the red wines for very long periods in oak. Until new regulations came into force, they were kept in BARRICA and bottled only immediately prior to shipment. The *bodega*'s new owner lovingly restored the old buildings, constructing a new fermentation plant as well as extending the vineyards so as to supply not just 40 per cent of the grapes, as in the past, but the whole requirement – thus making Murrieta a single-estate wine.

Pride of the *reservas* is the superb CASTILLO YGAY, one of the most sought-after and expensive of Spanish wines. It is made only in exceptional years – *see* CASTILLO YGAY for complete list. The quality of recent vintages has not always matched that of the older, but the ripe and fruity '89 saw a return to form. There are also round and luscious white and rosé wines.

Marqués de Riscal, Herederos del

r (p) res ☆☆☆→☆☆☆☆ *64, 65, 68, 70, 71, 73, 76, 78, 82, 86, 88, 89, 91, 92, 93, 94, 95*

Elciego (Rioja Alavesa). Founded in 1860 by Don Camilo Hurtado de Amézaga, the Marqués de Riscal, the *bodega* was designed by a *vigneron* from Bordeaux and was the first in the Rioja to use French methods for making its wines. Then, as now, a proportion of Cabernet Sauvignon was grown, although as elsewhere in RIOJA ALAVESA the preponderant grape is the Tempranillo.

The wines have always been light, stylish and elegant, and more in the style of claret than most Riojas. They have tended to be a little hard when young, but given time in bottle they age graciously, gaining both in fragrance and intensity of flavour. After some disappointing vintages during the mid-Seventies and early Eighties the wines have shown steady improvement and Riscal is again where it belongs – at the top of the ladder. It is difficult to describe vintages such as '52 and '38 as anything but perfect. The remarkable '22, deep in colour, gloriously fragrant and fruity and long in finish, is reminiscent of one of the best old *crus* from St-Emilion.

Riscal has also introduced an exclusive and very expensive Barón de Chirel, made with 50 per cent Cabernet Sauvignon, which ranks among the very best of all Riojas. The *bodega* possesses a library of all the vintages from its inception. The best of the older vintages of the present century were: 1910, '20, '22, '25, '38, '42, '43, '47, '50, '64, '65, '68 and '70.

Riscal makes a little rosé in the Rioja, but its excellent white wine is from Rueda, near Valladolid (*see* 'Castilla-León', page 55).

Marqués del Puerto, Bodegas

r (p w dr) res ☆☆→☆☆☆☆ *85, 87, 88, 89, 91, 93, 94, 95, 97*

Fuenmayor (Rioja Alta). Founded in 1972 as Bodegas López Agos, this is a small concern which makes its wines with some care. The name was changed to Bodegas Marqués del Puerto in 1983 and the firm now belongs to BODEGAS Y BEBIDAS. The red *reservas*, labelled as Marqués del Puerto or Señorío de Agos, have been much praised in Spain.

Martínez Bujanda, Bodegas

r p w dr res ★★→★★★★ *87, 89, 90, 91, 92, 94, 95, 96, 98*

Oyón (Rioja Alavesa). Founded in 1890, this family concern owns

375 hectares of vineyards and moved into one of the most modern and best-equipped wineries of the region in 1984. It exports a higher proportion of its wines than any other concern in Rioja.

One of its most successful wines is a very fruity young (or *joven*) red made in the manner of Beaujolais Nouveau, without time in oak. The *bodegas* also makes a white 100 per cent Viura which is fermented in barrel, an excellent young 100 per cent Garnacha red, and first-rate CONDE DE VALDEMAR *reservas*. *See also* Finca VALPIEDRA.

Martínez Lacuesta, Bodegas
r (p) w dr sw ☆→☆☆☆

Haro (Rioja Alta). This old-established *bodega* in the centre of Haro was founded in 1895 and remains in the family. The *bodega* has a sizeable capacity of some four million litres, with 7,000 oak BARRICAS for maturing the wines. At one time it owned vineyards and made its wine, but this is now bought from local cooperatives for maturation and bottling. Its red wines, once so familiar to travellers on Iberia Airlines, are of two types. The full-bodied CAMPEADOR, in Burgundy-type bottles, contains a high proportion of Garnacha, while the lighter Martínez Lacuesta is made with 75 per cent Tempranillo. The *reservas* and *gran reservas* of both types are often excellent wines.

Miguel Merino, Bodegas
res ☆☆→☆☆☆ 94, 95, 96, 97

Briones (Rioja Alta). This tiny new *bodega* has just 248 oak BARRICAS, but the wines are made with devotion by the owner, Miguel Merino, from grapes bought in from a single vineyard (94 per cent Tempranillo and 6 per cent others). These wines have been well-received in Spain.

Monte Real
r ☆☆☆

Among the best of the red wines made by Bodegas RIOJANAS, this is made with a high proportion of Tempranillo, both from CENICERO in Rioja Alta and from RIOJA ALAVESA.

Montecillo, Bodegas
r (p) w dr ☆☆→☆☆☆ 82, 86, 89, 90, 91, 94, 95

Navarrete (Rioja Alta). Founded in 1874, Bodegas Montecillo now belongs to the sherry firm of Osborne (*see* page 167). It owns 77 hectares of vineyards and a modern vinification plant near NAVARRETE, and *bodegas* for maturing its wines in CENICERO.

The wines are sold as Montecillo, Cumbrero and the excellent Viña Monty *reserva*.

Muerza, Bodegas
r (w dr) ☆☆ 89, 90, 91, 93, 94, 95, 96

San Adrián (Rioja Baja). Owned by Bodegas Príncipe de Viana (*see* 'Navarra and the Basque Country', page 120) the *bodega* makes sound and modestly priced RIOJA BAJA reds sold as Rioja Vega.

Muga, Bodegas
r w dr res ★★★ *85, 87, 88, 89, 90, 91, 94, 95*

Haro (Rioja Alta). This small, family firm was founded in 1926, but moved to a new *bodega* near the station in HARO in 1971. It is entirely unlike the great new *bodegas* constructed during the Rioja boom of the 1970s in that it started with only 500 BARRICAS – the minimum entitling it to export its wines – but such has been its subsequent success that the number has grown to 12,000. Everything is done in traditional style by a tiny and dedicated workforce, headed by the Muga brothers themselves, and its wines reflect the care that goes into their making – they are currently among the best in Rioja.

Those wines labelled as Muga, made with grapes grown in the firm's own vineyards and others bought from farmers in Abalos, are exceptionally light and fragrant, while the Prado Enea is a deeper-coloured, velvety and more fully bodied wine, sold in bottles with wax capsules. A new introduction is the superb Torre Muga ('94, '95), made with selected grapes (Tempranillo, Mazuelo, Graciano) from its own vineyards.

The firm also produces small quantities of a dry white wine and of a light sparkling wine made by the Champagne method (*see* 'Sparkling Wines', page 194).

Murua, Bodegas
r res ☆☆→☆☆☆☆ *90, 91, 94, 95*

Elciego (Rioja Alavesa). Small *bodega* making worthwhile, Alavesa-type red wines.

Nájera
On the hilly southern fringes of the RIOJA ALTA, west of Logroño, this picturesque little township is the site of a former residence of the Kings of Navarra; and the 11th-century monastery of Santa María contains the tombs of many of the kings and queens of Navarra, Castile and León.

Navajas, Bodegas
w dr r res ★★→★★★ *93, 94, 95, 96*

Navarrete (Rioja Alta). One of the best-selling brands in the UK, Navajas is known for its full and fruity red wines with vanilla oak. It also makes a fruity and first-rate white Viura aged in oak, and a cherry-red, vanilla-flavoured CRIANZA *rosado*.

Navarrete
Hill town and winemaking centre southwest of Logroño. It was the site of the battle in 1367 in which the Black Prince and Peter the Cruel defeated Henry of Trastamara, and possesses a fine 16th-century church and baronial houses.

Oak
The pioneer of the oak barrel for maturing wines, now in some ways the 'trademark' of Rioja, was Manuel Quintano, who, in 1787, encouraged a group of producers in LABASTIDA to make their

wines along French lines. The experiments were short-sightedly discontinued; and it was not until the phylloxera epidemic of the late 19th century, followed by an influx of *négociants* from Bordeaux, that ageing in oak became standard practice.

Because of its dense, even texture, which permits slow transpiration of oxygen, the favourite type of oak is American, though French oak from Nevers and Alliers is increasingly being used. Maturation is much faster in new barrels, and although the casks are systematically scoured, washed and disinfected after each racking of the wines (decantation from the lees), the pores of the wood gradually become clogged. It's a fact that goes largely unappreciated by visitors to the *bodegas*, who exclaim at the time the older, more traditional *reservas* spend in wood. Owing to the high cost of replacing them, some of the barrels in the older *bodegas* are over 50 years old.

Perhaps it is because the casks in the newer *bodegas* are so much richer in essential oils and resins, thereby adding an excessively oaky bouquet to the wines, that the canard about oak essence took hold. Such artificial extracts do exist, but no self-respecting *bodega* uses them; in fact, it would be heavily penalised if caught doing so. The fact that new concerns have invested millions of pounds in oak BARRICAS hardly supports the stories of its widespread employment.

Although maturation in oak, in combination with adequate bottle age, is essential in making good red wines, its use in making white Riojas has declined, since the producers found that it is a great deal less expensive to make the fresh, young white wines (so popular abroad) without maturing them in oak. Fortunately, there has been something of a return to oak-aged whites, and also to fermenting white wines in oak.

Oja, River
Tributary of the EBRO, flowing into it at HARO, which has given its name to the region.

Olarra, Bodegas
r (p) w dr sw res ☆☆

Logroño (Rioja Alta). Founded in 1972 by a group of Spanish industrialists. The *bodegas*, on the outskirts of Logroño and in the shape of a three-pointed star (symbolising the three subregions), are among the largest in the region, equipped with stainless-steel fermentation tanks and highly sophisticated computerised systems for controlling the flow of the must and other operations. Maturation is, however, carried out by traditional methods in 25,000 oak BARRICAS. Wines include white, rosé and red Añares and a young red Otoñal. Quality has been disappointing but is improving, and the Cerro Añon *reserva* is very good.

Ollauri
Small village in the RIOJA ALTA, just south of HARO, and the birthplace of Bodegas PATERNINA and BERBERANA, both of which still maintain their original cellars there for ageing their wines in bottle.

Ondarre, Bodegas
w dr r res ☆☆→☆☆☆☆ 93, 94, 95

Viana (Rioja Baja). Reliable wines, including a 100 per cent oak-aged white Viura and a 100 per cent Tempranillo *reserva*.

Oyón
Industrial town in the RIOJA ALAVESA, across the river from LOGROÑO and the home of the Bodegas EL COTO and FAUSTINO MARTINEZ.

Palacio, Bodegas
r (p) w dr sw ☆☆☆☆ 89, 90, 91, 94, 95, 96

Laguardia (Rioja Alavesa). Founded in 1894 by Cosme Palacio, the old *bodegas* was bought by Seagram in 1973 and moved to a modern *bodega* just outside LAGUARDIA, but saw a drastic decline in quality – probably because wine was bought in from co-ops. Since 1980, when the firm began making its wine, and after a management buy-out in 1987, standards have steadily improved. The Glorioso CRIANZA, *reserva* and *gran reserva* are now excellent wines. The young red *vino del año* ('wine of the year') is fresh and attractive and the Cosme Palacio is a first-rate wine.

Palacios Remondo, Bodegas
r w dr (p) res ☆☆→☆☆☆☆ 91, 94, 95, 96, 98

Mendavia (Rioja Baja). An old-standing family firm known for pioneering young varietal wines. When at their best the red Herencia Remondo *reservas* are both elegant and complex.

Paternina, Federico
r (p) w dr res ☆→☆☆

Haro (Rioja Alta). Founded in 1896 by Don Federico Paternina Josué, this was one of the largest and most successful firms in the Rioja, before its purchase by the RUMASA group and subsequent sale to Don Marcos Eguizábal. It has moved successively from the original cellars in OLLAURI to a larger *bodega* bought from a Haro cooperative and to the present great, modern plant, with its 40,000 BARRICAS capable of maturing 25 million litres of wine. The red BANDA AZUL CRIANZA is one of the best-known wines in Spain, but standards are not as high as before the takeovers. Probably the best wines are the white Banda Oro and the red Viña Vial *reservas*. *See also* CONDE DE LOS ANDES.

The glory of Paternina is its rare old vintages, kept in the deep cellars of the old *bodega* at Ollauri. No system of stars could do justice to such beautiful old wines as the 1902, '10, '20, '35, '47 and '59.

Ramón Bilbao
r res ☆☆

Haro (Rioja Alta). Maker of red wines, including a Viña Turzaballa *gran reserva*.

Real Divisa, Bodegas
r (p) w dr ☆☆→☆☆☆ 87, 90, 94, 95

Abalos (Rioja Alta). A *bodega* of some note in a small enclave of

RIOJA ALTA to the north of the Ebro, producing some worthwhile red wines made mainly from the Tempranillo and sold as Marqués de Legarda.

Remelluri, Granja de Nuestra Señora de
r (w dr) res ☆☆☆ 91, 93, 94, 95

Ribas (Rioja Alavesa). This small, family-owned *bodega* was founded by Don Jaime Rodríguez in 1968. With 70 hectares of vineyards planted high up on the slopes of the Sierra Cantábrica, it is one of the few in Rioja to make its wines entirely from its own grapes – a typical *coupage* being 90 per cent Tempranillo, 5 per cent Garnacha and 5 per cent Mazuelo and Graciano. Made by traditional methods, they are soft and fruity with a long finish and among the very best Riojas. Gifted oenologist Telmo Rodríguez has now introduced a white wine made from a variety of grapes other than Viura.

Remírez de Ganuza, Bodega
res ☆☆☆→☆☆☆☆ 92, 94,

Samaniego (Rioja Alavesa). The wines from this small *bodega*, founded by Fernándo Remirez in 1989, are made exclusively with hand-sorted grapes from old vines (90 per cent Tempranillo and 8 per cent Graciano) and are already among the most sought after wines from Rioja.

Rioja Alavesa
DO ca r (w dr) ☆☆→☆☆☆☆☆

The smallest of the three subregions of the DO Rioja, Rioja Alavesa is located in the province of Alava and extends north of the River Ebro, from near the Conchas de Haro to a line a little east of Logroño.

Because of the temperate climate, the southerly exposure of the vineyards and the composition of the soil, which is almost entirely calcareous clay, Rioja Alavesa produces some of the best wines from the whole region – in the opinion of many experts, *the* best. Another factor is the very high proportion of Tempranillo used in making the red wines. The main production centres are at LABASTIDA in the west, and ELCIEGO, LAGUARDIA and OYON towards the east. In general, the red Alavesa wines are big, fruity and soft (though one or two are very light) with a pronounced and characteristic Tempranillo nose, somewhat resembling that of Cabernet Sauvignon, but they mature more rapidly than those from Rioja Alta and do not last as long.

Rioja Alavesa also produces smaller amounts of white wine with a good acid balance, made mainly from Viura and Malvasía.

Rioja Alta
DO ca r (p) w dr sw ☆☆→☆☆☆☆☆

Together with RIOJA ALAVESA, the subregion of Rioja Alta produces the best Rioja wines. It lies within the province of La Rioja, extending (apart from a small northern enclave around ABALOS) south of the Ebro from the Conchas de Haro in the west to just beyond LOGROÑO in the east. The soils are more mixed than those of the Rioja Alavesa, comprising calcareous clay, ferruginous clay and alluvial silt. On the basis of this and of the microclimate, oenologists have subdivided the area, from west to east, into the zones of Cuzcurrita, HARO, San Asensio and CENICERO-FUENMAYOR. The wines from the wetter and hillier area of the west tend to be more acidic and lower in alcohol that those from Cenicero, where there is a transition in climate from humid to semi-arid and a change to predominantly calcareous soils, particularly suitable for growing the Tempranillo grape.

The main production centres are HARO in the west, CENICERO and FUENMAYOR in the centre, and NAVARRETE in the east.

Although the Tempranillo is the basic grape of Rioja Alta, as of Rioja Alavesa, traditionally its red wines contain a higher proportion of Mazuelo, Graciano and Garnacha, and tend to be brisker and fresher on the nose, a little more acidic and longer-lasting. As in Rioja Alavesa, the whites are made mainly from Viura and Malvasía, with some Garnacha Blanca. It is difficult to be more specific about the proportions, since the large *bodegas* sometimes use a blend of wines made from grapes grown both in the Rioja Alta and Rioja Alavesa.

Rioja Alta, Bodegas La
r (p) w dr res ☆☆☆→☆☆☆☆☆ *82, 89, 91, 93, 94, 95*

Haro (Rioja Alta). A medium-sized family concern founded in 1890, and one of the first to build a *bodega* in the hallowed area near the railway station in HARO, La Rioja Alta has consistently maintained the quality and prestige of its wines. It owns 300 hectares of vineyards, both in RIOJA ALTA and RIOJA BAJA, and possesses 55,000 BARRICAS for ageing its wines, made by strictly traditional methods. These include a characterful CRIANZA, Viña Alberdi (actually aged in oak for as long as many *bodegas*' *reserva* and now sold as a *reserva*); the fruity, full-bodied and velvety red VIÑA ARDANZA (named after one of the five families which founded the *bodega*); a lighter, very stylish Viña Arana; and the excellent 904 and 890 *reservas*. Its traditional white Rioja aged in cask, the Viña Ardanza Blanco Reserva, has been discontinued.

Rioja Baja
DO r (w dr) ☆→☆☆☆

The largest of the subregions of the DO Rioja, Rioja Baja extends from just east of LOGROÑO along the EBRO to ALFARO in the southeast. The larger part of the area lies in the province of La Rioja, south of the river, but there is also a narrow strip in Navarra to the north. The soils of Rioja Baja are almost entirely composed of alluvial silt and ferruginous clay; the climate is semi-arid, of the Mediterranean type, and the predominant grape is the red Garnacha Tinta, which yields musts high in alcohol and extract, but quick to oxidise. For these reasons the typical wines are coarser than those of the cooler and hillier RIOJA ALAVESA and RIOJA ALTA, and are often used for blending, to confer alcoholic degree and body. Nevertheless, the bold departure of Bodegas BERBERANA in planting Tempranillo and Viura in calcareous soils in the higher part of the area, particularly at Monte Yerga near Aldeanueva del Ebro, proved very successful.

The main centres of production are San Adrián, ALFARO, ARNEDO and Aldeanueva del Ebro, a sun-baked town which produces better asparagus and peppers than wine and is curiously named – it is not, as the name implies, either a hamlet, new, or near the Ebro.

The typical wines are full-bodied reds, high in alcohol and more akin to those of Ribera Baja (*see* 'Navarra', page 120) than the delicate growths of RIOJA ALTA or RIOJA ALAVESA.

Rioja Santiago, Bodegas
r p w res ☆→☆☆☆ *92, 94, 95, 96, 98*

Haro (Rioja Alta). Old-established firm with *bodegas* in HARO, just across the bridge over the EBRO, recently taken over by Bodegas LAN. The firm developed a large market in the US for its bottled *sangría*, labelled as Monsieur Henri; it was eventually taken over by its American distributor, Pepsi Cola, but has since reverted to Spanish control. Its best wines are the red Gran Condal and Vizconde de Ayala *reservas*.

Rioja Vega
r res ★★

Reliable red wine from Bodegas MUERZA.

Riojanas, Bodegas
r (p) w dr s/sw res ☆☆→☆☆☆ *82, 85, 87, 89, 91, 92, 93, 94, 95, 96*

Cenicero (Rioja Alta). This large and old-established *bodega* was founded in 1890 and built in a flamboyant style with a castellated keep. Advice from Bordeaux was taken and there were French technicians working there until the early years of the Second World War.

The *bodega* draws its grapes from both RIOJA ALTA and RIOJA ALAVESA, from some 200 hectares of vineyards owned either by the company or its shareholders and also from private farmers. Small amounts of selected Garnacha grapes from RIOJA BAJA are also used. Its wines include a dry white Canchales, a semi-sweet white Albina, and an inexpensive and very basic young red Canchales. It also makes good VIÑA ALBINA *reservas*; but perhaps the most interesting wines of all are the red MONTE REAL *reservas* which are made with a sizeable proportion (80 per cent) of Tempranillo from Rioja Alavesa.

Among the best of the older vintages were 1890, 1915, '22, '34, '42, '50, '56, '64, '66, '68 and '70.

Roda, Bodegas
res ☆☆☆→☆☆☆☆☆ *92, 94, 95, 96, 98*

Haro (Rioja Alta). Founded in 1989 by a Catalan couple, who decided that only in the Barrio de la Estación in Haro could they create their dream wines. The *bodega* makes only superb and costly *reservas*, all from hand-picked and sorted grapes from old vines vinified in French oak vats. Roda I has the edge on Roda II, but both are dark, concentrated and hugely fruity. A new premium Cirsión was introduced in 1998.

Rumasa

At its peak this great Spanish conglomerate, with extensive interests in banking, hotels and property as well as wines of all types, had taken over the important Rioja firms of PATERNINA, FRANCO-ESPAÑOLAS, LAN and BERBERANA. After its expropriation in 1983 the firms were first run by the government and finally sold to private interests, the first two to a Spanish businessman, Marcos Eguizábal, whose family is from the region. *See also* 'Sherry', page 170.

Salceda, Viña

r res ☆☆→☆☆☆ *89, 91, 92, 95, 96*

Elciego (Rioja Alavesa). The *bodega*, just beyond the bridge over the EBRO on the road from CENICERO to ELCIEGO, is of modern construction, dating from 1974. It is equipped with stainless-steel fermentation tanks, together with the traditional oak BARRICAS for ageing the wines.

Of medium size, Viña Salceda makes only red wine with a high proportion of Tempranillo: a Viña Salceda CRIANZA and Conde de la Salceda *reservas* and *gran reservas* are of good quality. The *bodega* has recently been taken over by the large Navarra firm of Julian CHIVITE.

San Mateo, Festival of

One of many such festivals in the wine-growing districts, the Fiesta de San Mateo begins in LOGROÑO on September 21st, rather before the official start of grape-picking on October 10th, and lasts for a week, with a uniformed band parading the streets, bullfights and firework displays in the Plaza del Espolón at midnight.

San Vicente de la Sonsierra

Picturesque village near LABASTIDA dominated by a ruined castle, with magnificent views over the River EBRO and across Rioja.

Santa Daría, Cooperativa Vinícola de

r w dr p ★★

Cenicero (Rioja Alta). Well-equipped cooperative, one of the best in the Rioja, bottling and selling its wines, ranging from *jóvenes* (young, unoaked) to *gran reservas*, under the label Santa Daría.

Santo Domingo de la Calzada

Just outside the DO Rioja, Santo Domingo, south of HARO, is on the old pilgrim route from France to Santiago de Compostela and its Parador is one of the most pleasant places to stay when visiting the region. The 12th-century cathedral incorporates an unusual feature: a live cock and hen housed behind a grille high on one wall, in commemoration of a miracle wrought by St Dominic, patron saint of pilgrims.

Sierra Cantabria, Bodegas
r res w dr p ☆☆☆ *90, 91, 94, 95, 96*
San Vicente de la Sonsierra (Rioja Alta). Small *bodega* known for its excellent young red Murmurón, made by carbonic maceration, and fruity and well-balanced red Sierra Cantabria.

Torre de Oña
DO r res ☆☆☆ *90, 91, 94*
Laguardia (Rioja Alavesa). Small *bodega* with 50 hectares located below the old walled town of Laguardia. It now belongs to LA RIOJA ALTA but it maintains its individuality. It makes only one wine: the red Barón de Oña *reserva*, which is delicate, complex and fruity, and aged in French oak.

Unión Vitivinícola *See* MARQUES DE CACERES

Valpiedra, Finca
res ☆☆☆→☆☆☆☆ *94, 95*
Cenicero (Rioja Alta). A state-of-the-art winery recently built by MARTINEZ BUJANDA in a bend of the Ebro near Cenicero, to produce premium quality single-vineyard *reservas*. The first (1994) vintage was outstanding – dense in colour, vividly fruity and aromatic, and long on the finish.

Viña Albina
r ☆☆☆
Well-known red wine from Bodegas RIOJANAS.

Viña Ardanza
r ☆☆☆
Consistently satisfying red Riojas, smooth, fruity and full-bodied, from Bodegas LA RIOJA ALTA.

Viña Bosconia
r ☆☆☆
Excellent Rioja from LOPEZ DE HEREDIA, using grapes grown in its Bosconia vineyards on the south bank of the EBRO.

Viña Pomal
r ☆☆→☆☆☆
Full-bodied red Rioja from Bodegas BILBAINAS made with grapes from its vineyards in Leza in the RIOJA ALAVESA.

Viña Real
r ☆☆☆
Excellent red RIOJA ALAVESA *reserva* from the COMPAÑIA VINICOLA DEL NORTE DE ESPAÑA, made in an outlying *bodega* in ELCIEGO.

Viña Tondonia
r w dr ☆☆☆→☆☆☆☆
First-rate and long-lasting red and white Riojas from Bodegas LOPEZ DE HEREDIA.

Viñedos de la Marquesa
r (w dr) res ☆☆ *91, 94, 95, 96*

Villabuena (Rioja Alavesa). Formerly known as SMS, the initials of three families: Samaniego, Milans del Bosch and Solana. Founded before 1900 and originally called the Marqués de la Solana, the *bodega* is now owned by the Milans del Bosch family and has a capacity of 300,000 litres and 1,400 oak BARRICAS.

The wines, all red, are made mainly with grapes grown in the 50 hectares of vineyards belonging to the family. Until 1981 the grapes were not de-stalked, so that the old wines, fermented in oak vats, are dark in colour and mature more slowly than most from RIOJA ALAVESA. Those currently available, labelled as Valserrano, have a hint of cedar in the nose and are fragrant, full-bodied, with a lot of fruit and a long, somewhat tannic finish.

Ygay
Hamlet in the Rioja Alta a little east of LOGROÑO. Since 1872 the cellars of *bodegas* MARQUES DE MURRIETA, a business established 20 years earlier, have stood on its outskirts on the Ygay estate.

WINE AND FOOD
It is perhaps a bit pretentious to talk of Riojan 'cuisine'. What the area offers is a range of genuinely regional dishes based on the excellent lamb, pork, kid and spicy *chorizo* sausage, and fresh vegetables in season. When André Simon first wrote about Rioja, he was, in fact, more enthusiastic about the vegetables than the wines, and it is still an experience to visit the great open market in Logroño.

The meals served to guests in the *bodegas* themselves, often in a great cellar lined with casks, are simple and well-designed to show off the wines, and usually begin with fresh local asparagus or a *menestra* of vegetables, followed by small lamb chops cooked over glowing vine shoots and ending with the ubiquitous *flan* (cream caramel) or the luscious peaches preserved in syrup. Such simple delights are not to be despised, however. When a few years ago the celebrated chef Paul Bocuse was engaged by the COMPAÑIA VINICOLA DEL NORTE DE ESPAÑA to prepare its centenary banquet, the story goes that, having sampled the *patatas a la riojana* (*see* below) prepared by the *bodega's* regular cook, he asked why he had been sent for.

Alubias con chorizo A rib-warming stew made with haricot or butter beans, chopped onions, garlic, olive oil and highly cured *chorizo* sausage, further seasoned with sweet paprika powder and parsley. This calls for a full-bodied two- or three-year-old red, or a *jarra* of the local house wine.

Bacalao a la riojana Dried cod cooked with olive oil, onions, garlic, strips of canned red pepper and sweet paprika powder. Drink one of the traditional oaky white Riojas with sufficient character to stand up to the rich assortment of flavours: for example, a white Tondonia from López de Heredia.

Cabrito asado Roast kid Rioja style. This is a good chance to show off the qualities of one of the many red *reservas*.

Callos a la riojana Highly spiced tripe, Riojan style.

Cardo Cardoon, a celery-like vegetable, served braised as a first course. Choose from among the many styles of white Rioja, perhaps one with oak, such as Monopole from CVNE.

Chorizo a la brasa *Chorizo*, the famous spicy cured pepper sausage, often homemade, and roasted whole. Since this is an extremely hot dish, a chilled glass of one of the young white Riojas, such as the Marqués de Cáceres or Faustino V, makes a refreshing accompaniment.

Chuletas de cordero al sarmiento Small lamb chops grilled over glowing vine shoots and served in the *bodegas* to set off the better reds and *reservas*.

Cordero lechal asado Milk-fed baby lamb roasted in a baker's oven. Choose the best red *reserva* you can run to, from Riscal, La Rioja Alta, López de Heredia, Muga, Riojanas, CVNE etc.

Espárragos Rioja Baja grows some of the best asparagus in Spain, which is served as a starter either with vinaigrette or mayonnaise. Take your choice of the dry white wines.

Malvices Tiny birds (red-wings) fried crisp and eaten whole. A light red Alavesa wine.

Melocotones en almíbar Particularly large and luscious local peaches preserved in syrup. Try a sweet or semi-sweet wine, such as the Diamante from Franco-Españolas.

Menestra de verduras a la riojana A mixed vegetable dish made from whatever happens to be in season, such as broad beans and peas, together with chopped onions, tomatoes, bacon or ham, seasoning and sometimes hard-boiled eggs. It is cooked in olive oil and light red wine. Try the Viñadrián *rosado* from Bodegas Gurpegui Muga.

Morcilla dulce *Morcilla* is a blood sausage akin to black pudding, but this version is made with cinnamon, other sweet spices and a little sugar. It is usually a first course, but anything but a sweet or semi-sweet white wine would seem tart.

Patatas a la riojana Potatoes in a clear orange-coloured sauce with *chorizo* sausage.

Picadillo A variant of *chorizo a la brasa*, the filling being ground, cooked and served hot. This calls for a chilled and cooling dry white: try Banda Dorada from Paternina, or the dry Lan.

Pimientos de piquillo rellenos a la riojana Regional variant on stuffed peppers, filled with a mixture of ground pork, beaten egg, nutmeg, garlic, parsley and a little pepper and salt, fried in hot olive oil and served in a piquant sauce. Order a full-bodied and robust red.

Pochas riojanas Substantial stew made from a local variety of haricot bean, allowed to fatten in the pod but not dried, and cooked with *chorizo*. Best eaten with a *jarra* of the local red house wine or a robust bottle of Rioja Baja.

Quesos (*cheeses*) The best local cheeses are the soft Camerano made from goats' milk and the Idiazábal from the Basque Country, semi-hard and made from unpasteurised ewes' milk.

Revuelto de ajos tiernos Eggs scrambled with tender young garlic shoots. An oaky or slightly oaky white Rioja, such as the CVNE Monopole, balances this very well.

Sopa de ajo con huevos A traditional Castilian garlic soup, seasoned with sweet paprika powder and thickened with bread and beaten egg. Better to leave the table wine for later and ask for a glass of *fino* sherry.

Tapas *Embuchados* (pork sausages), *lecherillas* (sweetbreads) and *champiñones a la plancha* (grilled mushrooms) are typical.

HOTELS

Arnedo Its hotels are the three-star Victoria and two-star Virrey.

Calahorra There is a comfortable *parador* here, the *Marco Fabio Quintiliano*.

Haro Now boasts a good hotel, *Los Agustinos*, housed in an old convent.

Logroño Recommended hotels are the four-star *Melia Bracos* and *Carlton Rioja*, the three-star *Ciudad de Logroño* and the new *Herencia Rioja*.

Santo Domingo de la Calzada *Parador*, converted from an old pilgrim hospice.

RESTAURANTS

Arnedo *Sopitas* (tunnelled into the cliff with individual dining alcoves; try the excellent *revuelto de ajos*).

Briones *Los Cuatro Arcos* (home cooking, modest prices, sensational *menestra* on Sundays).

Calahorra *Parador de Marco Quintiliano* (regional dishes and wines); *La Taberna de la Cuarta Esquina* (small restaurant with inventive cooking).

Ezcaray *El Echaurren* is probably the best restaurant in the region (vegetable soup, hake fillets in sauce, prawn croquettes).

Fuenmayor *Mesón Chuchi*, *Asador Alameda*.

Haro *Beethoven I, II* and *III* (good regional cooking, especially sweetbreads and *cocochas*); *Terete* (the classical Haro restaurant, in simple surroundings, serving marvellous roast baby lamb and with a long list of *reservas*. Now also selling take-away food).

Laguardia *Posada Mayor de Migueloa* (in an old baronial house).

Logroño *Avenida 21* (probably the best in Logroño); *Casa Emilio*; *El Señorío del Jamón*; *El Cachetero* (prestigious, but not what it once was); *Meridiana*; *Las Cubanas* (typical Riojan food, low prices with wine included); *Sidrería San Gregorio* (cider from the barrel, best beef in Logroño); *Robinson's English Pub* (for dancing and perhaps a late nightcap).

Oyón *Mesón de la Cueva* (good regional food served in atmospheric surroundings).

San Vicente de la Sonsierra *Casa Toni* (traditional dishes and specialities – breasts of quail in vermouth, truffles, venison and salmon).

Santo Domingo de la Calzada *El Rincón de Emilio* (extremely popular; its speciality is *callos a la riojana*).

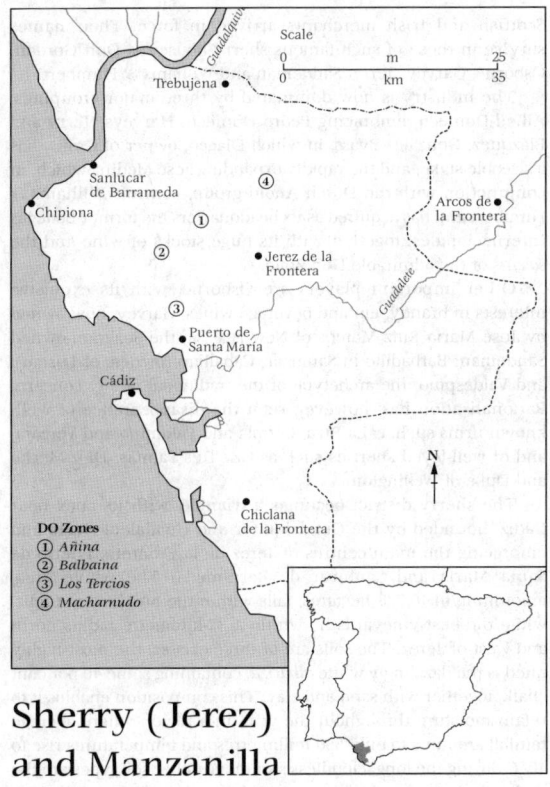

Sherry (Jerez) and Manzanilla

Sherry is, of course, the classical Spanish wine, and has long had particularly close associations with Britain. The great sherry boom took place with the active participation of British merchants, many of whom settled in Jerez. Further than this, the UK consumes more sherry than Spain and, closely followed by the Netherlands, is still the largest foreign market.

In common with most other fortified wines and spirits, sherry has recently suffered something of a setback – but this is not the first in its long history and its popularity and sales are again on the increase. A glass of chilled *fino* remains the most satisfactory preliminary to a meal – the least likely to interfere with what follows. For a wine of such character and one so expensive to make, sherry of all types remains extremely reasonably priced.

The wines were well-known even in Roman times, but it was Sir Francis Drake's raid on Cádiz in 1587 and the seizure of some 2,900 pipes (110-gallon barrels) which firmly established them in England. The British presence had begun to be felt after the expulsion of the Jews from Spain by the Catholic Monarchs in 1492; and during the late 18th and early 19th centuries, English,

Scottish and Irish merchants arrived in force. Their names survive in those of such famous sherry houses as Duff Gordon, Osborne, Garvey, Terry, Sandeman and Williams & Humbert.

The industry is now dominated by three major groupings: Allied-Domecq, embracing Pedro Domecq, Harveys, Terry and Blázquez; González-Byass, in which Diageo, owner of Crofts, has a sizeable stake; and the rapidly expanding José Medina which, in conjunction with the Dutch Ahold group, controls Williams & Humbert and has acquired as its headquarters the former Bodegas Internacionales, together with its huge stocks of wine and the *soleras* of the admirable Don Zoilo.

Other important players are Osborne, with its extensive interests in brandy, gin and beverage wines; Garvey, now owned by José María Ruíz Mateos of New RUMASA; the Seagram-owned Sandeman; Barbadillo in Sanlúcar; Caballero (owners of Lustau); and Valdespino, the archetype of the traditional family concern. Rationalisation has, however, seen the disappearance of well-known firms such as La Riva, Bertola and Palomino and Vergara, and of well-loved sherries such as CZ, Tres Palmas, Diez-Mérito and Duke of Wellington.

The sherry district occupies a triangle, with its apex near Cádiz, bounded by the Guadalquivír and Guadalete rivers and embracing the main centres of Jerez de la Frontera, Puerto de Santa María and Sanlúcar de Barrameda. The whole area, amounting to 10,723 hectares, falls within the province of Cádiz, while the best vineyards lie within a 32-kilometre radius north and west of Jerez. The soils are of three classes: the most highly rated is the dazzlingly white *albariza*, containing some 40 per cent chalk, together with sand and clay. This composition enables it to retain moisture throughout the year, in a region where average rainfall amounts to only 550 millimetres and temperatures rise to 40°C during the long, cloudless summers. Other soil types are the darker *barro* and a sandy *arena*, which are planted mainly with Moscatel grapes.

The sherry grape *par excellence* is the white Palomino, which grows best in the chalky *albariza* and is used for all the different types of sherry and almost exclusively for the *finos*. Next in importance is the Pedro Ximénez, which can, as in Montilla (*see* page 109), produce excellent dry wines, but is principally used in Jerez for sweet dessert wines. Smaller amounts of Moscatel are also grown for sweet sherries.

Sherry owes its entirely individual character to the method by which it is made. Unlike table wines it is matured with free access to the atmosphere, in a loosely stoppered cask with an air space above the liquid. This would ordinarily result in fairly rapid oxidation, were it not that the new wine spontaneously grows a *flor* (or 'flower') on the surface of the liquid.

This layer of yeasts both regulates the access of air to the must and eliminates harmful vinegar-producing bacteria. The growth varies according to the type of wine: it is thickest with *finos* (and even more so with the *manzanillas* from Sanlúcar de Barrameda) and less vigorous with the fuller-bodied *olorosos*, which are soon fortified to kill the yeasts and to protect the wine during its long physico-chemical maturation. The other difference between the making of table wines and sherry is that sherry is aged by the *solera* system: the progressive blending of older and younger wines. The *solera* consists of long rows of oak butts which are arranged in the *bodega* in tiers. Each row of butts or 'scale' contains wine of the same type but of different age. When wine is required for shipment or bottling, it is drawn off from the butts at the bottom containing the oldest wine. The contents are then made good from the 'scale' immediately preceding it in age, and so on through the system. In this fashion, there is regular 'refreshment' of older wine with younger, and as Richard Ford explained in 1846, 'houses are enabled to supply for any number of years exactly that particular colour, flavour, body etc, which particular customers demand'.

With few exceptions, then, there are no vintages in sherry, and a description such as 'Solera 1847' refers to the year in which the *solera* was first laid down.

The basic styles of sherry are the dry and light *finos*, such as Tío Pepe or La Ina, drunk chilled as an apéritif; the rather fuller *amontillados*, and the dark, fully bodied *olorosos*, the most maderised and fragrant of the wines. In their natural state *olorosos*, such as Río Viejo, are completely dry and are best drunk before a meal; but they are often blended with sweet wine to make a dessert sherry or Cream, of which one of the best known is Bristol Cream. This does not exhaust the possibilities, however, and other varieties such as *palo cortado*, Medium and Pale Cream are described in the A–Z listing.

Manzanilla from Sanlúcar de Barrameda, though made by similar methods and from the same grapes, is no longer officially allowed to be described as sherry.

In the past, it was very much a question of making the wine and then waiting to see how it would develop. Modern methods have enabled the *bodegas* to take these decisions at a much earlier stage; and in the latest of the continuous vinification plants, wine destined as a *fino* is drawn off after the lightest crushing of the grapes, which are then more firmly pressed to obtain the must for the *olorosos*.

In all essentials, sherry continues to be made along strictly traditional lines, but there have been many other innovations in recent years. González-Byass has instituted a programme for eliminating plant diseases by the cloning (vegetative reproduction) of virus-free vines, and the bacchanalian rite of treading the grapes with nail-studded boots has given way to modern horizontal or continuous presses. The wine is increasingly (but not always) fermented in temperature-controlled stainless-steel tanks rather than in butts, and is no longer shipped in cask, but bottled in the *bodega* first.

Quite apart from visits to the *bodegas*, the sherry region is a delightful one in which to spend a holiday. There are the Atlantic beaches of places like Puerto de Santa María, Rota and Chipiona; the great nature reserve of the Coto Doñana across the Guadalquivir; the rugged mountains and hunting of the Sierra de

Cádiz; the historic buildings of Cádiz and Sevilla; and by no means least, the superb seafood from the Bay of Cádiz. Jerez is at its best in the late spring, or in the early autumn at harvest time.

From the UK there are direct flights to Jerez; from elsewhere the quickest way to reach the area is to fly to Madrid and then on to Jerez by an internal flight or by the fast and luxurious high-speed train; alternatively, one may fly to Sevilla, 84 kilometres to the north by the A4 *autopista*, and hire a car. Once there, a car is not a necessity, as there is a local electric train to Puerto de Santa María and bus services to other places.

The larger *bodegas*, such as Pedro Domecq, González-Byass and Williams & Humbert, are well-organised for visits, which usually end with a generous tasting. Visiting hours are normally 9.30–13.00, but it is always advisable to check by letter or telephone beforehand. A letter of introduction from a wine merchant or shipper helps to smooth the way if you are planning to visit smaller establishments.

As to the vineyards, good views (as well as spectacular panoramas) can be found of the famous areas of Macharnudo and Carrascal to the north of Jerez by branching off the A4 from Sevilla at Las Cabezas and following the hilly by-road. Follow this almost lunar landscape of whitish sunbaked clay, by way of Lebrija and Trebujena and into Jerez.

Serving Sherry

Sherry is often ruined by improper serving and storage, especially fresh and delicate *finos* which are easily spoilt by oxidation. *All* sherries should be served in a glass tapering towards the top and large enough to be filled only a third or half full to allow for the development of the bouquet (*see* COPITA, page 160). *Fino* begins to deteriorate after about three months in bottle; and once the bottle is opened, the contents should either be drunk within three days or poured into a tightly corked half-bottle. Many of the complaints about popular *finos* arise from the habit of keeping half-empty bottles for weeks on the shelves of a warm bar.

Much the same applies to the lighter styles of *amontillado*, although they deteriorate more slowly. *Oloroso*, especially the sweetened ones, last much longer in bottle, and the rich dessert sherries sometimes improve because of the slow consumption of sugar, which gives them a dryish finish.

Fino and light *amontillado* should be served chilled, but not iced. The best thing is to leave the bottle in the refrigerator for a few hours before serving it; and the wine will also keep longer if stored in the refrigerator. Rather than suffer a lukewarm *fino* in a bar, it is better to ask for it to be poured into a larger glass and drink it 'on the rocks' – though chilling is preferable.

Oloroso, the fuller-bodied *amontillados* and creams should be drunk at room temperature.

Albariza

The best of the soils, white in colour and containing some 40 per cent chalk, the residue consisting of sand and clay.

Almacenistas
Small concerns which mature wine from their own vineyards or bought from individual growers. Such concerns do not sell direct to the public, but only to the large shippers for improving their commercial sherries. Fine-quality *almacenista* sherries are now much in demand, especially in the US. Emilio LUSTAU is the firm that has specialised in bottling and shipping them for retail sale.

Amontillado
Style of sherry, amber yellow in colour, with a dry, nutty flavour and of about 16 to 18 per cent strength. It takes its name from wines formerly prepared in Montilla (*see* page 105), and the genuine article is made by allowing a *fino* to age for a further period after the FLOR has died or been eliminated by addition of alcohol. Only completely dry wines may now be described as *amontillado*.

Amoroso
Traditional name, in Spanish 'loving', not now much used, for a smooth, sweet wine made by adding Pedro Ximénez wine and VINO DE COLOR to *oloroso*.

Añada
A young vintage wine as yet unblended in a CRIADERA. There has recently been an interest in unblended, single-vintage sherries, such as the magnificent old González-Byass *añadas* put on sale at Christie's in London.

Añina
District between Jerez de la Frontera and Sanlúcar de Barrameda, rated fourth of those with ALBARIZA soil.

Arcos de la Frontera
Picturesque town east of JEREZ, perched on a rocky crag above the River Guadalete. One of the region's most pleasant places to stay.

Arena
Reddish, sandy soil, containing some ten per cent chalk and the least favoured, except for the Moscatel vine.

Argüeso, Manuel de
Sanlúcar de Barrameda. Founded in 1822, this small firm now belongs to AR VALDESPINO and makes excellent Señorita *manzanilla*, Amontillado del Teatro and splendid PX El Candido.

Arrope
A non-alcoholic syrup, made by evaporating down must to 20 per cent of its original volume and used in making the VINO DE COLOR for sweet sherries.

Balbaina
This district to the west of Jerez is rated third in order of merit of those with ALBARIZA soil.

Barbadillo, Antonio

Sanlúcar de Barrameda. Founded in 1821, Barbadillo is the largest of the operations in Sanlúcar, with offices in the former bishop's palace and a complex of *bodegas* facing the church of Santa María in the centre of the town; even its *bodega nueva* ('new cellar') dates from 1850.

The firm owns vineyards in San Julián, and has gone into partnership with John HARVEY & Sons in the development of 1,000 hectares of new vineyards, as well as the most modern of vinification plants in Gibalbín, east of the A4 to Sevilla. However, it remains a family concern. The late Don Manuel Barbadillo was the doyen of *manzanilla* wines and wrote the most authoritative book on the subject.

Barbadillo makes a superb range of *manzanillas*, including a fresh and aromatic *manzanilla fina*; Solear and Eva *manzanilla pasadas*, resembling a *fino amontillado* from Jerez; Príncipe *amontillado*; a beautiful Cuco *oloroso*; and an exceptionally round and satisfying Eva Cream. It is also producing a fresh young table wine from Palomino grapes, labelled as Castillo de San Diego.

Barro

A mud clay containing up to ten per cent chalk, dark in colour because of its iron oxide, and second in quality of the soils.

Bienteveo

These rough shelters, made of poles thatched with *esparto* grass, are still occasionally to be seen in the vineyards and were formerly manned by armed guards, to prevent the depredations of thieves helping themselves to the ripe grapes. The literal translation is 'I see you well'.

Blázquez, Hijos de Agustín

Jerez de la Frontera. Old-established firm now owned by PEDRO DOMECQ, known particularly for its first-rate Carta Blanca *fino*; it also markets *finos*, *amontillados* and cream sherries under the labels of Don Paco, Carta Oro and Balfour, and makes the reliable and inexpensive Felipe II brandy. *See also* 'Spirits, Aromatic Wines and Liqueurs', page 200.

Bobadilla

Founded in 1879 and recently bought by OSBORNE, the firm is best known in Spain for its big-selling 103 brandy, but also makes worthwhile sherries, including a Victoria *fino*, Alcázar *amontillado*, Capitán *oloroso* and La Merced Cream. *See also* 'Spirits, Aromatic Wines and Liqueurs', page 200.

Bristol Cream

A proprietary name belonging to John HARVEY & Sons of Bristol, who decided during the 19th century to produce an even richer dessert sherry than the popular Bristol Milk by blending it with older *oloroso*. It is now the biggest-selling sherry in the world, with very large sales in the US.

Bristol Milk

Bristol has for centuries been one of the most important ports in the UK for the shipping of wines, and has imported dessert sherries under the name of Bristol Milk since the 17th century. The best-known labels are those of HARVEY and Avery's of Bristol.

Brown sherry

The English name for a dark dessert sherry, one which is usually of only very moderate quality.

Burdon, John William

John William Burdon, who began by working for DUFF GORDON, became one of the most successful 19th-century sherry shippers. The firm was eventually taken over in 1932 by Luís CABALLERO, which still markets a well-known range of sherries under the Burdon label. They include a crisp and fresh Dry Fino; a Medium Amontillado; a Pale Cream; and a raisiny Rich Cream.

Butt (bota)

The standard butt used for maturing sherry in the SOLERA is of 500 litres capacity, and is made of American oak. There are also larger butts, less pointed in shape, such as the *bocoy* of 600 litres. Butts have become increasingly expensive and represent an appreciable proportion of the cost of a wine which is more expensive than most to produce. Sherry butts are sometimes used for ageing Scotch whisky, but there is also a demand in Jerez for whisky casks for maturing sherry.

Caballero, Luís

Puerto de Santa María. The Caballero family was making wines in CHIPIONA as long ago as 1795 and shipping them from 1830. In 1932, by way of a takeover, the firm became the successors to John William BURDON, whose firm was one of the most successful of the English enterprises in Jerez during the 19th century. Apart from the Burdon sherries and its own well-known Pavón and Puerto *finos*; the nutty Tío Benito *amontillado*; and the Benito range of Pale Dry *amontillado*, Pale Cream and Cream, it also makes one of the most popular *ponches* (*see* page 200). Caballero also owns Emilio LUSTAU, famous for its *almacenista* sherries.

Cádiz

Capital of the province embracing the sherry region, Cádiz, south of Jerez de la Frontera on a peninsula connected by a stone causeway, is one of the most stylish of Spanish cities. The only city not captured by Napoleon during the Peninsular War, it is a place of white houses, narrow streets and handsome squares, shaded gardens and a wide promenade with views out to the Atlantic. Its port is now the main centre for shipping sherry. Cádiz also claims to be the gastronomic capital of Andalucía. The waters of its bay and the surrounding coast supply fish and shellfish in great variety, and its *freidurías*, where you can buy them freshly fried to take away, were the forerunners of the British fish-and-chip shop.

Camera

A wooden box containing a candle for judging the clarity of the wine against the light.

Canoa

A wedge-shaped funnel traditionally used for transferring wine from one BUTT to another.

Capatáz

The cellarman at a *bodega*, his knowledge and experience is all-important in the operation of the SOLERA.

Carrascal

District to the immediate north of Jerez, whose ALBARIZA soils are rated second in order of merit.

CAYD

Sanlúcar de Barrameda. Founded 100 years ago by the Bozzano family, which was of Italian descent, the *bodega* was sold in 1969 to the local Cooperativa de Campo Virgen de la Caridad, which was by then supplying most of its wine. This embraces 1,000 members with vineyards in the locality; and the combined capacity of the cooperative and the original *bodega* amounts to some 30,000 butts.

The musts were formerly fermented in cement *tinajas* (*see* 'Montilla-Moriles and Málaga', page 110), the first of which were in fact constructed by craftsmen from Montilla, but these have now been replaced by stainless steel. Some of the musts develop as typical *manzanillas* including Bajo de Guía and Sanluqueña *finas*, and others as the Cayd *fino*, *amontillado*, medium and cream.

Chiclana

Village on the border of the sherry district south of Cádiz, which produces wine in large quantity, but not of the highest quality. Its *finos* are sometimes blended with the less expensive sherries.

Chipiona

Seaside town on the coast road from Sanlúcar de Barrameda to Puerto de Santa María. Its ARENA vineyards are noted for their Moscatel, used in some of the sweet dessert wines.

Copita

The tall glass, narrowing towards the top, used for tasting sherry. It should be filled only a third to a half full, so that the full aroma of the wine may be appreciated. The small Elgin glasses habitually used in bars, pubs and restaurants, and filled to the brim, are entirely unsuitable for sherry, since the wine needs space and air for the nose and flavour to develop properly. If you are served sherry in an Elgin or small thistle glass, ask for it to be poured into a tulip-shaped brandy or wine glass.

When travelling in the sherry area, it is well worth bringing back a set of *copitas* or the larger *catavinos*.

Cream sherries

These sweet dessert wines are of two types. The dark, full-bodied mahogany-coloured variety is made by sweetening an *oloroso* with a sugary must prepared from Pedro Ximénez and other grapes left to dry in the sun. The base wine for pale creams is a *fino* or Pale *amontillado*, which is blended with a sweet, concentrated must. *See also* AMOROSO, BRISTOL CREAM and BRISTOL MILK.

Criadera

The literal meaning of the word is 'nursery', and it is used to describe the series of butts from which wine is drawn off to 'refresh' or replenish a SOLERA.

Croft Jerez

Jerez de la Frontera. Croft is one of the oldest names in the port trade, but has been associated with sherry only since 1970, when IDV (International Distillers and Vintners, now part of Diageo), which had fallen heir to the company by way of WA Gilbey, decided to set up Croft Jerez to supply its large requirements of sherry. Starting from scratch, the company planted more than 375 hectares of vineyards and in 1975 opened the Rancho Croft on the outskirts of Jerez, whose handsome, traditionally styled buildings, with a capacity of 50,000 butts, house one of the most modern of sherry establishments.

Thanks to a new vinification plant and well-organised handling procedures, the firm operates efficiently with only 70 workers, and at a time when other firms are finding themselves in financial difficulties, it is one of the most flourishing in Jerez.

Its largest-selling sherry is the sweet Croft Original Pale Cream; Croft Particular is along similar lines but medium to dry and there is a new high-quality Croft Limited Edition containing old *oloroso*. Other labels are a light, dry and elegant Delicado *fino* and a first-rate and moderately priced *palo cortado*.

Crushing *See* ZAPATOS DE PISAR

Delgado Zuleta

Sanlúcar de Barrameda. Prestigious Sanlúcar firm, founded in 1719 and most celebrated for its fragrant MANZANILLA PASADA, with which King Alfonso XIII is known to have toasted the crew of one of his submarines while it was submerged in the Bay of Santander.

Diez-Mérito

Jerez de la Frontera. Diez Hermanos, a company of French origin, was founded in 1876. It absorbed the old-established firm of the Marqués de Mérito before itself being taken over by the RUMASA group and, subsequently, by the entrepreneur Marcos Eguizábal.

The firm's magnificent Fino Imperial and superb Victoria Regina *oloroso* have been discontinued and Diez-Mérito now exists in little but name, marketing only a Brandy de Jerez.

Don Fino
Popular *amontillado* from SANDEMAN.

Don Zoilo
This superior range of sherries was formerly made by Zoilo RUIZ MATEOS, the flagship of the expropriated RUMASA group in Jerez; it is now made and sold by José MEDINA who took over the *soleras*. The best known of the range is the round and aromatic *fino*, one of the best in its class.

Double Century
The best known of PEDRO DOMECQ's cream dessert sherries.

Dry Fly
Proprietary name belonging to English shipper Findlater Mackie Todd. It was first used before the Second World War to describe its superior Findlater's Fino, which could not be protected by registration. More recently, Findlater has been marketing a very popular, somewhat sweeter apéritif sherry under the same name.

Dry Sack
A medium sherry, the most popular of the wines from WILLIAMS & HUMBERT, sold in a distinctive sack – though the name, of course, is derived from the old English name for sherry (*see* SACK).

Duff Gordon
Puerto de Santa María. The company was founded in 1768 by a Scot, Sir James Duff, who was British Consul in Cádiz at the time. The firm flourished and in 1833 his son, Cosmo Duff Gordon, entered into partnership with Thomas Osborne of the sherry firm of the same name.

OSBORNE finally bought out the interest of the Duff Gordon family in 1872, but, in addition to its own sherries, has continued to market the Duff Gordon wines under that name, though they are sold only abroad and are not found in Spain itself.

Made in the original *bodegas*, they embrace a wide range, including the Fina Feria; No 28 Oloroso (popular in the US, Canada and Japan); the popular El Cid medium-dry *amontillado*, and Santa María cream. Also makes a brandy and a Special Spanish Brandy.

El Cid
Big-selling *amontillado* from DUFF GORDON.

Fiesta de la Vendimia
The famous wine festival held in Jerez de la Frontera in mid-September to celebrate the beginning of the vintage. Dedicated each year to a different country or city where sherry is popular, this colourful affair embraces flamenco, bullfighting and horse shows, and culminates in the pressing of the first fruits on the steps of Collegiate Church, a ceremony presided over by the Queen of the Vintage and her attendants in traditional costume, chosen from the prettiest girls in Jerez.

Fina
A light, dry MANZANILLA from Sanlúcar.

Fino
The lightest, driest and most delicate sherry, a pale straw colour and of 15 to 18 per cent strength – the present tendency is to market lighter, less alcoholic *finos*. It develops beneath the FLOR until final fortification and is at its fragrant best when freshly bottled. Once opened, it should be served chilled and drunk within a few days.

Fino Quinta
Excellent *fino* from OSBORNE.

Flor
A film of yeasts of the genus *saccharomyces* growing spontaneously on the surface of certain types of sherry, especially *finos*, during their maturation in SOLERA. It protects the wine from undue oxidation or conversion to vinegar and develops most thickly on wines aged in old butts.

Florido, Bodegas César
Chipiona. Small firm making the excellent Moscatel Especial from locally grown grapes.

Fortification
The addition to a wine of alcohol or brandy. When deficient in alcohol, *fino* sherries are lightly fortified at an early stage, and *olorosos* more strongly to kill the FLOR. *Finos* destined for export are further fortified before shipment or bottling with a 50 per cent mixture of alcohol and mature sherry to prevent the reappearance of the *flor*.

Garvey
Jerez de la Frontera. Famous sherry house founded by William Garvey, who emigrated from Ireland in 1780 and set up business in Sanlúcar de Barrameda about 1797. His *bodegas* were long among the biggest in Jerez and are impressive even by modern standards, with an *oloroso* SOLERA ranged along the side of an arcaded patio a quarter of a mile long.

The firm was acquisitioned in 1979 by RUMASA, which fastidiously restored the old family mansion and also constructed a new vinification plant and further large *bodegas* for maturing the wine on the outskirts of Jerez. After the collapse of Rumasa in the early 1980s the firm was government controlled for a while, but it has been re-acquired by the former head of Rumasa, José María Ruíz Mateos.

The wine is now fermented in stainless steel. Of its excellent sherries, the best known is the San Patricio *fino*, named by William Garvey after the patron saint of Ireland. Other wines from this sherry house include the aromatic and fully flavoured Tío Guillermo *amontillado*, the dry Ochavico and medium-dry Long Life *oloroso*, as well as the sweet Flor de Jerez cream sherry.

González-Byass

Jerez de la Frontera. One of the largest and most important of the sherry firms, González-Byass is still family controlled. The company was founded in 1835 by Don Manuel María González Angel, who later took into partnership the firm's London agent, Robert Blake Byass.

The head of the firm until his death some years ago, Don Manuel González Gordon, Marqués de Bonanza, was one of Jerez' most distinguished figures, and wrote one of the best books on its wines; *Sherry, The Noble Wine* (1972). The Byass family some time ago sold their interest in the firm, but there is now renewed British participation in the form of a large holding by Diageo.

The old *bodegas* in the centre of the town, alongside those of PEDRO DOMECQ, are vast in size: the famous 'La Concha', designed by Gustave Eiffel, houses 12,400 butts and the more modern 'Tío Pepe' *bodega*, on three floors, a further 30,000; but even these are dwarfed by the modern vinification plant of 'Las Copas' on the road to Cádiz, with its capacity of 60,000 butts. A quaint characteristic of the older *bodegas* is the small mice which inhabit them, carefully protected and fed – on sherry, of course.

TIO PEPE is the biggest-selling *fino* in the world and deservedly so, since it remains one of the driest and most elegant. Other popular wines are the newly introduced Manzanilla Rocío; Elegante dry *fino*; La Concha *amontillado*; Alfonso dry *oloroso*; San Domingo Pale Cream; Nectar Cream and Noë PX.

González-Byass also makes a magnificent old Amontillado del Duque and some superb old *olorosos* in limited quantity, such as the dry Apóstoles Oloroso Muy Viejo and two very old dessert sherries, the Matúsalem and Solera 1847 *oloroso dulce*. Both of these are almost black in colour with a deep maderised nose and a dryish bitter-sweet finish, since most of the sugar has been consumed over the years. Their ultimate sherry is the newly-introduced Millennium Oloroso. *See also* page 203.

Guadalete, River

The Guadalete River, which flows into the Bay of Cádiz, fairly closely follows the eastern boundary of the fan-shaped sherry-producing region.

Guadalquivír, River

The River Guadalquivír flows into the Atlantic at Sanlúcar de Barrameda and forms the western boundary of the sherry region, dividing it from the salt marshes of the famous wildlife reserve of the Coto Doñana.

Harvey, John

Jerez de la Frontera. The old Bristol company of John Harvey & Sons had its origins in an earlier company founded in 1796, with which the Harvey family became associated in the early 19th century. Long famous as a sherry shipper and particularly for its BRISTOL MILK and BRISTOL CREAM, it is now part of Allied-Domecq. It was not until 1970 that it established its own vineyards and *bodegas* in Jerez by buying the old-established firm of Mackenzie & Co. It later acquired the adjoining large *bodegas* of the Marqués de Misa, and in 1973 began developing much larger vineyards in association with GARVEY and BARBADILLO.

The continuous vinification plant which John Harvey operates at the Gibalbín vineyards with Barbadillo is one of the region's most modern. More recently, Harvey's acquired the ex-RUMASA firms of PALOMINO & VERGARA, and Fernando A DE TERRY, subsequently sold to PEDRO DOMECQ.

The old Misa *bodega* is one of the most impressive in Jerez, and a perennial attraction for visitors in the beautiful gardens of the old Mackenzie *bodegas* is the pool with its Mississippi alligator.

Apart from the world-famous BRISTOL CREAM, Harvey's markets an extensive range of sherries, including the less expensive Luncheon Dry Fino, and Club Amontillado. At the top end of the range, BRISTOL MILK is a better sherry than Bristol Cream, and the 1796 wines – Fine Old Amontillado, Palo Cortado and Rich Old Oloroso – are all first-rate.

Hidalgo y Cía, Vinícola

Old-established Sanlúcar firm and makers of the light and graceful La Gitana *manzanilla*, soft and deep Palo Cortado Viejo and first-rate new Pastrana *manzanilla pasada*.

Infantes de Orleans-Borbón, Bodegas de los

Founded by the Duke of Montpensier in 1886, the firm is now 50 per cent owned by BARBADILLO. Among its well-made sherries are the Alvaro *manzanilla* and first-rate Botánico *amontillado*.

Jerez de la Frontera

Jerez (or Xérès) de la Frontera is the capital of the sherry region and, in its corrupted English form, has given its name to the wine. The town was probably founded by the Phoenicians and was much fought over during the period of the Moorish occupation – hence the suffix of *de la Frontera* granted by King John I in 1380 (there is another Jerez de los Caballeros on the borders of Portugal). Its wines were well-known in Roman times; but the trade greatly increased with the settlement of foreign traders, mostly English, after the expulsion of the Jews in 1492 and the massive participation of English, Scottish and Irish shippers, many of whom remained in the area, during the late 18th and 19th centuries.

With its old castle and walls, narrow streets and attractive white Andalucían houses, its great roofed market and innumerable *bodegas*, often set in decorative gardens, it is a most attractive place to stay, especially in late spring or autumn.

La Goya

First-rate *manzanilla pasada* made by DELGADO ZULETA.

La Guita

Classic *manzanilla pasada* made by PEREZ MARIN.

La Ina

PEDRO DOMECQ's big-selling and excellent *fino*, which is a shade less dry than some other examples.

Los Tercios

Reputed vineyard area with ALBARIZA soil, to the southwest of JEREZ and adjoining that of BALBAINA.

Lustau, Emilio

Jerez de la Frontera. Family-owned until recently, but now taken over by Luís CABALLERO, Lustau occupies *bodegas* incorporating part of the old city wall. It also owns a large modern *bodega* on the outskirts of Jerez and is one of the concerns which best weathered the recent recession through its policy of selling well-made own-brand sherries. Its branded sherries in various styles are first-rate wines and include Puerto *fino*; Los Arcos *amontillado*; Peninsular Palo Cortado; very rare Emperatriz Eugenia *oloroso*; Vendimia Cream; and a luscious Emilin dessert Moscatel. What has particularly caught the imagination of sherry drinkers is the ALMACENISTA range of sherries from small, individual stock-holders, rarely seen abroad until Lustau began selecting, bottling and shipping them for retail sale. As from 1995, Lustau began selling 'single cask' sherries, limited to 600 bottles, from its ALMACENISTAS, the first being the dry *oloroso* from Pilár Aranda.

Macharnudo

Rated the best of the ALBARIZA areas, Macharnudo lies on high ground north of Jerez. At its centre is Macharnudo castle, familiar to enthusiasts of PEDRO DOMECQ sherries from its picture on the labels. The firm still uses the castle, which was built during the 17th century, for receptions.

Manzanilla

A pale, crisp and very dry *fina* with a salty tang from SANLUCAR DE BARRAMEDA, made in a SOLERA sometimes containing as many as 14 SCALES. The word is also used in Spain for camomile tea, from which it is probably derived because of a certain similarity in flavour. *Manzanillas* owe their special characteristics to the atmospheric conditions and the special methods of operating the SOLERAS in Sanlúcar.

Not all the wines matured in Sanlúcar emerge as *manzanillas*, and *manzanilla* musts aged in Jerez develop as normal *finos*.

Manzanilla pasada

An old and mature *manzanilla*, which resembles a light and very dry *amontillado*.

Medina y Cía, José

Jerez de la Frontera. The company was formed fairly recently by the progressive acquisition of *bodegas* in Sanlúcar de Barrameda and Jerez de la Frontera by the Medina family. Besides José Medina the group now includes Luís PAEZ, PEREZ MEGIA and

WILLIAMS & HUMBERT and is one of the biggest concerns in Jerez. Through its Dutch partners, the Ahold group, it is the largest exporter of sherries to Holland and Germany.

As a new base for its growing operations, José Medina recently acquired from Marcos Eguizábal the extensive installations of the former Bodegas Internacionales, together with most of its stocks of wine. These include the famous DON ZOILO *solera*. Medina also markets a complete range of sherries under its own label.

Medium sherry

An increasingly popular term for a sherry which is akin to an *amontillado*, but a little sweetened and made in a different way – from a blend of wines rather than by ageing *fino*. Superior brands, like those from SANDEMAN, are made by blending fine *amontillado* with Pedro Ximénez.

Mitad y mitad

A mixture of alcohol and mature sherry in equal proportions which is used for fortification.

Oloroso

The darkest, softest, fullest-bodied and most fragrant of the styles of sherry, containing up to 24 per cent alcohol. It is matured without FLOR and in its natural state is completely dry, but is often blended with Pedro Ximénez wine and VINO DE COLOR for making sweet dessert sherries.

Osborne y Cía

Puerto de Santa María. Founded in 1772, still in family hands. The largest firm in Puerto de Santa María, Osborne bought the important DUFF GORDON in 1872 and has since launched sister concerns in Portugal, Mexico and the Rioja (*see* 'Montecillo', page 141).

Osborne's old *bodega* in Puerto de Santa María, built in 1837, is one of the most beautiful in the region; and the modern vinification plant, where the wine is fermented in horizontal rather than vertical tanks to approximate more closely to the traditional butt, is among the most advanced.

The wines include the excellent Fino Quinta, very dry, with a greenish cast and almond-like taste; the nutty Coquinero *amontillado*; the dry Bailén *oloroso*; and Osborne cream. The firm is also the largest maker of Spanish brandy and spirits. *See also* 'Spirits, Aromatic Wines and Liqueurs', pages 205-6.

Pajarete, Paxarete

Pedro Ximénez wine used for sweetening certain styles of sherry.

Palo cortado

Style of sherry between an *amontillado* and *oloroso*. Having 17.5 to 23 per cent of alcohol, it is classified as *dos* (the weakest), *tres* or *cuatro cortados*, according to body and age. Genuine *palo cortado* is a beautiful wine possessing great depth and fragrance – and it is always expensive.

Palomino & Vergara

Jerez de la Frontera. This family firm, which was founded in 1765, occupied *bodegas* (now demolished) in the middle of Jerez. The *bodegas*' centrepieces were the great glass-domed offices with the original mahogany and gilt counter and fitments.

Palomino & Vergara was one of the largest of the firms taken over by RUMASA, and was later sold to John HARVEY and subsequently dismantled. The SOLERAS of its best-known wine, the light, dry Tío Mateo *fino*, have been sold to REAL TESORO.

Pedro Domecq

Jerez de la Frontera. Pedro Domecq is the oldest of the large *bodegas* and the biggest single firm in the region, with extensive vineyards in MACHARNUDO and elsewhere, and dozens of *bodegas* between Jerez, Puerto de Santa María and Sanlúcar de Barrameda. In the oldest, 'El Molino', built in 1730, there are butts laid down centuries ago and dedicated to historical figures such as Pitt, Nelson and Wellington. The firm was founded by an Irish emigrant in 1730, but greatly expanded by the Domecq family from the Basses Pyrenées in association with its English agent, father of the writer John Ruskin. The firm was sold in 1994 to the British Allied-Lyons (also owner of John HARVEY) which, in view of the importance of the acquisition, has since been re-named Allied-Domecq. Don José Ignacio Domecq, who died in 1997, was one of the great sherry tasters and authorities of his generation; and the family maintains ties with Britain, among other things mounting one of the world's crack polo teams from among its members.

The firm makes an excellent Rioja (*see* page 135) and has extensive interests in Mexico, where it produces both beverage wines and vast quantities of brandy and tequila. It is in fact one of the largest brandy makers in the world. *See* 'Spirits, Aromatic Wines and Liqueurs' (page 206).

Apart from the famous *fino* LA INA, Domecq's other sherries include one of the best dry *olorosos*, Río Viejo; Botaina (old *amontillado*); Capuchino (*palo cortado*); a superb Sibarita *oloroso*; the popular Double Century Cream; and an older and even richer Celebration Cream and Venerable.

Pérez Marín, Hijos de Rainera

Sanlúcar de Barrameda. This small firm, founded in 1850, has long been known for making some of the best *manzanilla*. Its Bodegas La Guita took the name from the habit of a former member of the family, Domingo Pérez Marín, of refusing to sell his wine except for cash – *guita* in local slang. Its most famous wine is the delicious La Guita *manzanilla pasada*, an old and very fragrant *fina* on the point of conversion to *amontillado*. The other speciality is a *vinagre de yema*, a sherry vinegar made in *solera* and of quite astonishing fragrance and fruitiness.

Pérez Megía, Hijos de A

Sanlúcar de Barrameda. Dating from 1821, the firm was in the fifth generation of the family which founded it when, fairly recently, it was bought by José MEDINA. It makes a complete range: Alegría is one of the leading *manzanillas*, and Jalifa a top-quality *amontillado*, made in the *soleras* laid down by the founder.

Plastering

The light dusting of the grapes with gypsum (calcium sulphate) before vinification, a process strongly attacked in Victorian times, but beneficial and leading to improved acidity in the musts.

Puerto de Santa María

Next in importance of the sherry towns to JEREZ, Puerto de Santa María is particularly noted for its *finos*, *amontillados* and brandy, and was the main port for shipping sherry until it was supplanted in the 1920s by its larger neighbour, Cádiz. It is a pleasant, open place with wide streets and houses with grilles and *miradores* and an impressive bull ring built by the Osborne family. There are good beaches in the vicinity, served by resort hotels (*see* page 175) and on the outskirts is the lush Casino Bahía de Cádiz.

PX

Abbreviation for the Pedro Ximénez grape, which is used mainly for sweet wines in Jerez.

There is a legend that the vine originated in the Canaries, was thence taken to the Rhine and brought to Jerez by one Pieter Siemens, a soldier of the Emperor Charles V, in the 16th century. Unfortunately, this seems more picturesque than true.

Raya

A term employed in classifying musts and also used to describe less delicate styles of *oloroso*.

Real Tesoro

Jerez de la Frontera. The firm, formerly known as the Herederos del Marqués del Real Tesoro, takes its name from the first *marqués*, who gained the title ('Royal Treasure') by using his own silver to forge cannonballs while in command of a fleet for the Royal Treasury.

The *bodega* was founded by a descendant of the *marqués* in the late 19th century. One of the smaller family firms, it is particularly noted for an excellent *manzanilla* and a good, natural, unsweetened, nutty *amontillado*. Real Tesoro was fairly recently bought by José Estévez who, in a period of recession and with the profits from an enterprise producing sand for glass-making, has constructed an impressive brand-new *bodega* and continues the business under the name of Real Tesoro. The biggest-selling of Real Tesoro's brands is the popular Tío Mateo *fino*, of which the SOLERA was acquired from John HARVEY after the takeover of PALOMINO & VERGARA.

Refreshment

The replenishment of the butts of a SOLERA with younger wine as the most mature wine is drawn off.

Rota

Village on the coast west of Jerez, once known for its red Rota Tent wine, but now the site of a great US naval base.

Ruíz Mateos, Zoilo

Founded as a small wine company in ROTA in 1857, Ruíz Mateos was the springboard for the vast RUMASA empire, to which, in abbreviated form, it gave its name.

The company moved to Jerez in 1930 and later acquired the handsome mansion of La Atalaya, formerly belonging to the Vergara family of PALOMINO & VERGARA, as administrative headquarters both for itself and the whole of RUMASA's sherry group. La Atalaya also housed the magnificent Museum of Clocks and Watches founded by José María Ruíz Mateos, the president of RUMASA; the mansion is now a municipal museum.

The SOLERAS of Ruíz Mateos' magnificent DON ZOILO sherries have been acquired by José MEDINA, who now markets the wines.

Rumasa

The early steps in the formation of Rumasa have been described under RUIZ MATEOS, and the company embarked on the high road to fortune when it signed a contract with John HARVEY & Sons of Bristol for supplying all its large requirements of sherry.

After breaking with Harvey's, José María Ruíz Mateos, the younger son of the founder, Don Zoilo, moved to Madrid and set about forming what was to become the largest grouping in Spain, embracing banks, insurance, shipping, chemicals, hotels and property as well as foreign business.

However, Rumasa lost none of its early interest in wines and gained control of 35 per cent of the *bodegas* in Jerez: RUIZ MATEOS, Unión de Exportadores de Jerez, WILLIAMS & HUMBERT, PALOMINO & VERGARA, Marqués de Misa, Pemartín, Varela, Bertola, Otaolaurruchi, Diestro, Lacave, Diez Morales, Valderrama & Gordon, Bodegas Internacionales, GARVEY and TERRY. In Rioja, the company took over Paternina, Bodegas Franco-Españolas, LAN and Berberana; in Montilla, Monte Cristo and Pérez Barquero; and in Penedès, the sparkling wine firms of Castellblanch, René Barbier, Conde de Caralt and Segura Viudas. Among its foreign acquisitions, the company included the Augustus Barnett chain of off-licences in England.

Rumasa overstretched itself and in 1983 was expropriated lock, stock and barrel by the government, which took over the running of the different enterprises, finally selling them. This was the subject of prolonged litigation, with José María Ruíz Mateos seeking refuge abroad for a time. The last of the companies to be returned to private ownership was Williams & Humbert, and José María has since re-entered the trade by buying José de SOTO and GARVEY.

Sack

Old name for sherry (and also for Málaga and Canary wines), probably originating in the 15th century and derived from the Spanish *sacar* (to draw out).

San Patricio
One of the best-known *finos*, made by GARVEY.

Sánchez Romate Hermanos
Jerez de la Frontera. This old-established firm is supplier to the Spanish royal family. Its sherries, which have long been noted for their quality, include the NPU *amontillado*, an unblended SOLERA wine of great quality; Marismeño *fino*; Don José *oloroso*; and Iberia cream.

Sánchez Romate is, however, most famous for its Cardenal Mendoza brandy (*see* page 201).

Sandeman-Coprimar
Jerez de la Frontera. The firm was founded by a Scot, George Sandeman, who started business as a shipper in London about 1790, acting as agent for DUFF GORDON and later setting up his own establishments in Oporto and Jerez. Until its takeover by Seagram, it remained a family firm. One of the largest concerns in JEREZ, it makes its wines scrupulously and by traditional means, although they are no longer vinified in cask as they were.

Big-selling wines are its DON FINO; Character *amontillado*; and Medium Dry, made by blending *amontillado* with PX; and Armada cream, a first-rate dessert wine. In limited amounts it also makes some quite exceptional wines, such as the Royal Ambrosante *palo cortado* and the dry and sweet Imperial Corregidor and Royal Corregidor *olorosos*.

Sanlúcar de Barrameda
Town west of JEREZ at the mouth of the Guadalquivir estuary, famous for its dry *manzanillas*. A picturesque place with a wide beach opposite the wildlife reserve of Las Marismas, it has several good seafood restaurants and a few small, characterful hotels.

Scale
Term used of a SOLERA to denote a row of butts containing wine of similar type and age.

Sobre tabla
Young wine which has been racked free of the lees and is ready for use in a CRIADERA.

Solera
Derived from the Latin *solum*, or Spanish *suelo* (meaning a floor), the word in its narrower sense applies to the BUTTS at floor level from which sherry is withdrawn for bottling or shipment.

More loosely, the word is used for the whole assembly of butts in which sherry is matured, including those of the CRIADERA from which the *solera* proper is replenished. The butts are arranged in tiers of SCALES containing wine of identical type, but progressively younger in age. In limited amounts and from time to time the wine is taken from the last row of butts, or *solera* proper. As wine is drawn off, the butts are topped up with rather younger wine, and each scale is in turn 'refreshed' or replenished from that immediately preceding it in age. This procedure is known as 'working the scales', and is feasible because the younger wine rapidly takes on the characteristics of the older.

Soleras for producing *fino* require more scales, perhaps five, than those used in making the fuller-bodied *oloroso*; and the most complicated are those used in SANLUCAR DE BARRAMEDA for making *manzanilla*, which can have up to 19.

Soto, José de

Jerez de la Frontera. Apart from its sherries, which include the Manzanilla Juncal, Fino Soto and Fino Ranchero, Amontillado Maravilla, Oloroso la Espuela and Cream, the old family firm was the first to make a *ponche* (*see* 'Spirits, Aromatic Wines and Liqueurs', page 206), and its brand remains one of the best: drier than the others, with hints of chocolate and herbs. Soto was recently bought by José María Ruíz-Mateos, formerly of RUMASA.

Sunning

In the past, it was standard practice to lay out the grapes on *esparto* grass mats and to sun them briefly. Thanks to improved methods of judging the optimum time for picking, sunning is now mainly used for grapes intended for sweet wines and the effect is to concentrate the amount of sugar in the must.

Terry, Fernando A de

Puerto de Santa María. This large firm, which is also a brandy maker on a big scale, was founded in 1883 by the descendants of an Irish family which had settled in Spain as long ago as 1500. In 1981 the founding family sold both the *bodegas* and famous establishment for raising the white Cartujano horses to a Catalan finance house, then acting for RUMASA; the company, with its huge complex outside Puerto de Santa María, was later acquired by John HARVEY and now belongs to Allied-Domecq.

Of its various sherries, only Maruja *manzanilla* survives. It makes brandy on a large scale (*see* 'Spirits, Aromatic Wines and Liqueurs', page 207).

Tío Pepe

The world's largest-selling *fino*, made by GONZALEZ-BYASS, and one of the driest, of consistently high standard.

Valdespino, AR

Jerez de la Frontera. Old-established Spanish sherry house, whose *bodegas* and patios are among the most beautiful in Jerez – the older *bodegas* were once part of an ancient monastery. Its methods are strictly traditional, the wines are still fermented in oak BUTTS, and their quality is testament to the care with which they are made.

The sherries include a classic single-vineyard Inocente *fino*; a dry macho Tío Diego *amontillado*; an older and superb Don Tomás *amontillado*; and a raisiny Pedro Ximénez Solera Superior. In the

US, where the firm's wines are sold under the name of Hartley and Gibson, the range comprises *manzanilla*, *fino*, *amontillado*, dry *oloroso* and cream.

This is one of the oldest of the sherry firms, which until recently belonged to the Valdespino family, who have been making wine in the area since the 14th century. However, the concern has just been sold to José Estévez of REAL TESORO.

Venencia

An instrument used for withdrawing samples of sherry from the BUTT. In JEREZ, it consists traditionally of a small silver cup on a long whalebone handle; in SANLUCAR DE BARRAMEDA, where it is even more important not to disturb the FLOR, the cup is smaller and the *venencia* is made in one piece out of a bamboo cane. *Venencia*s are now made with plastic handles and stainless-steel cups.

Vino de color

A dark-coloured wine used for blending with certain brown and dessert sherries and made by fermenting a sugary boiled-down must (ARROPE) with a proportion of new must.

Williams & Humbert

Jerez de la Frontera. The firm was founded in 1877 by Alexander Williams, until then working as a clerk for WISDOM & WARTER. It subsequently became one of the most important in Jerez. A jewel in RUMASA'S crown, it was the last of the sherry companies acquired by the expropriated colossus to be returned by the government to private ownership. It now belongs to José MEDINA.

Its *bodegas* are among the most picturesque in Jerez, and points of interest for visitors are the splendid coaches and harnesses. Until 1979 the office of the British Vice-Consul was located within the *bodega*.

Its most popular wine is the DRY SACK *amontillado*; it also makes the well-known Canasta Cream and Walnut Brown, and a first-rate Dos Cortados *palo cortado*, while Pando (sometimes erroneously thought to have been named after the P & O shipping line) is a good *fino*. Williams and Humbert is now the supplier of sherries to Marks & Spencer.

Wisdom & Warter

Jerez de la Frontera. The company was founded in 1854 by two Englishmen, of whom *Punch* once wrote, 'Wisdom sells the wine, Warter makes it.' The firm, now controlled by GONZALEZ-BYASS, markets a wide range of sherries, including Fino Los Buhos, Manzanilla la Canoa, very rare Solera *amontillado*, Merecedor Oloroso and Wisdom's Choice Cream.

Zapatos de pisar

Old-fashioned cowhide boots, studded with flat tacks and formerly used in crushing the grapes. Crushing is now carried out in horizontal presses, either mechanical or pneumatic, or in yet more modern vinification plants by a continuous process, in which a first light crushing produces musts for *finos* and later, heavier pressing for the fuller-bodied *olorosos*.

WINE AND FOOD

On gastronomic maps of Spain, Andalucía is often labelled the *zona de los fritos* or 'region of fried food'; and high on the list of such dishes must come the fries of mixed fish, sometimes called *parejas* in Cádiz – this being the name of the dish cooked by the fishermen while at sea in their boats.

Cooking in the sherry region is very much oriented towards fish and seafood, available in great variety from the Bay of Cádiz and the nearby Atlantic coastline. In places such as Sanlúcar de Barrameda the shellfish is magnificently fresh and the lobsters, for example, are large enough to serve a party of six. Another great speciality is the *gazpachos* or cold soups. Sherry vinegar is one of the best and fruitiest of vinegars – it is a great adjunct in salad dressing and other dishes. Apart from the delicious iced cakes and fruit tarts from the sweet trolley, by far the most popular sweet is *tocino de cielo* (*see* page 112). Sherry is, not surprisingly, often used in cooking, and it is also usual to drink a chilled *fino* throughout the meal rather than a table wine.

Acedías fritas Fried baby soles.
Barbujitos Small fresh anchovies, fried.
Bistec salteado al Jerez Steak sautéed with sherry.
Boquerones de la Isla Fried fresh anchovies, locally caught.
Cañaíllas de la Isla A sea-snail typical of the coast. It is lightly boiled and eaten cold, the sharp tail of one snail being used to extract the meat from the others.
Cazón Baby shark, marinated with paprika and vinegar.
Consomé al Jerez Consommé with sherry, usually 'fortified' with an extra dose at the table!
Coquinas al ajillo Cockles in garlic sauce.
Dorada a la sal Gilthead baked in a thick paste of sea salt, which is removed by the waiter at the table.
Fritura gaditana A mixed fry of small fish.
Gazpacho andaluz Cold, uncooked soup containing chopped tomatoes, cucumber and green peppers, together with olive oil, vinegar and garlic. Breadcrumbs may either be used in making it or served on the side.
Helado de pasas con PX A particularly delicious ice cream made with raisins and served with sweet Pedro Ximénez sherry poured over it.
Jamón de Jabugo The best and most fully flavoured type of the highly cured *jamón serrano*, from a village near Huelva. Like Bayonne or Parma, it is either eaten on its own or served with melon, usually as a first course.
Macedonia de frutas naturales Fresh fruit salad served in the fruits' own juices, laced with sherry.
Naranjas acaramelizadas Fresh oranges, cut up and served in a syrup containing caramel.

Paire Scabbard fish, cut into steaks and grilled.
Pijotas A tiny fish fried crisp in olive oil.
Pipirrana con gambas Prawns cooked in a sauce of tomatoes and peppers.
Puntillitas Minute inkfish, dipped in a light batter and fried in olive oil.
Riñones al Jerez Calves' kidneys, sliced and sautéed in olive oil and served in a tomato sauce containing sherry.
Salchichas al Jerez Fried sausages, flavoured with sherry and served with squares of fried bread.
Salpicón de mariscos Cold fish and shellfish salad with scampi, monkfish and lobster, dressed with a sauce which contains sherry vinegar.
Sopa de pescado gaditana A rich fish soup akin to *bouillabaisse*.
Tortilla suflé A sweet soufflé omelette.
Urta a la roteña *Urta* is a fish for which there is no translation. It feeds on shellfish, acquiring great flavour, and is a speciality of Rota, on the coast west of Jerez, where it is often cooked with a rich sauce of tomatoes and red peppers.

HOTELS

Arcos de la Frontera *Parador Arcos de la Frontera*, with splendid views over the gorge.
Cádiz The quietest, most pleasantly situated hotel is the *Atlántico*, in a garden at the far tip of the peninsula, overlooking the ocean. It belongs to the Parador chain, its only disadvantage is a long walk through the narrow streets to the centre (and back again!) and it would be an adventurous driver who took the car.
Jerez de la Frontera The best hotels are the four-star *Royal Sherry Park* and *Hotel Jerez*, both of which possess large gardens and swimming pools, and the three-star *Avenida Jerez*.
Puerto de Santa María boasts the luxurious *Monasterio de San Miguel* (a converted monastery), the Yacht Club and *Meliá Caballo Blanco*.
Sanlúcar de Barrameda has a few small but characterful hotels: *Doñana*; *Los Helechos*; and the *Posada del Palacio*.

RESTAURANTS

Arcos de la Frontera *Parador de Arcos*; *El Convento* (with a pretty patio for outdoor dining).
Cádiz *El Faro* (the best in Cádiz, splendid range of locally caught fish and sophisticated cooking, such as stuffed cuttlefish and peppers stuffed with *bacalao* or dried cod); *Ventorrillo del Chato* (period charm, well-cooked Andalucían dishes, such as oxtail in *oloroso*, and a long wine list).
Jerez de la Frontera *La Mesa Redonda* (small, sophisticated restaurant belonging to a member of the Valdespino family who does the cooking and marketing); *El Bosque* (charming surroundings, international cuisine and some well-cooked Andalucían dishes, good wine list); *Tendido* (opposite the bullring, local fish dishes and good wine list); *El Abaco* in the Hotel Royal Sherry Park.

Puerto de Santa María *El Faro del Puerto* (branch of the famous *El Faro* in Cádiz); *La Goleta* (spacious restaurant outside the town); *La Terraza* (luxurious restaurant of the Casino Bahía de Cádiz, international cooking).

Sanlúcar de Barrameda *Mirador Doñana* (beach restaurant serving tapas and the excellent local seafood); *Bigote* (once small and select and serving superbly fresh seafood, this has been greatly enlarged and is now something of a *caravanserai*).

Valencia and Murcia

The eastern area along the Mediterranean coast, known as the Levante, embraces the three DOs of Utiel-Requena, Valencia and Alicante within the autonomy of Valencia, and Jumilla, Yecla and Bullas in Murcia. For bulk production the Levante is second in importance only to La Mancha. The city of Valencia is home to a number of large wineries with the very latest equipment, drawing from the region in general for grapes or wine. Clean and drinkable light table wines are supplied to the world and the *bodegas* specialise in blending wines to their customers' specification.

The traditional wines are Mediterranean, full-bodied, spicy and high in alcohol. The alcoholic strength of the wines from Yecla and Jumilla may in part be explained by the fact that the black Monastrell grape, so typical of the regions, was largely unaffected by phylloxera, and the vines are not usually grafted on to American stocks as in other parts of Spain and the rest of Europe. Monastrell is also the grape *par excellence* of Alicante, though a certain amount of white wine is made from Verdil. Perhaps the best of the Levante wines are the *rosados* from the upland region of Utiel-Requena, made from the black Bobal grape. On top form, these are among Spain's most attractive rosés: pale, very light, fruity, fragrant and refreshing. The commercial *bodegas* in Valencia draw largely on the wine from Utiel-Requena for their blends – the Swiss firm of Schenk, for example, maintains a *bodega* there and buys from the cooperatives – and there is a gentlemen's agreement that wine from any of the three demarcated regions of the autonomy of Valencia may be labelled and shipped as DO Valencia. Not surprisingly, in a part of the country famous for its dessert grapes, there is also some luscious Moscatel from the coastal area.

Tourists in resorts such as Alicante, Benicasím, Benidorm, Calpe and Javea will certainly profit from choosing the local growths and the house wine in the restaurants, rather than Rioja.

Agapito Rico, Viñedos
DO r ☆☆→☆☆☆ *94, 95, 98*
Jumilla (Murcia). DO Jumilla. Founded in 1989, this small *bodega* makes some of Spain's best *vinos jóvenes* in the unlikely region of Jumilla, especially the '98 Carchelo wines (100 per cent Merlot, 100 per cent Syrah, and a blend of Merlot with Monastrell and Tempranillo). Also produces excellent *crianzas* ('95).

Alicante
Alicante, with a mild climate and marble-paved promenade, lined with palms and facing the port, is the best base for visiting the local *bodegas* and also those of the somewhat inaccessible regions of YECLA and JUMILLA in the mountainous hinterland of Murcia.

Alicante
DO r p (w dr sw) ☆→☆☆
This demarcated region, extending to 14,874 hectares and producing 15.3 million litres of wine in '97/'98, is divided into two subregions. The maritime zone on the coast around Calpe, Javea and Denia makes sweet Moscatel.

The larger and more important central zone lies in the hills around Villena, Pinoso and Monóvar and produces a light rosé, a VINO DE DOBLE PASTA, and full-bodied reds high in alcohol, made with some 90 per cent Monastrell. Small amounts of white wine are also made from 85 per cent Verdil.

Alicante, Bodegas Cooperativas de
DO r p w dr ★★
Petrer (Alicante). DO Alicante. Large cooperative formed in 1987 and accounting for half of the DO wine from the region, made by its 3,000 members. Of its reliable wines, the best are the Monastrell/Tempranillo Viña Alone red; a luscious Alone Moscatel (Alone was the Greek name for Alicante); and a very good Marqués de Alicante, made from Tempranillo, Monastrell and Cabernet Sauvignon.

Alto-Turia
w dr ☆☆
Subdivision of the DO VALENCIA located in the high northwest of the province, and producing white wines of some quality. Fruity,

lightly acidic with a greenish cast and containing some 11.5 to 13 per cent alcohol, they are made with the Merseguera grape.

Benicarló
VC r ☆

A prime favourite in the 19th century for lacing less robust French wines, the red wine of Benicarló has virtually disappeared, owing to the expense of replanting with grafted vines after phylloxera. The small town of Benicarló, which has a comfortable seaside *parador*, is close to the picturesque and sea-girt Peñíscola, whose castle was the refuge of the last of the Anti-Popes, Pedro de Luna.

Bleda, Bodegas
DO r p w dr g ★★

Jumilla (Murcia). DO Jumilla. The *bodega* was founded in 1917 by the father of the present owner and was the first in the region to bottle its wines (in 1936).

The white Castillo Jumilla, made from 100 per cent Macabeo, and the rosé containing 100 per cent Monastrell are worthwhile young wines for early consumption, as are the red blends of Monastrell and Tempranillo.

Carcelén NCR, Asensio
DO r p w dr ☆→☆☆

Jumilla (Murcia). DO Jumilla. Maker of sound, but typically full-bodied Jumilla wines high in alcohol, labelled as Sol y Luna, Pura Sangre, Bullanguero and Acorde.

Casa de Calderón
DO r p g

Requena (Valencia). DO Utiel-Requena. This small *bodega*, which is attractively set islanded among its vineyards, is owned by the Mompó family and makes some superior Requena wines, among them a port-like *generoso*. *See also* VINIVAL.

Castaño, Bodegas
DO r p w dr ★★→★★★ 95, 96, 97, 98

Yecla (Murcia). DO Yecla. Well-equipped *bodega*, the best in Yecla, labelling its wines as Hecula. Most of these are light for the region, made with Tempranillo, Monastrell, Merlot and Cabernet Sauvignon and around 12°-12.5° by volume of alcohol, as are Pozuelo and Castaño. The young red Castaño, made by carbonic maceration, is clean, very fruity and well-structured.

Castellón de la Plana
VC r w dr ☆

The province of Castellón de la Plana, north of Valencia, was once a prolific producer of wines, including the famous BENICARLO. After the PHYLLOXERA epidemic it was replanted with hybrids, yielding coarse, 'foxy' wines frowned on by INDO. Because of the expense of replanting with grafted varieties, vineyards have been progressively abandoned.

The 1,000 hectares which remain have been demarcated as the VC San Mateo, and they produce mainly a white wine of high alcoholic degree in small wineries where conditions are often anything but sanitary.

Castillo de Liria
DO w dr r p ★→★★

The label used by large-scale exporter Vicente GANDIA PLA for its range of pleasant table wines.

Cheste
DO w dr ☆→☆☆

Formerly a DO in its own right, Cheste, lying between VALENCIA and UTIEL-REQUENA, has been incorporated in the DO VALENCIA. It is a prolific producer of dry and somewhat earthy white wines of 12.5 to 15 per cent, neutral and without a great deal of character.

Clariano
DO r w dr ☆

Subdivision of the DO Valencia in the extreme south of the province bordering Alicante. It produces both red and white wines of 11 to 13 per cent, the best of which are the reds made from the Monastrell grape.

Eval, Bodegas
DO r (p g) ☆☆

Villena (Alicante). DO Alicante. Large modern *bodega* making reliable López de la Torre reds, matured in oak, from a blend of the Monastrell and Cencibel (Tempranillo) grapes.

Fondillón
DO g ☆☆☆

Famous *generoso* from Monóvar, west of Alicante. It is aged in *solera* and emerges copper-coloured, aromatic, fairly sweet and somewhat like a light *oloroso* sherry. Very little is now made.

Gandía Pla, Vicente
DO w dr r p ★→★★

Valencia. Large-scale exporter with huge state-of-the-art plant at Chiva, west of Valencia, making inexpensive and very drinkable Castillo de Liria wines. Also a top-quality Ceremonia ('96) made from Tempranillo and Cabernet Sauvignon.

García Carrión, Bodegas J
DO r p w dr ☆→☆☆

Jumilla (Murcia). DO Jumilla. Private firm making good Jumilla wines, mainly red. Best is the delicious Castillo de San Simón.

García Poveda, HL
DO r (p w dr sw) res ★→★★

Villena (Alicante). DO Alicante. Sizeable family concern with *bodegas* at Villena in the hills behind Alicante. Costa Blanca red, white and rosé; Marquesado red, white and rosé; Costa Blanca Moscatel. The firm also makes a range of vermouths, full-bodied in character like the other wines. *See also* page 203.

Gutiérrez de la Vega, Bodegas
DO w dr sw p r ☆☆→☆☆☆ *94, 96, 97*

Parcent (Alicante). DO Alicante. Output is minute and the wines, in big demand, are hugely expensive, but individual and excellent. There's a dry white 100 per cent Moscatel Romano; a Rojo y Negro made from Merlot, Garnacha and Cabernet; and the intriguing sweet Casta Diva Cosecha Miel ('98) and Catavina Tender ('97), both 100 per cent Moscatel de Alejandría, the latter *pétillant*.

Hybrids

The district around CASTELLON DE LA PLANA, BENICARLO and Vinaroz supplied red wine to France during the PHYLLOXERA epidemic of the late 19th century, but after it had itself been affected, vines were replaced with American hybrids. Many survive on peasant plots, but government regulations forbid their use in new plantations.

Irrigation

Because of the low rainfall, irrigation is permitted in JUMILLA and YECLA, but only on a limited scale and during the winter.

Jumilla
DO r (w dr) ☆→☆☆

The demarcated region extends to 42,650 hectares with a production in '97/'98 of 19.9 million litres of wine. The traditional wines were dark, full-bodied reds containing up to 18 per cent alcohol. Apart from the heat of its long summers, the other reason for this high alcohol content is that, because of the high content of chalk and organic material in the soils, the region was largely unaffected by the PHYLLOXERA aphid, and it is one of the few areas in Spain or in Europe where vines are still grown ungrafted. The wines are now being lightened by earlier picking and better winemaking, and Spain has discovered that the Monastrell grape when properly handled can yield dark and fragrant wines, to rival those of Ribera del Duero and the New World. See AGAPITO RICO and CASA CASTILLO.

La Purísima, Cooperativa Agrícola
DO r p w dr g ☆

Yecla (Murcia). DO Yecla. The livelihoods of the thousands of smallholders in Yecla have long depended on this huge co-op, which vinifies their grapes. In the mid-1980s it exported vast amounts of basic bulk wine, but has undergone a severe crisis as demand fell away and consumers required something better. It is hoped that modernisation will result in better wines and a revival of its fortunes.

Levante

Name given to the strip stretching along the Mediterranean coast of Spain from the Cabo de Gato, just east of Almería, to the delta of the Ebro in the north.

Mendoza, Bodegas Enríque

DO r res w sw ☆☆→☆☆☆☆

Alfaz del Pi (Alicante). DO Alicante. Good red wines made from 100 per cent Cabernet Sauvignon, 100 per cent Merlot and blends with Pinot Noir. Also a pleasant Moscatel.

Murviedro, Cavas

DO r p w dr

Requena (Valencia). DO Utiel-Requena. Label for very drinkable Valencian wines from Bodegas SCHENK. The white is made with Merseguera and Moscatel; the rosé with Bobal and Garnacha; and there are different *crianza* reds made with Monastrell and Bobal, and Monastrell and Tempranillo (from Utiel-Requena).

Phylloxera

Certain areas of the Levante (JUMILLA and YECLA) were wholly or partially unaffected by this insect pest of the vine and still grow ungrafted vines, while others, like CASTELLON DE LA PLANA, were replanted with American hybrids and have never fully recovered.

Poveda, Salvador

DP r p w dr g ☆→☆☆☆☆

Monóvar (Alicante). DO Alicante. Family concern with *bodegas* in the hills, making some of the best Alicante wine; albeit full-bodied and high in alcohol, notably the red and rosé Viña Vermeta and the outstanding dessert FONDILLON 1970.

Quiles, Primitivo

DO r p w sw g ☆☆→☆☆☆☆

Monovar (Alicante). DO Alicante. Founded in 1780, this family firm is famous for its Moscatel and FONDILLON. It also produces modern-style wines, but the best are the magnificent El Abuelo *rancio generoso* and Fondillón, made in *solera*, and the Primitivo Quiles Moscatel Extra.

Roch, Julia e Hijos

DO r (p) ☆☆

Jumilla (Murcia). DO Jumilla. Young *bodega* founded in 1991, with 230 hectares of vineyard planted with the native Monastrell, as well as Cabernet Sauvignon and Syrah. Makes young wines labelled as Casa Castillo from Monastrell/Tempranillo, and also *crianzas*, including a 100 per cent Tempranillo, which bode well for the future.

San Isidro, Cooperativa

DO r (p w dr) res ★→★★

Jumilla (Murcia). DO Jumilla. Huge, well-equipped and well-run modern cooperative. Apart from its fresh, young Sabatacha white and rosé, and a young red San Isidro made by carbonic maceration for immediate consumption, it also makes good oak-aged reds with 12.5° to 14° of alcohol under the labels of Sabatacha, Gemina and San Isidro Gran Noval.

Schenk, Bodegas
DO r p w dr sw res ★→★★

Valencia. DOs Valencia and Utiel-Requena. This Spanish arm of the large Swiss concern buys wine from the whole Levante area and from as far afield as La Mancha. Apart from elaborating and shipping wines for supermarkets and own-label purchasers, it bottles good, standard Valencian wines under the label Cavas MURVIEDRO, Estrella, Los Monteros, Las Lomas and Aldea.

Señorío del Condestable, Bodegas
DO r p w dr ★★ 94, 95, 96, 98

Jumilla (Murcia). DO Jumilla. An outpost of Bodegas y Bebidas (formerly Savín, *see* page 132) making a particularly pleasant red Señorío de Robles, and 100 per cent Monastrell Vilamar.

Utiel, Cooperativa Agricóla de
DO r ☆ *p* ☆☆

Utiel (Valencia). DO Utiel-Requena. One of the best of the large cooperatives in the region, making a thick black VINO DE DOBLE PASTA for blending, a normal red wine, and light, pale and fragrant Castillo de Utiel, Sierra Negrete and Vega Infante rosés.

Utiel-Requena
DO r p ☆→☆☆

At the western extreme of the province of Valencia, with an area of 38,900 hectares and a production in 1997-'98 of 20 million litres. Utiel-Requena is an upland extension of the central plateau.

The traditional wines, which are made from 90 per cent of the black Bobal grape with smaller amounts of Cencibel (Tempranillo) and Garnacha, are of three types: a thick, almost black VINO DE DOBLE PASTA for blending (of which progressively less is being produced); a pale, light and delicious rosé; and a sturdy *tinto*, or red wine. Another increasingly important activity is the large-scale production of grape juice.

Valencia

Valencia, the third city of Spain, surrounded by its orange and lemon groves, is the queen of the Levante, and despite the devastations of the Napoleonic and Civil Wars there still remain parts of the old walls with their gates and turrets, and narrow streets flanked with balconied houses. Its *fallas*, celebrated in mid-March with bonfires and processions of giant effigies in the street, is one of the liveliest Spanish fiestas.

Valencia is the headquarters of numerous huge export houses, shipping wine in bulk all over the world; and its Grao ships more wine than any other port in Spain. It is the natural base for visits to the neighbouring vineyards and to those of UTIEL-REQUENA.

Valencia
DO (r) w dr sw ☆→☆☆

The demarcated region, of 17,355 hectares and producing 59.6 million litres of wine in '97/'98, incorporates the former DO

CHESTE and the subregions of ALTO TURIA, CLARIANO and VALENTINO. It produces more white wine than red, mostly of typical Mediterranean type: earthy, full-bodied, strong and low in acid.

Valentino
DO r dr (w) ☆→☆☆

The largest of the subregions of the DO VALENCIA, to the west of the city in the centre of the province and incorporating the former DO CHESTE. The principal white grape varieties are Merseguera, Malvasía, Moscatel, Pedro Ximénez and Planta de Pedralba; and the best wines are the dry whites made from Merseguera and Pedro Ximénez and the sweet Moscatels. Reds are made from Garnacha Tinta and Tintorera.

Valsangiacomo, Cherubino
DO w dr r p ☆☆

Valencia. DO Valencia. Reputed exporter of regional wines, such as the Vall de Sant Jaume range and the superior Marqués de Caro wines.

Vinival, Bodegas
DO r p w dr sw ☆

Valencia. DO Valencia. Vinival was founded in 1969 to handle bulk wines from across the Levante, from the old-established firms of Garrigos, Mompó, Techendorff and Steiner. The majority shareholder is now Bodegas y Bebidas (formerly Savín, *see* 'Rioja' page 132). It operates from a huge, brick-built, cathedral-like building near the port. With its capacity of 30 million litres, it ships huge quantities of sound, spicy Mediterranean-type wine. The best of the big-selling Torres de Quart range is the soft rosé; much the best of its wines are the rosé and red Viña Calderón.

Vino de doble pasta

Much of the wine from UTIEL-REQUENA and ALICANTE is made in an entirely individual fashion. The grapes are destalked and lightly crushed, and after a few hours in the vat to extract colour from the skins the must is pumped off into a fresh vat, where fermentation continues *en blanc* to produce a light, fragrant and delicate rosé. The original vat is then topped up with a further load of crushed grapes, and continued fermentation produces a *vino de doble pasta*. This is thick in extract, black in colour and with up to 18 per cent alcohol; not for consumption, but for blending with thinner wines such as those from Galicia.

With the growing demand for lighter wines, production is decreasing in favour of grape juice.

Yecla
DO r (w) ☆→☆☆

The demarcated region, which extends to 3,500 hectares and produced 1 million litres of wine in '97/'98, neighbours that of JUMILLA in the hills of Murcia, and its vineyards produce very similar wines. As in Jumilla, the impact of the phylloxera epidemic was far less severe than in other parts of Spain, and 40 per cent of the predominant Monastrell grapes are still grown ungrafted. The typical wines are dark, full-bodied reds containing up to 18 per cent alcohol. With a drop in the demand for bulk wine, exports have fallen dramatically in recent years, and attempts are now being made to produce lighter wines. See Bodegas CASTAÑO.

WINE AND FOOD

Like all the coastal areas of Spain, the Levante offers a magnificent variety of fish and shellfish; but the region in general, and Valencia in particular, is known above all for its rice dishes, especially the world-renowned *paella*.

The fertile *huertas*, known as the gardens of Valencia, are famous for their oranges and also for their vegetables, of which good use is made in cooking. Alicante almonds are used to make nougats or *turrones*.

It is one of nature's ironies that hot regions, where one most appreciates lighter wines, produce the strongest, and colder areas the lightest. At least in its rosés from Utiel-Requena the Levante has a wine that goes admirably with fish and light food. Oddly enough, a full-bodied red wine goes better with *paella* than a white, though one of the spicy Valencian whites will also stand up to its mixture of definite flavours.

Arroz abanda Fish and shellfish cooked with onions, bay leaf, saffron, olive oil and seasoning, and served with rice which takes on the flavour by being boiled in the fish stock. It is accompanied with *alioli*, a thick garlic sauce.

Arroz 'Empedrat' Popular with the workers in the *turrón* factories of Jijona, this is also known as *arroz de fábrica* ('factory rice') and is made with haricot beans, garlic, tomatoes, parsley and rice.

Bacalao a la valenciana Dried cod cooked in the oven with rice, fish broth, tomato purée, onions, grated cheese, butter and hard-boiled eggs.

Conejo a la valenciana Young rabbit stewed with green peppers, black peppercorns, garlic, parsley and olive oil.

Empanadillas valencianas Small pasties filled with a tuna and tomato sauce mixture, before being fried crisp in olive oil or baked in the oven.

Faves al tombet Fresh broad beans cooked with lettuce, artichoke hearts, garlic shoots, red paprika, vinegar and bread.

Guisantes al estilo valenciano A delicious dish of fresh peas cooked with garlic, pepper, onions, thyme, white wine, bay leaf, olive oil and saffron.

Paella valenciana Saffron-flavoured rice, cooked simply with fish and shellfish or with a variety of other ingredients, such as chicken, meat and fresh vegetables. It is usual in Spain to drink red rather than white wine with *paella*.

Potaje valenciano A thick soup containing chickpeas, spinach, sweet paprika, lemon, parsley, onions, garlic and egg yolks.

Sopa a la valenciana A thick soup made with a variety of fresh vegetables, rice, onions and parsley, cooked in ham stock.

Sopa de mariscos levantina Valencian version of *bouillabaisse* with shellfish, vegetables, saffron, bay leaf, tomatoes and garlic. It is served in two parts: first the broth with croûtons, and then the shellfish with a cold sauce.

Turrón Nougat. *Turrón de Alicante* is a hard, brittle tablet made of toasted and coarsely chopped almonds, honey and egg whites. *Turrón de Jijona* is a softer confection containing ground almonds, ground pine kernels, sugar, coriander and egg yolks.

HOTELS

Alicante The best hotels are the *Grand Sol*, *Almirante* and *Covadonga* in the city itself, and the five-star *Sidi San Juan* in the holiday resort of Playa de San Juan on its outskirts.

Valencia has many luxury hotels such as the *Astoria Palace*, *Meliá Valencia Palace* and *Husa Reina Victoria* – but my own favourite is the old-fashioned three-star *Inglés*, opposite the best ceramic museum in Spain, in the palace of the Marqués de Dos Aguas.

RESTAURANTS

Alicante *Maestra* (excellent rice dishes); *Darsena* (with 73 rice dishes on its menu); *Nou Manolín* (good *tapas*, reasonable prices and a wonderful cellar).

Castellón de la Plana *Rafael* (at the port, guaranteeing the very freshest fish and seafood); *Tasca del Puerto* (first-class ingredients; seafood and rice dishes).

Murcia *El Rincón de Pepe* (Murcia is a good-ish drive from Jumilla and Yecla, but worth the trouble as El Rincón is quite simply one of the best restaurants in Spain).

Requena *Mesón del Vino* (regional dishes and wines. Excellent roast lamb, and good *tapas* in the bar).

Valencia *Eladio* (frogs' legs with fresh broad beans, marinated salmon, aubergine stuffed with shellfish); *Albacar* (sophisticated modern cooking); *Oscar Torrijos*; *Rias Gallegas* (Galician cuisine); *El Angel Azul* (try the monkfish with mushrooms).

Sparkling Wines

Manufacture in Spain of sparkling wines by the Champagne method was begun by Don José Raventós, whose family firm of Codorníu is now one of the world's largest producers of this wine. The wines were initially known as *champaña*, but producers in Reims rightly objected that the name should be applied only to wines produced in Champagne; and they are now referred to as *cava*, a word also used, rather than *bodega*, to describe the establishments in which they are made.

Since February 1986 *cava* has been the subject of a DO which, in deference to the pundits of the EU and unlike most of the others, demarcates a patchwork of dissimilar regions, municipalities and villages in different parts of Spain where it may be produced. These include areas, sizeable and minuscule, in the provinces of Girona, Barcelona (including the whole of the area in Penedès demarcated for still wines), Tarragona, Lleida (Lérida), Zaragoza, Navarra, La Rioja and Alava, with others in Burgos, Valencia and Badajoz likely to follow. However, 99 per cent of *cava* – and all the best – is made in Cataluña, with probably over 75 per cent in and around Sant Sadurní d'Anoia in the Penedès, where it originated.

The grape varieties used in Cataluña are mainly the white Xarel-lo, giving alcoholic strength and colour; the Macabeo (or Viura), contributing freshness and fruit; and the Parellada, grown up the hill slopes, conferring acidity and delicacy of nose. Chardonnay is increasingly grown and used for *cava*; outside Cataluña it is generally made with 100 per cent Macabeo. Pink wines (never in the UK referred to as rosé in the context of sparkling wines) are made with a proportion of the black Cariñena or Garnacha Tinta.

In modern installations the must is extracted in horizontal presses and vinified in temperature-controlled stainless-steel tanks; elaboration then follows the classical methods of Champagne. The young wine is dosed with a solution of sugar and with cultured yeasts, filled into stout Champagne-type bottles, temporarily corked and left for a period of years in deep underground cellars until the sugar has been converted into carbon dioxide and alcohol. The bottles are then, over a period of months, gradually upended, so the fine sediment falls towards the neck of the bottle, which is finally frozen and uncorked, and the plug containing the sediment is forcibly expelled by the pressure of gas inside. A *licor de expedición* containing a little sugar is added; the bottles are then recorked and allowed to rest before being labelled and despatched.

The large *cavas* have now rationalised the process by using *girasoles* to promote the descent of the sediment, forklift trucks and pallets for stacking the bottles in cellars, and electronic systems for locating batches of bottles and bringing them to the bottling line for *dégorgement* (the removal of the temporary corks) and labelling. But none of these handling processes affects the elaboration or the quality of the wine – as romantics would sometimes have one believe. Such differences as do emerge between Champagne and *cava* result from the character of grapes and soil, not from the method of manufacture.

Not all *espumosos* (or sparkling wines) are made by the same method as Champagne, which is now, in EU jargon, described as the *método tradicional*. There are also sparkling wines whose second fermentation takes place, not in individual bottles, but in large pressurised tanks known as *cuves closes* or, in Spain, *gran-vas*. This process produces acceptable wines, albeit with a larger and shorter-lasting bubble, but still a great deal better than the *gaseosos*, made simply by pumping carbon dioxide into still wine. The *vinos de aguja*, or 'green wines', which develop a more subdued bubble or *pétillance* as the result of a naturally occurring secondary fermentation, are described in the chapter on Galicia.

Endless discussions compare the relative merits of *cava* and Champagne. In my experience *cava* tends to be softer, fuller in flavour and fruitier in nose; Champagne has more edge and finesse. Conventional wisdom is that no one of any experience fails to tell the difference, but that most discriminating of Spanish winemakers, Miguel Torres, notes that 'the *cavas* of Sant Sadurní d'Anoia have frequently been judged superior to their French homologues'. They are certainly less than half the price. The only sensible thing is to enjoy Spanish *cava* as a sparkling wine in its own right.

In 1997-8 143 million litres of *cava* were made, of which 74 million were exported, so its production is a most important facet of the Spanish wine industry.

Styles of Sparkling Wine

In increasing order of sweetness, Spanish sparkling wines are labelled as follows.

Brut de Brut	Very dry	Seco	Fairly dry
Brut Nature	Very dry	Semiseco	Semi-dry
Brut Reserva	Very dry	Semidulce	Semi-sweet
Vintage	Very dry	Dulce	Sweet
Brut	Dry		

Rosado, or rosé, indicates a pink wine.

Agustí Torelló
DO 94, 95, 96
Sant Sadurní d'Anoia (Barcelona). DO Cava. Small family firm whose *cavas* are among the most reputable in Spain. Top is the very expensive brut natural Kripta Gran Reserva ('94) made from Macabeo, Parellada and Xarel-lo and presented in a bottle resembling the traditional amphora. The Agustí Torelló Mata brut natural and the brut are also first-rate wines, and reasonably priced for their high quality.

L' Aixertell
Brand name for a big-selling *cuve close* sparkler made by the Unión de Cellers del Noya, a company jointly owned by FREIXENET and Bodegas y Bebidas *(see* page 132).

Ampurdán, Cavas del
DO

Perelada (Girona). Under the same management as the Castillo de PERELADA, well-known for its *cava* wines. Since it makes still wines in Cataluña (*see* page 64) and sparklers by the *cuve close* method, Spanish regulations require that it be housed in a separate building across a public highway. Its Perelada was the subject of the famous 'Spanish Champagne' case.

Bilbaínas, Bodegas
DO

Haro (Logroño). DO Cava. One of the leading producers of Rioja (*see* page 131), Bodegas Bilbaínas also makes sizeable amounts of Royal Carlton Brut Nature by the *método tradicional*, using Viura and Malvasía grapes. The wines are made in deep cellars beneath the *bodega* by the most traditional methods, clearance after second fermentation taking place in PUPITRES and *dégorgement* being effected manually. The wine is dry and of good quality, but rather fuller in flavour than those from Cataluña. It is sold widely in the north of Spain, though not in competition with the *cavas* from its new owners Codorníu, in Cataluña.

Canals and Nubiola *See* CASTELLBLANCH

Castellblanch
DO

Sant Sadurní d'Anoia (Barcelona). DO Cava. When Castellblanch was founded by Don Jerónimo Parera Figueras in 1908, it was a family concern with only three employees and an annual turnover of 100,000 bottles. Expansion took place rapidly under Don Jerónimo's son, and after Rumasa (*see* page 170) acquired the company in 1974, output was boosted to ten million bottles, made by the *método tradicional* or in *cuves closes*. The firm is now part of the FREIXENET group. Its wines are sold as Brut Zero, Dos Lustros, Gran Castell and Topacio; and under the Canals and Nubiola labels.

Castilla la Vieja, Bodegas de Crianza

Producers of an excellent Brut Natural Palacio de Bornos made by the Champagne method. It is one of the absurdities of the *reglamento* covering sparkling wines that because it is made with 100 per cent Verdejo, this delicious wine may not be called *cava*. *See also* 'Castilla-León', page 47.

Cava

Meaning 'cellar', the word is used both to describe an establishment in which sparkling wines are made by the Champagne method, and such wines themselves – now the subject of a DO.

Champaña

Name long used for Spanish wines made by the Champagne method until, in deference to the French protests, the Spanish government forbade it.

Chandon
DO

Sant Cugat Sesgarrigues (Barcelona). DO Cava. It says much for the name *cava* (and reflects the difference in price of grapes in Cataluña and Reims) that Moët & Chandon set up shop in the Penedès, and is making good NV wines with a blend of Chardonnay and traditional native grapes.

Codorníu
DO

Sant Sadurní d'Anoia (Barcelona). DO Cava. It was Don José Raventós of the family firm Codorníu, winemakers since 1551, who in 1872 began the manufacture of sparkling wine by the Champagne method in Spain, after studying practices in Reims. Today, Codorníu is one of the two largest firms in the world to make wines of this type. The *cavas* and family mansion are situated in decorative gardens above 24 kilometres of underground cellars. The original buildings, designed in *fin de siècle* style with echoes of Gaudí and including an old press house converted into a wine museum, have been declared a National Monument; and the former labelling hall is now a reception area for the 160,000 visitors who descend on the *cavas* each year.

Cordorníu has vineyards of its own but buys large quantities of grapes from 1,000 regular suppliers in the area. These are pressed in a modern band press and vinified in batteries of temperature-controlled 20,000-litre stainless-steel tanks, with subsequent elaboration by the *método tradicional*. The best wines are the Gran Codorníu Brut; Jaume Codorníu made with Chardonnay, Parellada and Macabeo; the fresh Anna de Codorníu, with 85 per cent Chardonnay; and Non Plus Ultra, from 40 per cent Chardonnay and traditional native grapes. *See also* RAIMAT.

Conde de Caralt
DO

Sant Sadurní d'Anoia (Barcelona). DO Cava. This firm was making *cava* in Cataluña long before it made still wine. Once part of the Rumasa group (*see* page 170), it now belongs to FREIXENET. Its dry, light sparkling wine is bottled under the label Conde de Caralt.

COVIDES (Cooperativa Vinícola del Penedès)
DO 96, 97

Sant Sadurní d'Anoia (Barcelona). DO Cava. Large co-op making and exporting good *cava* under the labels of Duc de Foix and Xenius.

Espumoso
Spanish name for sparkling wine.

Ferret, Cavas
DO 92, 95, 96

Guardiola de Font-Rubí (Barcelona). DO Cava. First-rate wines, including Esequiel Ferret, Ferret Reserva and Ferret Novissim *gran reserva* ('92) from a small firm which has won many awards.

Florit, Mas
DO 97

Torrelles de Foix (Barcelona). DO Cava. Small firm founded in 1984, maker of a first-rate extra brut Mas Florit ('97), from 70 per cent Parellada and 30 per cent Macabeo.

Freixenet
DO

Sant Sadurní d'Anoia (Barcelona). DO Cava. Freixenet, founded in 1915, with its acquisitions of CONDE DE CARALT, CASTELLBLANCH and SEGURA VIUDAS, is about equal in size to CODORNIU and, between them, the two concerns are responsible for at least 80 per cent of all the *cava* from PENEDES.

The Freixenet plant at Sant Sadurní is one of the most modern in the Penedès, and the wine is vinified at low temperature in huge stainless-steel tanks of 600,000 litres capacity. Freixenet was also the first of the *cavas* to introduce GIRASOLES. Thanks to these innovations and the highly advanced handling and bottling equipment, it has been able to hold down the price of its *cava* wines without detriment to quality. The Freixenet group is currently the largest exporter of Spanish sparkling wines to the United State, where it sells around 17 million bottles. It also makes sparkling wine in Mexico and California, and owns the Champagne house of Henri Abelé.

Apart from splendid vintage wines, such as the Cuvée DS 1990, named in honour of Doña Dolores Sala, widow of the company's founder Don Pedro Ferrer Bosch, the best of the wines are the Freixenet Vintage Brut Reserva Real, the very dry and light Brut Nature, and popular Cordon Negro. It also markets the less expensive Carta Nevada and Cremant Rosé.

Gaseoso

The cheapest (and nastiest) form of sparkling wine, made by pumping pressurised carbon dioxide into still wines. It also describes 'fizzy' lemonade and aerated mineral drinks generally.

Girasol

A large octagonal metal frame on a faceted base that holds 504 bottles. Increasingly used in *cavas* in place of the traditional PUPITRE, to effect the descent of the sediment after the secondary fermentation takes place.

The frame, with its complement of bottles, may be swung round in a few seconds by a couple of men; FREIXENET, which was the first of the *cavas* to introduce it on a large scale, claims that it gives more consistent results than the PUPITRE. Most of the *cavas* in Cataluña have begun to use the device, and it has also been tried out in Reims by the French Champagne-makers.

Girona

This province in the northeast of Cataluña produces sizeable [amounts] of sparkling wine, most of it made by the Castillo de [Perela]d Cavas del AMPURDÁN.

González y Dubosc
DO

Sant Sadurní d'Anoia (Barcelona). DO Cava. This well-known firm is owned by the sherry-maker González-Byass. The cava wines, light, dry and fresh and very reasonably priced, are marketed in the UK under the name of Jean Perico.

Gramona
DO 92, 93, 95, 96

Sant Sadurní d'Anoia (Barcelona). DO Cava. Family firm founded in 1921 and one of the most respected cava-makers. Its brut natural, extra brut and brut are made from blends of the native Xarel-lo, Macabeo and Parellada, and are labelled Tres Lustros ('93), Reserva Brut ('96), Celler Batlle ('95) and Impérial ('95). There is also a Rosado made from 100 per cent Pinot Noir.

Gran-vas

Spanish name for *cuve close*. With this type of sparkling wine, second fermentation takes place in large closed tanks pressurised to eight atmospheres, and lasts for four to five months according to temperature, usually −5°C. The wine is then filtered and bottled under pressure. Although the wines do not possess such a fine or lasting bubble as those made by the Champagne method, they are a great deal more acceptable than GASEOSOS and make pleasant party drinking. To avoid the possibility of such wine being passed off as *cava*, Spanish regulations require that it may not be made in the same building. Corks from *cava* wine bear a star on the bottom, and *gran-vas* a small black circle.

Grapa

A metal hook used for securing the temporary cork during the second fermentation. *Grapas* and corks have now been largely replaced by crown caps.

Hill, Cavas
DO 93

Moja (Barcelona). DO Cava. Apart from its still Catalan wines (*see* page 70), the firm produces a range of good *cavas*, including Reserva Oro, Brut de Brut, Brutísimo and Rosado Hill.

INVIOSA
DO

Almendralejo (Badajoz). DO Cava. Very drinkable Bonaval *cava*, made with 100 per cent Macabeo from the unlikely Extremadura.

Juvé y Camps
DO 94, 95, 96

Sant Sadurní d'Anoia (Barcelona). DO Cava. Sparkling-wine producer of repute, making limited amounts of a superior CAVA made from free-run juice, a favourite of the Spanish royal famil The labels used are: Reserva de la Familia ('96), Gran Re Grand Cru, 100 per cent Chardonnay Milésime ('94) a

Licor de expedición

A solution of sugar in brandy and old white wine, used to top up the bottles after completion of the second fermentation and removal of the temporary cork. It is the amount of sugar in the *licor* which determines the style of the finished wine. A dry brut will contain only two per cent, while the sweet sparklers, which tend to be popular in South America, are dosed to the extent of 12 to 20 per cent. In general, the best sparkling wines are the driest, because defects cannot be masked by excessive sweetening.

Licor de tiraje

A solution of sugar in white wine added before the second fermentation. It is from the breakdown of this sugar into alcohol and carbon dioxide by the action of special yeasts that wines made by the Champagne method derive their sparkle in the bottle.

Lleida

The province of Lleida (Lérida), set in the northwest of Cataluña, produces sizeable amounts of *cava*. See RAIMAT.

Marqués de Monistrol
DO

Sant Sadurní d'Anoia (Barcelona). DO Cava. The CAVAS are at Monistrol de Noya, just outside Sant Sadurní, and are among the most picturesque in the area, with a flagged patio and old wine press overlooked by the parish church. Although the company, which has been making CAVA wines since 1882, is now controlled by the Riojan Bodegas Berberana, it is still very much a family concern, with ten of the families who work in the CAVAS and vineyards living on the estate.

Monistrol owns 450 hectares of vineyards and makes three million bottles of wine annually, most of it *cava* and much of it exported to Italy. The driest and most elegant of its sparkling wines is the Gran Tradición Extra Brut. The company also produces Brut Gran Reserva de la Familia and Gran Reserva de la Familia Rosé. *See also* 'Cataluña', (page 71).

Masachs, Josep
DO

Vilafranca del Penedès (Barcelona). DO Cava. A sizeable family firm currently producing some three million bottles yearly in its ultra-modern plant.

The best of the firm's wines are the extra brut Carolina de Masachs, Josep Masachs and Louis de Vernier, and the brut Gran Vernier, Josep Masachs and Louis de Vernier.

Mascaró, Antonio
DO 92, 93

Vilafranca del Penedès (Barcelona). DO Cava. Small and old-established family firm with cellars in the heart of Vilafranca, making liqueurs and an excellent brandy (*see* page 205) as well as still and good *cava* wines. Its Brut and Gran Brut wines contain a high proportion of Parellada (with small additions of Macabeo and Macabeo/Xarel-lo) and are correspondingly fresh and fruity. *See also* 'Cataluña', page 71.

Mestres Sagües, Antonio
DO
Sant Sadurní d'Anoia (Barcelona). DO Cava. One of the smaller family firms in the Penedès, making good sparkling wine by the *método tradicional*, now available in the UK under the labels Clos Damiana, Clos Nostre Senyor, Coquet and Mestres Rosado.

Método Tradicional
The approved Spanish name for the traditional Champagne method by which *cava* wines are made.

Mont Marçal (Manuel Sancho e Hijos)
DO 91, 93
Castellví de la Marca (Barcelona). DO Cava. Made only from free-run juice and from the traditional grape varieties Parellada, Xarel-lo and Macabeo, Mont Marçal Brut Natural and Mont Marçal Brut are first-rate wines, elegant and very dry.

Muga, Bodegas
DO
Haro (Logroño). DO Cava. One of the most scrupulous in its methods of the Riojan *bodegas* (*see* page 142), Muga some time ago revived an old Riojan tradition by making a *cava* wine. Made from 100 per cent Viura, Conde de Haro is a bone dry, fruity and characterful wine in its own right – though nobody would confuse it with Champagne.

Nadal, Cava
DO 93, 95
Pla del Penedès (Barcelona). DO Cava. Small family firm with 110 hectares of vineyards, and a well-equipped modern winery making a first-rate Extra Brut Salvatge ('93) and a clean and elegant Ramon Nadal Giro ('93).

Parxet
DO
Santa María de Martorelles (Barcelona). DO Cava. Sizeable producer of *cava* within the tiny DO Alella (*see* 'Cataluña', pages 63-4), making a fresh and fruity Brut Nature Chardonnay and also a first-rate Parxet Brut Nature from a traditional blend of Macabeo, Parellada and Pansà Blanca (Xarel-lo).

Penedès
Penedès as such is *not* demarcated for producing *cava* as it is for still wines (*see* pages 72-3). However, all the individual municipalities within the DO Penedès are also entitled to make *cava* by the *método tradicional*, and 95 per cent of *cava* now originates from this area.

Many of the scores of *cavas* in and around Sant Sadurní d'Anoia and Vilafranca del Penedès are small, family firms which sell direct to visitors, who descend upon the area from Barcelona in their hordes at weekends to tour the *cavas* and taste the wines.

Owing to the fact that, in the last decade, the number of *cavas* with DO has increased from 65 to upwards of 250, it is no longer practical to print the names of firms other than those included in the A–Z listing.

Perelada, Castillo de
DO 93, 96, 97

Perelada (Girona). DO Cava. Winemaking traditions at Perelada, on the verges of the Pyrenees, date from the 12th century, when the Carmelite monks planted the first vineyards. To this day the cellars lie beneath the 14th-century church of Carmen de Perelada, with its delicately arcaded patio, and the crenellated castle built shortly afterwards. The old buildings house a splendid library, a museum of glassware and ceramics and an extensive wine museum. More recently, a casino has been opened in the castle – dare one suggest, to promote the consumption of its excellent sparkling wines?

Like the associated Cavas del AMPURDAN, the Castillo de Perelada also produces still wines. About 50 per cent of the grapes are from its own vineyards (the rest being brought from local farmers), and the wine, carefully made by the Champagne method, is binned away to undergo its second fermentation in deep cellars underneath the former orchard.

The best of the wines is the extra brut Gran Claustro, which, with five to six years in the cellars, emerges dry, soft and flowery. The other wines in its range are the Brut Nature, excellent extra brut Chardonnay, Castillo de Perelada brut and *rosado*.

Pupitre

In the production of sparkling wine, the traditional method of coaxing both the sediment and the fine suspended matter into the neck of the bottle after the second fermentation is to place the bottles, neck first, into the oval holes of a *pupitre*. This is a large wooden frame in the form of an inverted 'V'. The bottles are regularly given a shake and a slight angular twist by hand, and the inclination of the *pupitre* is gradually altered, so that the bottle ends up almost on its head, with the solid matter gathered against the bottom of the cork.

Raïmat
DO

Raïmat (Lleida). DO Cava. The Raïmat Chardonnay made by a subsidiary of CODORNIU, with the grapes grown on its estate outside LLEIDA, is one of the best of all *cavas*.

The wines also include Brut Nature and Blanc de Blancs, both made from a blend of Chardonnay, Macabeo and Xarel-lo; a 100 per cent Chardonnay; and a good Gran Brut made from Chardonnay and Pinot Noir.

Raventós i Blanc, Josep María
DO 93, 94

Sant Sadurní d'Anoia (Barcelona). DO Cava. Josep María Raventós left the family firm of CODORNIU in the mid-Eighties, to make his own CAVA on the basis of 100 hectares of inherited vineyards. The Raventós i Blanc Reserva Brut Natural and the other wines are aimed at the top of the market.

Reserva Mont-Ferrand
DO 94

Blanes (Girona). DO Cava. Good *cavas* from Girona. The Nature contains Chardonnay as well as Xarel-lo/Macabeo/Parellada, and the Rosado is made from Monastrell and Garnacha.

Rioja

In the full flush of the Rioja boom of the late 19th century, various of the newly founded *bodegas* set about making sparkling wine, using the Champagne process, from the local white Viura and Malvasía grapes. Some were more successful than others, but the Compañía Vinícola del Norte de España (*see* page 130) was so successful that it actually started a sister establishment in Reims. Although this lasted only three years, CVNE long continued to supply the French Champagne-makers with Rioja for making their wines during the period when they were suffering from the after-effects of the phylloxera epidemic.

There has been a revival in the making of sparkling wine in Rioja, where various areas are demarcated under the DO Cava; in addition to Bodegas BILBAINAS and Bodegas MUGA, Bodegas OLARRA and Bodegas FAUSTINO-MARTINEZ are both making brut CAVA from 100 per cent Viura.

Roura
DO

Alella (Barcelona). DO Cava. Good *cava* made with Xarel-lo/Chardonnay from a winery reputed for its still Alella wines. Best is the Brut Natural Roura 5*.

Rovellats, Cavas
DO 93, 95, 96

San Martí de Sarroca (Barcelona). DO Cava. Small family firm making limited amounts of exclusive and expensive *cava*, stocked by some of the leading restaurants in Spain. Wines are produced under the labels Brut Especial and Brut Imperial and there are two *gran reservas*, Brut Nature and the Gran Cru Masía S.XV, produced in minuscule amounts. There is also a Rosé Brut from Monastrell and Tempranillo.

San Sadurní de Noya
(Catalan Sant Sadurní d'Anoia)

Now spelt on roadsigns in the Catalan form of Sant Sadurní d'Anoia, this little town west of Barcelona is the headquarters of the Spanish sparkling wine industry, with *cavas* on every street.

Segura Viudas
DO

Sant Sadurní d'Anoia (Barcelona). DO Cava. Once the flagship of the companies formerly within Rumasa (see page 170), making sparkling wine by the *método tradicional* and now part of the FREIXENET group. The nucleus of the modern winery is an old house picturesquely situated on the road from Sant Sadurní to Igualada, with Montserrat (see 'Cataluña', page 72) as a backdrop. Some of the grapes are grown on the 110 hectares of surrounding vineyards, the rest are bought from local growers.

The most delicate of Segura Viudas' wines are dry, light and fresh and among the best of all Spanish *cavas*. They are the Brut Natural Reserva Heredad and Aria. Other marks are the Brut Vintage, Brut, Rosé, Dry and Medium Dry.

Serra, Jaume
DO

Vilanova i La Geltrú (Barcelona). DO Cava. Good brut *cavas*, including a first-rate Brut Vintage 1994.

Sunflower
English translation of GIRASOL.

Vallformosa, Masía
DO 94, 96

Vilobí del Penedès (Barcelona). DO Cava. Family firm making stylish brut *cavas*. See also 'Cataluña', page 80.

Ventura, Jané
DO 95

El Vendrell (Tarragona). DO Cava. Well-known for its still wines (see Cataluña, page 80), the firm also produces good extra brut, brut and rosé *cavas* from the traditional Xarel-lo, Parellada and Macabeo blend.

Vilafranca del Penedès
Vilafranca is primarily a centre for making still wines (see 'Cataluña', pages 80-1) but a number of the *cavas* are located there. It is also the headquarters of the official regulatory body for sparkling wines, the Consejo Regulador de los Vinos Espumosos.

WINE AND FOOD
Manufacture of sparkling wines centres on Cataluña, especially Penedès, and details of regional cooking and restaurants are given in the chapter on Cataluña (see pages 81-3).

Spirits, Aromatic Wines and Liqueurs

Sherry is so much an image of Spain that foreigners are often surprised to learn that a great deal more of it is drunk outside the country than in, especially in Britain, the Netherlands and the northern European countries. In Spain itself, brandy, most of it produced in Jerez, is much cheaper and more popular. Sales of sherry have, in fact, declined in recent years, a fall aggravated by the increasing fashion among the younger generation for imported spirits, vermouths and liqueurs, and brandy has been the salvation of some of the big sherry houses.

The Spanish learned about distillation from the Moors. Alcohol was first used in medicine by the Catalan-born Arnold of Vilanova, and Spanish brandy was first shipped from Cataluña in the 17th century. Until the early 19th century its main use in Jerez was for the fortification of sherry, and the first Jerez brandies were not sold on any scale by the sherry houses until the mid-19th century. They were made by what is now known as the Charentais method, perfected in Cognac, by distillation of wine in a simple pot-still, in effect a copper kettle with a coiled condenser. This takes place in two stages: the raw spirit is then matured in oak casks. It is still the method used for the best and most refined Spanish brandy; but the great bulk of inexpensive Spanish brandy is made by 'continuous' distillation of wine in tall, steam-heated columns in the manner of grain whisky, a more economical and productive industrial process. The resulting *holandas*, or 65 per cent grape spirit, made in distilleries all over Spain, are then diluted with water and aged in oak casks.

In Jerez, which produces 95 per cent of Spanish brandy, maturation takes place in a *solera* (*see* page 171-2) and involves the trademark periodic 'refreshment' of the older spirit with the younger. The aeration and quicker maturation gives rise to brandies quite different in character from those made in Cataluña or France, where there is no such frequent transfer from cask to cask. Jerez brandy has an oaky charm of its own, but it is so distinctive that it is not sensible to make direct comparisons with Cognac or Armagnac.

In 1987 a new DO was set up for Brandy de Jerez, as it is officially known, and a *consejo regulador* established to administer it. The main provisions are that only brandy made in Jerez de la Frontera, Puerto de Santa María and Sanlúcar de Barrameda qualifies for DO and that it must be made by traditional methods from *aguardiente de vino* (grape spirit) and matured in *criaderas* and *soleras* as in making sherry, or by static maturation in a single barrel, as in making an *añada* or vintage sherry. In ascending order of quality and depending on the time of maturation and on the content of aldehydes, esters and higher alcohols the *reglamento* defines three types of Brandy de Jerez: *Solera*, *Solera Reserva* and *Solera Gran Reserva*, the last of which must be matured for more than three years and contain more than 300

Cointreau
This famous orange-flavoured liqueur was formerly made for the house of Cointreau by Cavas MASCARÓ in Vilafranca del Penedès. It is still made in Vilafranca, but by a Spanish subsidiary under the close supervision of the French firm.

Coñac
To the legitimate discomfort of producers in Cognac, Spanish brandy is widely known in Spain as *coñac*. This is certainly no fairer than the dubious labelling of sherry-type wines from Cyprus and elsewhere as 'sherry', a practice the Jerez houses are, unsurprisingly, vehement in denouncing. The makers of Spanish brandy are therefore careful to label their product as 'brandy' or Brandy de Jerez.

Conde de Osborne
A very old mature *solera gran reserva* brandy made by OSBORNE and presented in white ceramic bottles designed by Salvador Dalí.

Cuarenta y Tres
A sweet, light-yellow, vanilla-flavoured liqueur, rather resembling Southern Comfort in taste, made by Diego Zamora in Cartagena. Its name means 'forty-three'. Sweet as it is, Spaniards often drink it as an apéritif.

Don Narciso
Delicate and aromatic brandy, a blend of seven- and ten-year-old spirits and one of the best from Spain, made and matured by the Charentais method by Cavas MASCARÓ in Vilafranca del Penedès.

Dubonnet
The popular French apéritif, made under licence in Barcelona and differing little from the original.

DYC
Spanish-made whisky produced in a distillery near Segovia, now owned by PEDRO DOMECQ, where the water and grain are considered to be most like those of the Scottish Highlands. It is not of the quality of the original and has made limited headway against the imported Scotch, which is widely obtainable in Spanish supermarkets and grocers.

Escat
Barcelona firm making a wide range of spirits, including vodka, gin, *anís*, *pastís*, advocaat, kirsch, rum (known in Spain as *ron*), together with crème de menthe, cherry and apricot brandies, and a liqueur made with bananas from the Canary Islands.

Espléndido
DO
The youngest of the range of brandies from the famous and old-established sherry firm of Garvey, in Jerez de la Frontera.

Capa Negra
DO
Jerez brandy made by the sherry firm of Sandeman-Coprimar in Jerez de la Frontera.

Cardenal Mendoza
DO
Jerez brandy made by the sherry firm of Sánchez Romate and labelled 'Cardinal' in the US. First produced in 1887, this *solera gran reserva* brandy is aged in *oloroso* casks and is one of the best from Jerez, exceptionally smooth and fragrant.

Carlos I
DO
The most refined of the brandies made by PEDRO DOMECQ in Jerez, and though very slightly on the sweet side, it is light and spirituous, more resembling a French Cognac than most Jerez brandies and more suited to northern tastes.

Centenario
Made by TERRY and sold in bottles with a yellow net, this popular Brandy de Jerez currently ranks number two in sales.

Chartreuse
Although many well-known French liqueurs are made under licence in Spain, Chartreuse was more firmly rooted, since from 1903 to 1940, during the exile of the monks from La Grande Chartreuse, it was made exclusively in Tarragona. The distillery was directly supervised by the three fathers who share the closely guarded secret of its recipe, and who spent January to May in Tarragona and the rest of the year in Voiron, in the French Alps.

It is said that 130 herbs (many procured locally) were used for making the Green Chartreuse, and rather fewer for the Yellow. The difference between the French and Spanish versions was minimal, though in my experience the Spanish was slightly drier – and also, of course, like all Spanish-made liqueurs, vastly less expensive. I write in the past tense, since the Tarragona distillery was closed in 1991.

Chinchón
One of the best brands of ANIS, made by a subsidiary of González-Byass in the small town of Chinchón, southeast of Madrid. It was named after a 17th-century Marquesa de Chinchón, wife of a governor of Peru, who in 1638 discovered the medicinal properties of quinine, giving her name to the cinchona tree from the bark of which it is obtained and, indirectly, inspiring the fabrication of VINOS QUINADOS, drunk as tonics.

Cinzano
Cinzano, in its different varieties, is made under licence in Vilafranca del Penedès and, with Martini, is the most widely drunk VERMOUTH in Spain.

Bénédictine
Famous French liqueur made under licence in Spain.

Bilbaínas, Bodegas
This is virtually the only *bodega* in the Rioja to produce that *rara avis*, a Riojan brandy that can stand alongside its still and sparkling wines. Its Imperator has a vinous, oaky nose, is completely dry, but it tastes of little except oak, and the finish is short. *See also* pages 131 and 189.

Blázquez, Hijos de Agustín
DO
Well-known sherry firm, makers of FELIPE II, one of the drier and least manipulated of the Jerez brandies.

Bobadilla
DO
Sherry firm now owned by OSBORNE and best-known for its brandies: Solera 103 White Label, aged for six months, pale and delicate; Solera 103 Black Label *solera reserva*; and Gran Capitán *solera gran reserva*, which is a blend of brandies between three and (remarkably) eighty years old.

Brandy
As explained in the introduction to this section, most Spanish brandy is made from HOLANDAS, a grape spirit of 65 per cent alcohol. This is produced by distilling wine (in the manner of grain whisky) in a continuous still and maturing the raw spirit in *solera* (*see* 'Sherry and Manzanilla', pages 171-2). The better Catalan bran-dies, and also a few of the premium Jerez marks, are however made by the Charentais method in pot-stills.

A large proportion of commercial Spanish brandies are sweeter and more caramelised than their French counterparts and have therefore made less impact to date in international markets other than Latin America.

Brandy 103
DO
Popular Jerez brandy made by the sherry firm BOBADILLA, which in turn is owned by Osborne, Spain's largest producer of spirits.

Caballero, Luís
Sherry concern located in Puerto de Santa María and maker of one of the best brands of PONCHE, Caballero, which is sold in eye-catching silvered bottles.

Calisay
Quinine-based liqueur, a speciality of the Barcelona area, which may be drunk either as a *digéstif* or, with ice and with or without fruit (such as lemon, orange and maraschino cherries), as an apéritif. A dash of Calisay much enlivens fruit salads. *See also* MOLLFULLEDA, page 205).

milligrams of non-alcohol per 100 centilitres of absolute alcohol. Another popular spirit is *aguardiente*, made by distilling the pips and skins remaining from the fermentation of wine. Akin to the French *marc* or Portuguese *bagaceira*, this is a somewhat fiery liquid best left to those who have learned to stomach it.

Spain also produces a gamut of liqueurs, many of them household names marketed internationally by foreign companies and made under licence in Spain, by the maceration of fruits and herbs in alcoholic solution and subsequent distillation. Firms in Jerez and Cataluña make very respectable gin and vodka by the traditional methods. Vermouth is made in large amounts, much of it under licence, by the preparation of herbal extracts and their blending with white wine. The native *anís* is first-rate; and tonic wines and spirits containing quinine extract, of which the best known are Jerez-Quina and Calisay, are something of a speciality and are made in Jerez, Málaga and Barcelona.

Aguardiente

Aguardiente is defined by the Estatuto de la Viña, del Vino y de los Alcoholes as 'natural alcohol with a strength of not more than 80 per cent', distilled from vegetable materials. It therefore constitutes a wide variety which includes the HOLANDAS used for the manufacture of brandy and known as *aguardiente de vino*, as well as other varieties distilled from fermented fruits and cereals.

However, over the counter of a bar, *aguardiente* means *aguardiente de orujo*, a popular and potent spirit distilled from the grape skins and pips left over from the fermentation of wine in the manner of the French *marc* or Portuguese *bagaceira*. It is made all over Spain and is not normally branded, but poured from an unlabelled bottle – a fact that, combined with its well-deserved reputation for strength, intimidates many tourists.

Alvear

Apart from Montilla (*see* page 105), Alvear produces brandy, made from HOLANDAS and matured in *solera* after the fashion of the Jerez brandies and the fortified wines of the area. The inexpensive Secular is fruity, with a raisiny nose and peppery finish. The more refined Senador and PRESIDENTE are oakier and more aromatic, and the Presidente Alvear Gran Reserva has a very dry finish.

Amer Picon

The well-known orange-flavoured bitters, manufactured under licence in Spain.

Anís

Aniseed-flavoured liqueur corresponding to the French *anisette*. The best Spanish *anís*, such as CHINCHON and ANIS DEL MONO, is of excellent quality.

Anís del Mono

One of the best and most popular brands of ANIS, made by Bosch y Cía, a subsidiary of OSBORNE, in Badalona near Barcelona.

Felipe II
DO

Pleasant and inexpensive Jerez brandy made by Agustín Blázquez in Jerez de la Frontera.

Fontenac
One of the best brandies from Miguel TORRES in Vilafranca del Penedès. It is made by the Charentais method and is aged in French style rather than in *solera*; it is hence less oaky than Brandy de Jerez, and more along the lines of an Armagnac.

Fundador
DO

Fundador was one of the first Jerez brandies and was put on sale to the public by PEDRO DOMECQ in 1874, some 20 years after Don Pedro Domecq Lustau had been so struck with the quality of a batch of HOLANDAS accidentally left in cask that he decided on systematic production of a brandy.

To foreign tastes, Fundador remains one of the most agreeable of the inexpensive brandies, since it is grapier and less sweetened than many of its competitors. Perhaps this explains why it is the export leader.

García Poveda, HL
Makers of a range of Costa Blanca vermouths, fully flavoured and spicy in comparison with those from France and Italy. The firm also produces table wines from the Alicante area (*see* 'Valencia and Murcia', pages 180-1).

Garvey
DO

Famous sherry house, now owned by José María Ruíz Mateus, and producer of, in ascending order of age and refinement, Espléndido, Gran Garvey and RENACIMIENTO brandies.

González-Byass
DO

As well as the famous sherries, González-Byass produces three brandies: SOBERANO, the medium-priced INSUPERABLE and, in very limited amount, the exquisite LEPANTO *solera gran reserva*.

Gran Duque de Alba
DO

Premium-quality *solera gran reserva* Brandy de Jerez formerly made by Diez-Mérito and now by Williams & Humbert.

Holandas
Grape spirit containing 65 per cent alcohol and made by the continuous distillation of wine. It is produced in various districts of Spain, especially La Mancha, Extremadura and Huelva. This spirit is subsequently diluted with water and aged, either in *solera* or cask, to make brandy.

Honorable

An exceptional brandy made by Miguel TORRES in Vilafranca del Penedès, by double distillation in copper pot-stills and a long maturation in French oak.

Independencia
DO

Dark, velvety and sweet, this is a premium *solera gran reserva* brandy from the sherry house of OSBORNE.

Insuperable
DO

The big brother of SOBERANO from GONZALEZ-BYASS, smoother and more aromatic.

Jerez-Quina

Popular tonic wine, made with sherry, macerated cinchona bark and the peel of Seville oranges, and regularly administered to Spanish children and convalescents.

Larios

Larios makes good Málaga (*see* page 107), but in Spain it is a household word for its gin, sold in bottles with a red and yellow label that have a marked likeness to that of the export Gordon's. Though not of quite the same quality as good London gin, it is entirely acceptable with mixers. The firm also produces the 1866 Gran Reserva brandy, Triple Seco orange liqueur, and rum.

Lepanto
DO

Soft, mellow and fragrant, but entirely Jerezano in character, this expensive *solera gran reserva* brandy from GONZALEZ-BYASS, sold in a cut-class decanter, is exceptional.

Liqueurs

Most of the best-known French liqueurs are made under licence is Spain (*see* COINTREAU, BENEDICTINE, MARIE BRIZARD) and differ little from the originals – except they are much cheaper and therefore popular with travellers. There are also numerous separately listed firms making fruit brandies, crème de menthe, kirsch and also some native liqueurs with a foreign following (*see* PONCHE, CUARENTA Y TRES, PACHARAN).

Lustau, Emilio
DO

Sherry firm whose *solera reserva* and *solera gran reserva* brandies are sold as Señor Lustau.

Magno
DO

Made by OSBORNE in Puerto de Santa María, Magno is a brandy that spends four to five years in *solera*. Dark in colour, smooth,

Frutos Villar, Bod. 48, 49, 54
Fuencaliente 28
Fuenmayor 136, 146, (R) 152
Fundador 203, 206
Funes 118

Galicia 11, 12, 91-102
Gallega, Bod. 94
Gandesa, Co-op Agrícola 70, 79
Gandía Pla, Vicente 180
García Carrión, Bod. J 180
García, Mariano 50
García Poveda, HL 180-1, 203
Garidells 70
Garnacha Blanca 21, 61, 115, 126
Garnacha Peluda 61
Garnacha Tinta 20, 61, 115, 126, 187
Garvey 154, 163, 202, 203, 206
gaseoso 188, 191
Gemina 182
generoso 15, 85-7
Geria, La 29
Gerona 59
Getariako Txakolina 12
Gewürztraminer 61
gin 199, 207
girasol 187, 191
Girona 187, 191
Glorioso 144
Godello 92
Godeval SAT 94
González y Dubosc 192
González Byass 154, 155, 156, 157, 164, 203, 204, 207
Gonzalo de Berceo 131
Gotim Bru 67
Gracia Hnos 107
Graciano 115, 126
Gramona 192
Gran Alanis 93
Gran Barquero 109
Gran Campellas 22
Gran Canaria (H, R) 32
Gran Capitán 200
Gran Castell 189
Gran Civet 70
Gran Claustro 67, 195
Gran Colegiata 48
Gran Condal 147
Gran Coronas Mas La Plana 70, 80
Gran Duque de Alba 203
Gran Feudo 117, 118
Gran Irache 118
Gran Licor de Naranja 205
Gran Muruve 49
Gran Recosind 77
gran reserva 15
Gran Toc 70
Gran Verdad 42
Gran Vernier 193
gran-vas 15, 188, 192
Granbazán 93
Grandes Bod. 49
Grans Muralles 80
grapa 192
grape varieties 11, 12

hybrids 45, 52, 181, see also introductions to regional sections
Gregorio, Miguel Angel 129
Grupo Sindical de Colonización No 795 49
Guadalete, River 164
Guadalquivir, River 164
Guadalupe 84, 87, (H, R) 90
Guelbenzu, Bod. 118
Güímar, Valle de (DO) 13, 28
Guitián Godello 94
Gurpegui 136
Gurpegui Muga, Bod. Luís 136
Gurpegui Muga, Luís 118
Gutiérrez de la Vega, Bod. 181

Haro 136-7, 146, (H, R) 152
Hartley and Gibson 173
Harvey, John 154, 158, 159, 164-5
Hecula 179
Heredad 197
Herencia Remondo 144
Hervás 85
Hidalgo y Cía, Vinícola 165, 206
Hijos de Francisco Vallejo 87
Hill, Cavas 70, 192
holandas 85, 198, 199, 200, 203
Honorable 204, 207
Hormilleja 137
Huelva 87, (R) 90
Huesca (R) 25

Iberia 171
Icod 28
Ijalba, Viña 137
Imperator 200
Imperial 134
Impérial 192
Imperial Corregidor 171
INCAVI 70
Independencia 204, 205
Infantes de Orleans-Borbón, Bod. de los 165
Inocente 172
Insulares Tenerife, Bod. 28-9
Insuperable 203, 204
INVIOSA 192
INVIOSA, Bod. 87
Ipagro 111
Irache, Bod. 118
irrigation 181
Ismael Arroyo 49-50
Iturbe, Don Javier Bilbao 131

Jalifa 169
Jaloco 88
Janus 49
Jarandilla de la Vera (R) 85, 87, 90

Jean Perico 192
Jerez de la Frontera 12, 153-76, 198, (H, R) 175
Jerez-Quina 199, 204
Jerez/Xérès/Sherry y Manzanilla-Sanlúcar de Barrameda (DO) 13, 14
Jerte 85
Jesús Nazareno, Bod. Co-op 95
Jesús Nazareno, S Co-op Vitivinícola 107
joven afrutado 106
JR 108
Jumilla (DO) 13, 177, 181
Juncal 172
Juvé y Camps 192

Kraliner 76
Kripta 188

La Antique 50
La Aurora 109
La Concha 164
La Coruña (R) 102
La Gitana 165
La Goya 165
La Granja Remelluri 46, 116
La Guita 165, 168
La Ina 155, 166, 168
La Invencible, Co-op 37
La Mancha (DO) 11, 13, 35, 38
La Merced 158
La Palma (DO) 13, 27, 29
La Purísima, Co-op Agrícola 181
La Rioja Alta 124, 149
La Riva 154
La Serna 134
La Vicalanda 131
Labastida 137
Labastida, Unión de Cosecheros de 137
labels 12-14
Lagar de Cervera 95
Lagar de Fornelos 95
lagos 12
lágrima 107
Laguardia 137 (R) 152
Lagunilla, Bod. 130, 138
Lalanne, Bod. 22-3
Lama, Bod. 107
LAN, Bod. 138
Lanciano 138
Lanzarote (H, R) 32
Lanzarote (DO) 13, 27, 29
Lapatena, Bod. 95, 97
Lar de Barros 87
Lar de Lares 87
L'Arc Cabernet 81
Larios 104, 107, 204
Larouco 100
Las Campanas 116, 121
Las Lomas 183
Las Palmas 29
Las Torres 80
Laura Lalanne 23
L'Avi Arrufi 73
laws, wine 12-14
Lazarillo 40
León 44, 45, 50, (H, R) 58

Index

Conde de la Cortina 106
Conde de Haro 194
Conde de Osborne 202, 205
Conde de la Salceda 148
Conde de Siruela 48, 49
Conde de Valdemar 134, 141
Condes de Albarei 94
consejo regulador 13-14
Conti, Celler Oliver 68
Contino 134
copita 160
Coquet 194
Coquinero 167
Córdoba 106, (H) 112, (R) 113
Cordon Negro 191
Cordorníu 187, 190
Corella 117
Corral, Bod. 134
Corte Real 89
cosecha 15
Cosecheros Abastecedores 38
Cosecheros Alaveses 130, 134
Cosecheros des Vino del Ribeiro 94
Cosme Palacio 144
Costa Blanca 180-1, 203
Costers del Segre (DO) 13, 14, 62, 68-9, 70, 74
Costers del Siurana 69
Coto de Imaz 135
COVIDES 69, 190
Cream 15, 155, 161
crema 16
Crema de Lima 206
Cremant Rosé 191
Cresta Azul 64
criadera 161, 198
criado por 15
crianza 134-5
Crismona 106
Cristalino 78
Croft Jerez 154, 161
Crucillón 21
Cruz Conde, Bod. 106
Cruz García 128
Cuarenta y Tres 202
cuatro cortado 167
Cuatro Rayas 45
Cubillo 139
Cuco 158
Cueva del Granero 37
Cumbrero 135, 141
Cune 134, 135
Curaçao 205
Cuvée DS 191
Cuzcurrita 146
CVNE see Cía Vinícola del Norte de España
CZ 154

Dalmau Hnos. 69
Dariña, Bod. 48
Daroca 22
De Muller, SA 64, 69
De Payva 87
dégorgement 187
Dehesa de los Canónigos, Bod. 48
Dehesa del Carrizal 37

Delgado Zuletta 161, 165
denominación específica 14
denominación de origen (DO) 8, 12-13, 15
denominación de origen calificada (DOCa) 12
denominación de origen provisional (DOP) 12
Diamante 136
Díaz e Hijos, Jesús 36, 37
Diego Zamora 202
Diez-Mérito 154, 161
Diogenes 109
Dolç de l'Obac 69
Dom Berenguer Tinto, Solera 1918 69
Dom Joan Fort, Solera 1865 69
Domecq, Bod. 135, 139
Dominio de Conte 132
Dominio de Pingus 48
Don 111
Don Alvaro 54
Don Aragón 24
Don Bueno 107
Don Darius 135
Don Fino 162, 171
Don Hugo 135
Don Jacobo 134
Don José 171
Don Narciso 202, 205
Don Paco 158
Don Ramón 21
Don Suero 56
Don Tomás 172
Don Zoilo 154, 162, 167, 170
Doña Mencía 107
Dorado 61 45
dos cortado 167, 173
Dos Lustros 189
Double Century 162
Dry Fly 162
Dry Sack 162, 173
Dubonnet 202
Duc de Foix 69, 190
Duff Gordon 154, 162
Duke of Wellington 154
dulce 15
dulce color 105, 107
Dulce Viejo 107
Duque de Estrada 39
Duque de Sevilla 21
Durius 48
DYC 202, 208

Ebro, River 117, 135
Ederra 131
Eguizábal, Don Marcos 136, 144, 148, 161, 167
El Abuelo 182
El Barco de Valdeorras 100
El Candido 157
El Cid 162
El Coto de Rioja 130, 135-6
El Galayo 49
El Hierro (DO) 13, 27
El Lomo 27-8
El Monte (DO) 13
El Naranjo 107
El Preludi 75
elaborado por 15
Elciego 136
Eléctrico 111

Elegante 164
embotellado por 15
Emilin 166
Emperatriz Eugenia 166
Empordà-Costa Brava 65
enate 21
Entrena 128
Escat 202
Esmeralda 79
Espléndido 202, 203
espumoso 15, 188, 190
Estación de Viticultura y Enología 18
Estatuto de la Vino y de los Alcoholes 13
Estola 36
Estrella 183
Etiqueta Negra 99
Etxaniz Txakolina 117
Eva 158
Eval, Bod. 180
EVENA 115, 117
Extremadura 84-90
Extrísimo Seco 65
Ezcaba, Chacolí Tinto de 117
Ezcaray (R) 152

Fabiola 108
Falces 118
Falset, Comarca de 69, 78
Fariña, Bod. 48, 54
Faustino, Bod. 136
Fefiñanes, Bod. del Palacio de 94
Felanitx 30
Felipe II 158, 200, 203
Fermoselle 49
Fernández, Alejandro 48, 49, 53
Ferrer, José L 28
Ferret, Cavas 190
Festival Cream 161
Fiesta de la Vendimia 162
Figueres (R) 83
Fillaboa, Granxa 94
Fin de Siglo 95
Fina 163
Fina Feria 162
Finca Dofí 64
fino 15, 104, 107, 153, 154, 155, 163
Fino Capatáz 105
Fino Quinta 163, 167
Fino Ranchero 172
Fino Soto 172
Flaherty, Ed 37
flor 16, 45, 53, 84, 86, 88, 104, 154, 163
Flor de Jerez 163
Flor de Montilla 110
Flor de Pingus 48
Flores, Bod. 28
Florido, Bod. César 163
Florit, Mas 191
Fondillón 180
Fontenac 203, 207
Forner, Don Enrique 139
fortification 163
Franca Roja 28
Franco-Españolas, Bod. 136
Fransola 70, 79
Freixenet 191

Borsao Borja, Bod. 21-2
Bosch y Cía 199
Bosconia 139
bota 159
Botaina 168
Botánico 165
Brandy 103 158, 200
Brandy de Jerez 198
Bretón y Cía, Bod. 132
Briñas 137
Briones 132, (R) 152
Brisel-Godello 100
Bristol Cream 155, 158, 164, 165
Bristol Milk 159, 164, 165
Brown sherry 159
Brut 15, 188
Brut de Brut 188
Brut Nature 188
Brut Reserva 188
Brut Zero 189
Bullanguero 179
Bullas (DO) 12, 177
Burdon, John William 159
Burgos 187, (R) 58
butt 159

Caballero, Luís 154, 159, 200, 206
Cacabelos 47
Cáceres 85-6, (R) 90
Cádiz 154, 159, (H, R) 175
Calahorra 132, (H, R) 152
Calatayud (DO) 12, 21, 22
Calatrava, Campo de 36
Calisay 199, 200, 205
Callejo, Bod. Félix 47
Cambados 93, (H) 101, (R) 102
Cambrils (R) 83
camera 160
Campeador 141
Campillo, Bod. 132
Campo de añejamiento 66
Campo de Borja (DO) 12, 21, 22
Campo Grande 45
Campo Hermoso 94
Campo de Tarragona 66, 78
Campo Viejo, Bod. 132-3
Can Ràfols del Caus 66-7
Canals and Nubiola 189
Cañamero 84, 86, 88
Canaries 26-33
Cañas, Bod. Luís 133
Canasta Cream 173
Cancionero 107
canoa 160, 173
Cantabria 44, 115, 116
Capa Negra 201
capataz 160
Capitán 158
Capuchino 168
carbonic maceration 115
Carcelén NCR, Asensio 179
Cardenal Mendoza 171, 201
Cardinal 201
Cariñena 61, 187
Cariñena (DO) 12, 20, 21, 22
Carlos I 201, 206
Carlos II 206
Carlos VII 105
Carlos Serres, Bod. 133

Carolina de Masachs 193
Carrascal 156, 160
Carricas, Bod. 116
Carrión, Hijos de Miguel 35, 36
Carta Blanca 158
Carta Nevada 191
Carta Oro 158
Carta de Oro 131, 133
Carta de Plata 131, 133
Cartojal 108
Casa de Calderón 179
Casa Castillo 182
Casa Gualda 36
Casa de la Viña 36, 41
Casa del Vino 137
Casar de Santa Inés 51
Casar de Valdaiga 47, 51
Casta Diva Cosecha Miel 181
Castaño, Bod. 179
Castel de Fornos 93
Castell d'Orcau 68
Castell del Remei 67
Castellblanch 189
Castellón de la Plana 179-80, (R) 186
Castilla la Vieja, Bod. de Crianza 47, 189
Castilla-La Mancha 34-43
Castilla-La Mancha Vino de la Tierra 37
Castilla-León 44-58
Castillo de Alhambra 37, 42
Castillo de Almansa 40
Castillo de Calatrava 42
Castillo de Cuzcurrita 133
Castillo Irache 118
Castillo Jumilla 179
Castillo de Liria 180
Castillo de la Mancha 42
Castillo de Manzanares 42
Castillo de Monjardin 116
Castillo de Montblanc 68
Castillo de Monterrei 96
Castillo de Mudela 42
Castillo de Perelada, Cavas del 64, 67
Castillo de Sajazarra 158
Castillo de San Diego 158
Castillo de San Simón 180
Castillo de Tiebas 121
Castillo de Utiel 183
Castillo Ygay 133, 140
Cataluña (DO) 13, 21, 59-83, 187, 198
Catavina Tender 181
catavino 160
Catedral de León 56
Caus 67
cava 14, 15, 187-8, 189
Cava (DO) 12, 14, 187, 189
CAYD 160
Cayetana Blanca 84
CB 105
Cebreros 44, 47
Ceclavin 85
Celler Batlle 192
Cenalsa 120
Cenicero 133, 146
Centenario 201
Centro Españolas, Bod. 37
cepa 15
Ceremonia 180

Cerro Añon 143
Cervantes, Bod. 37
chacolí 16, 116-17
Chacolí de Guetería (DO) 12, 116
Chacolí de Vizcaya (DO) 13, 116-17
Champagne method 187-8, 194
champaña 187, 189
Chandon 190
Character amontillado 171
Charentais method 198, 200
Chartreuse 201
Chaves, Bod. 93
Cheste 180
Chiclana 160
Chinchón 201
Chipiona 160
Chivite, Bod. Julián 117, 118
Chueca, Iñaki 117
Cigales (DO) 13, 44, 45, 47-8
Cilleros 85-6
Cintruénigo 117
Cirsión 148
Ciudad Real 37
Ciurana, Jaume 70
clarete 8, 15, 47, 51, 52, 55, 87
claretes de aguja 46
Clariano 180
claros 52
clásico 78
climate 10
Clos Damiana 194
Clos Gebrat 81
Clos Martinet 71, 74
Clos Mogador 67, 74
Clos Nostre Senyor 194
Clos de l'Obac 67, 69, 74
Club Amontillado 165
Cobos, Bod. 109
Cointreau 202
Colegiata 48
Collar Perla 80
Collar Rubí 80
Collar Zafiro 80
Colleccio 63
Compañía Vinícola del Norte de España (CVNE) 124, 134, 135, 149, 196
Compañía Vinícola del Sur 104, 106
Con Class, Bod. 48
con crianza 15, 134
coñac 202
Conca de Barberà (DO) 13, 62, 67-8, 70
Conca de Tremp, Comarca de la 68
Concavins, Bod. 68
Condado, Co-op Vinícola del 86
Condado de Haza 48
Condado de Huelva (DO) 13, 84, 86
Condado de Niebla 86-7
Conde de Alacha 133
Conde de los Andes 134, 144
Conde de Caralt 68, 190

Index

The following abbreviations apply: Bod. Bodega; Cía Compañía; Co-op Cooperativa; DO denominación de origen; Hnos Hermanos. (H) and (R) denote hotel and restaurant recommendations.

Abadía Retuerta 45
Abadía de San Campio 92, 99
Abalos 128
Abellan, Sucesores de Alfonso 35
abocado 14
Abona (DO) 12
Abuelo Nicolás 21
Acorde 179
Adegas das Eiras 92
Agapito Rico, Viñedos 178
Agarimo 94
AGE, Bod. Unidas 128, 130, 132
Agedas Ladairo 95
Agramont 115
Agricola Castellana Sociedad Co-op 45
Agro de Bazán 93
aguardiente 16, 199, 206
aguardiente de orujo 17, 199, 205
aguardiente de vino 198, 199
Agusti Torelló 188
alambrado 129
Alanis, Bod. 93
Alava 123, 187
Alavesa 134
Alavesas, Bod. 129
Alba de Bretón 132
Albali, Viña 35, 40
albariza 154, 156
Albatros 78
albero 103, 105, 111
Albet i Noya 63
Albor 129
Alcañón 21
Alcázar 158
Aldea 183
Aldeanueva, Viñedos de 129
Alegría 169
Alella (DO) 12, 62, 63-4
Alella Vinícola, Can Jonc 64, 71
Alfaro 129
Alfonso 164
Alicante 178, (H, R) 186
Alicante (DO) 12, 177, 178
Alicante, Bod. Co-op de 178
Alión, Bod. y Viñedos 45-6
Allende, Finca 129
Allozo 37
almacenistas 157, 166
Almagro (R) 43
Almansa (DO) 12, 35
Almendralejo 84
Almirantazgo de Castilla 47
Alone 178
Alta Pavina, Bod. 46
Altar Wine 64
Alto Aragón, Viñedos y Crianzas del 21
Alto-Turia 178-9

Alvaro 165
Alvaro Palacios 64, 74
Alvear 104, 105, 199, 206
Amadeus 98
Amadis 64, 74, 76
Amandi 93
Amavia 100
Ambrosio Velasco 119
Amer Picon 199
Amézola de la Mora, Bod. 129-30
amontillado 14, 104, 105, 155, 157
Amontillado del Duque 164
Amontillado del Teatro 157
amoroso 14, 157
Ampurdán, Cavas del 64, 189
Ampurdán-Costa Brava (DO) 12, 65
añada 157, 198
Añares 143
Andalucía 11
añejado por 15
añejo 14
Añina 159
anis 199, 201, 206, 207
Anis del Mono 199, 205
anisette 205
año 14, 15, 126
Anoia, Comarca de 65
Antaño, Bod. 46
Antequera 105, (H) 112, (R) 113
Antic Castell 70
Apóstoles Oloroso Muy Viejo 164
Araceli 106
Aragón 20-5
Aragón y Cía 105-6
Aragonesas, Bod. 21
Aranda de Duero, (R) 58
ARCO-Bodegas Unidas 130
Arcos de la Frontera 157, (H, R) 175
arena 157
Arganda 36, 42
Argüeso, Manuel de 157
Aria 197
Armada 171
Armonioso 38
Arnedo 130, (H, R) 152
aromatic wines 198-208
arrope 75, 157
Artadi 130
Artés, Cellers Co-op d' 73
Artium 73
Asman Abocado 105
Asunción 105
Augustus 74
Aureo Semidulce, Solera 1954 69
Avery 159
Axarquia 106
Ayuso, Bod. 36
Azpilicueta 128
Azumbre 45

Bacchus 111
Bach, Masía 65
Badajoz 84, 187, (R) 90
Baena 107
Bailén 167
Baix Ebre-Montsià, Comarca de 65
Baja Montaña 114, 116
Bajo de Guia 160
Baladí 103
Balandra 76
Balbaina 157
Balbour 158
Banda Azul 130, 144
Banda Oro 144
Bañeza, La 46, 50
Barbadillo, Antonio 154, 158, 206
Barcelona 59, 63, 65-6, 187, (H, R) 83
Barón de Chirel 130, 140
Barón de Eroles 21
Barón de Ley 130
Barón de Oña 130, 149
barrica 130
Barril, Masía 66, 74
barro 158
Basa 46
Baso 116
Basque Country 114-5
Bayona (H) 101
Belchite 21
Benavente 46
Benavides 106
Bénédictine 200
Benefique 107
Benicarló 179
Benito 159
Berberana, Bod. 39, 48, 130, 139
Beronia, Bod. 131
Bertola 154
bienteveo 158
Bierzo (DO) 12, 44, 45, 46-7
Bilbaínas, Bod. 131, 149, 189, 200
Binissalem (DO) 12, 14, 26, 27
Bizkaiko Txakolina 13
blanco 8, 15
Blázquez, Hijos de Agustín 154, 158, 200, 203
Bleda, Bod. 179
Boabdil 106
Bobadilla 158, 200, 206
Bobal 177
bocoy 159
Bodegas y Bebidas 36, 132
Bollullos par del Condado 85
bombona 66, 75
Bonaval 192
Bordejé, Bod. 21
bordelesa 132
Bordón 136
Bornos, Palacio de 47
Borruel, Bod. 21

Vinos quinados
These tonics or medicated wines containing quinine extract are drunk either for pleasure or given to children and invalids. *See also* JEREZ-QUINA.

Vodka
Spanish vodka, like gin, is produced in sizeable amounts in Jerez and the Barcelona area, and is inexpensive and of acceptable quality – certainly when drunk with mixers.

Whisky
It is now more chic among Spaniards to drink whisky than sherry and it has recently outstripped even brandy in sales, with the young tending towards whisky and Coca-Cola. Most of the best-known brands of Scotch, less expensive than in their homeland, are readily available – as also are some American and Canadian whiskeys. The home-produced DYC whisky is also sold in large amounts.

Zoco
Best known of the brands of PACHARAN, the sloe liqueur from Navarra.

Ricard
Well-known French *pastis* made under licence in Reus, in Cataluña.

Rives
A good-quality Spanish gin made by OSBORNE.

Soberano
DO

The biggest-selling Brandy de Jerez, made by GONZALEZ-BYASS in Jerez. Like FUNDADOR, it is less sweetened and caramelised than many and will thus appeal to foreign visitors more than the darker varieties popular with the Spaniards themselves. An honest-to-goodness young brandy, remarkably inexpensive, especially when bought in litre bottles; the taste for it grows!

Sol y sombra
Literally 'sun and shade', a mixture of brandy and ANIS. Often mixed by aficionados as one part brandy to two of ANIS.

Terry, Fernando A de
DO

Less caramelised than it once was, the regular Centenario Terry, in a bottle with a yellow net, is extremely popular in Spain. The older and more refined Solera 1900 is still on the sweet side.

Torres, Miguel
Together with MASCARO, Torres produces the best Catalan brandy. The range, in order of age, comprises Torres 5 and Torres 10 made by the *solera* system; and FONTENAC, Miguel Torres, Miguel Torres Black Label and HONORABLE premium brandies, made by the Charentais method on the premises and subsequently aged in oak for long periods. I have attended blind tastings where it proved extremely difficult to distinguish the Black Label from good VSOP Cognac. *See also* page 79.

Vermouth
Vermouth, much of it produced under licence in Cataluña (CINZANO and MARTINI for example), is produced on a large scale in Spain. The only ways in which Spanish-made vermouths differ from their Italian namesakes is in the local white wine used for their manufacture – which is a relatively unimportant factor in comparison with the herbal extract – and in price. There is also a wide variety of purely Spanish vermouths, produced mainly in Cataluña and along the east coast. These tend to be heavier and fuller in flavour.

Veterano
DO

Jerez brandy made by OSBORNE and known across the country, if only because of the roadside hoardings with their large black bull. Dark in colour and somewhat sweetened and caramelised, it currently ranks number three in order of sales in Spain.

Pacharán

A delicious liqueur with a base of ANIS which is made from sloes in Navarra. The most widely available brand is ZOCO.

Pedro Domecq
DO

One of the first firms to make brandy in Jerez, Pedro Domecq maintains a huge store for ageing its brandies in *solera* and, taking into account its vast Mexican operation, is probably the biggest manufacturer in the world, with a worldwide output of 12 million cases. In ascending order of age and quality its labels are FUNDADOR, Carlos II and CARLOS I. Domecq also makes an ANÍS *dulce* and a sweet lime liqueur, the Crema de Lima.

Pernod

The well-known aniseed-flavoured drink is made under licence in Tarragona.

Ponche

First produced by the sherry firm of José De Soto in 1888, *ponche* is a blend of brandy and herbs. Often flavoured with orange, it is enjoyed by those with a taste for something sweeter than brandy but less sticky than a liqueur, and it fills an uncluttered gap in the market – its silvered bottles also stand out on the shelves. The largest selling variety, claiming some 80 per cent of the market and with a fragrant orange nose, is CABALLERO. De Soto's *ponche* remains one of the best, since it is more aromatic and less sweet than some. Other Jerez producers are OSBORNE, Hidalgo, Valdespino, BOBADILLA, Barbadillo and J Ruíz y Cía, makers of the excellent Ponche Español.

Presidente

The best of the brandies from the Montilla firm of ALVEAR.

Queimada

Galician speciality made by setting alight AGUARDIENTE in a white chinaware bowl. When the blue flame subsides, the liquid is, surprisingly, stone cold. More elaborate versions are made, especially at Christmas, by pouring the spirit into an earthenware *cazuela*, adding roasted coffee beans, slices of fresh lemon and maraschino cherries, burning off some of the alcohol and ladling the potent concoction into glasses.

Quinine

Quinine-based apéritifs and liqueurs are widely produced and very popular in Spain. *See also* JEREZ-QUINA, CALISAY, VINOS QUINADOS and CHINCHON.

Renacimiento
DO

Smooth and very old *solera gran reserva* brandy made by GARVEY of Jerez and sold in a cut-glass decanter.

aromatic and a little sweet, it commands half of the domestic market in the popular medium-priced *solera reserva* range.

Marie Brizard
Perhaps the most famous of French *anisettes*, this is made under licence at Pasajes in the Basque Country.

Martini
Martini, especially in the sweet and bitter-sweet varieties, is extremely popular in Spain and is made in Barcelona.

Mascaró, Cavas
Mascaró, a small family concern in Vilafranca del Penedès (see page 71), has long provided some of the best Catalan brandy. Made by the Charentais method and aged along French lines, it is more reminiscent of Cognac or Armagnac than the Brandy de Jerez. The regular Mascaró is light, smooth and fragrant, and is in my opinion much superior to most three-star Cognacs – as well as being a great deal less expensive. The older DON NARCISO is made from a blend of Macabeo, Xarel-lo and Parellada grapes vinified in the *cava* itself.

Mascaró also produces a vodka and a superior gin, made with alcohol distilled from sugar beet and juniper berries from the Penedès. For many years, the firm made COINTREAU for sale in Spain and now produces its own Curaçao, the Gran Licor de Naranja, a pleasant liqueur made by steeping dried orange peel from Spain, Algeria, Haiti and Italy in alcoholic solution and then distilling it.

Mollfulleda, Destilérias
Large firm with its distillery in Arenys de Mar near Barcelona, specialising in the quinine-based CALISAY. Apart from this, it also produces rum, gin, kirsch and a range of liqueurs – orange, peppermint, coffee, cocoa and others.

Montulia, Bodegas
Apart from Montilla (see page 108), Montulia also makes ANIS and a range of *solera* brandies.

Orujo
Popular name for the fiery *aguardiente de orujo* distilled from grape skins and pips (see AGUARDIENTE).

Osborne y Cía
DO
This famous sherry firm is the largest producer of spirits in Spain, making VETERANO, MAGNO and INDEPENDENCIA brandies. All tend to be dark in colour and somewhat sweetened and caramelised to the Spanish taste. Its CONDE DE OSBORNE *solera gran reserva* is even older and mellower than Independencia. Osborne also makes the biggest-selling PONCHE and produces RIVES gin and vodka in a plant outside Puerto de Santa María, and ANIS DEL MONO in Barcelona.

León, Comarca de 50, 55
León, Jean 70-1
Lepanto 203, 204
Lepe 87
Lérida (or Lleida) 59, 62, 187, 193, (R) 83
L'Ermita 64
Les Terrases 64
Levante 11, 177, 181
Líbano, Señorío de 138
Lichine, Alexis 39, 135
licor de expedición 187, 193
licor de tiraje 193
liqueurs 8, 198-208
Logroño 123, 138, (H, R) 152
Long Life 163
López Agos, Bod. 140
López de Heredia, R Viña Tondonia 124, 138-9, 149
López Hnos 104, 107-8
López de la Torre 180
Los Arcos 166
Los Buhos 173
Los Cobales 106
Los Curros, SAT 50
Los Llanos, Bod. 37-8, 41
Los Monteros 183
Los Tercios 166
Louis de Vernier 193
Luberri 139
Lucenta 108
Luncheon Dry Fino 165
Luque, Bod. 107
Lustau, Emilio 157, 166, 204

Machurnado 156, 166
maderisation 75
Madrid 34, 38, (H, R) 43
Magaña, Bod. 118
Magdala 79
Magnificat 65
Magno 204-5
Málaga 108, (H) 112, (R) 113
Málaga (DO) 8, 11, 13, 103-13
Mallorca 26, (H) 32, (R) 33
Malmsey 61
Málón de Echaide 119
Malumbres 118
Malumbres, Bod. Vicente 118-19
Malvasía 61, 115, 126
Malvasía El Grifo 27
malvina 45, 52
Manacor 29
Manchuela (DOP) 35, 38
Manuel Quintana 137
Manzanares (R) 43
manzanilla 15, 153, 155-76
  pasada 166
  Rocío 166
Maravilla 172
Marfil 64, 71
María del Valle 107
Marie Brizard 205
Marismeño 171
Marius 40
Marqués de Alella 71, 72
Marqués de Alicante 178
Marqués de Aragón 24
Marqués de Arienzo 139
Marqués de Badajoz 88
Marqués de Cáceres, Unión Vitivinícola 139

Marqués de Caro 184
Marqués de Castañaga 39
Marqués de Figueroa 94
Marqués de Griñón 39, 48, 130, 131, 139
Marqués de Legarda 145
Marqués de Monistrol 71, 130, 193
Marqués de Murrieta, Bod. 124, 139-40
Marqués del Puerto, Bod. 132, 140
Marqués de Riscal, Herederos del 53, 56, 124, 130, 136, 140
Marqués de Roméral 128
Marqués de la Sierra 105
Marqués de la Solana 150
Marqués de Velilla 49
Marqués de Villamagna 133
Marquesado 181
Martin Codax 95, 100
Martínez Bujanda, Bod. 134, 140-1
Martínez Lacuesta, Bod. 132, 141
Martínez Payva, Bod. SAT 87
Martini 205
Maruja 172
Mas de l'Alba 81
Mas Borás 71, 79
Mas Martinet Viticultors 71, 74
Masachs, Josep 193
Mascaró, Antonio 193-4
Mascaró, Cavas 71, 202, 205
Masia Hill 70
Matanegra 84, 88
Matúsalem 164
Mauro, Bod. 50, 54
Mauro Toro 50
Mazuelo 115, 126
Medina, Bod. 88
Medina del Campo 46
Medina y Cía, José 166-7
Megía, Luis 39
Méndez Siverio, Juan Jesús 29
Mendoza, Bod. Enrique 182
Méntrida (DO) 13, 14, 35, 39
Merecedor Oloroso 173
Mérida 84, 88, (H, R) 90
Mesoneros de Castilla 50
Mesquida, Jaume 27, 29
Mestres Rosado 194
Mestres Sagües, Antonio 194
método tradicional 15, 188, 194
Miajados 85
Miguel Merino, Bod. 141
Milésime 192
Millennium Oloroso 164
Milmanda 68, 71-2, 79
Minguillar 107
Miño, Condado de 95
Miño, River 91, 95
Miserere 69, 74
mistela 75
mitad y mitad 167
Mollet de Perelada, Co-op de 72
Mollfulleda, Destilerías 205
Mollina 108

Monasterio de Tentudia 89
Monastrell 61, 177
Mondéjar (DO) 13, 35
Monje, Bod. 29
Monopole 134
Monsieur Henri 147
Mont Marçal 194
Mont-Plané 116
Montánchez 84, 88
Monte Cristo 106, 108
Monte Ory 118
Monte Real 141, 147
Montearruit 107
Montebuena 137
Montecillo, Bod. 135, 141
Monterrei (DO) 13, 92, 95, 96
Monterrei, Co-op de 96
Montilla 108, (R) 113
Montilla-Moriles (DO) 8, 11, 13, 103-13
Montisierra 108
Montonec 61
Montserrat, Monastery of 63, 72
Montulia, Bod. 108, 205
Morales, Bod. Co-op de 50
Morgadio, Bod. 96
Moriles 108
Morriones, Francisco 121
Mosen Cleto 21
'mountain wine' 109
Moure, Adegas 96
Moza Fresca 95
Mozaga, Bod. 30
Muerza, Bod. 141
Muga, Bod. 142, 194
Murcia 11, 177-86, (R) 186
Murmurón 149
Murua, Bod. 142
Muruve 49
Murviedro, Cavas 182, 183

Nadal, Cava 194
Nájera 142
Nava del Rey 51, 53
Navajas, Bod. 142
Navalcarnero 39, 42
Navarra 123
Navarra (DO) 11, 13, 114-22, 187
Navarrete 142
Navarro, Bod. 109
Navisa Industrial Vinícola Española 109
Nectar Cream 164
Nekeas, Bod. 119
Noë PX 164
Non Plus Ultra 190
NPU 171
NR 109
Nuestra Señora de la Cabeza, Co-op 39
Nuestra Señora de la Manjavacas, Co-op 40
Nuestra Señora de la Oliva 118
Nuestra Señora del Portal 73
Nuestra Señora del Romero, Co-op 119
Nuestro Padre Jesús del Perdón, Co-op 40
No 28 Oloroso 162

Index

Oak 142-3
oak maturation 11
Ochavico 163
Ochoa, Bod. 115, 119
Ochoa, Don Javier 117
Oja, River 143
Ojo de Llebre 35, 61
Olarra, Bod. 143
Olite 119, (H, R) 122
Olivella Sadurní 72
Oliver, Miguel 27, 30
Ollauri 143
oloroso 15, 104, 109, 154, 155, 167
Oloroso la Espuela 172
Ondarre, Bod. 144
Ondarrubi Beltza 116
Ondarrubi Zuri 116
Onix 81
Onomástica 133
Ontinar 119
Orense 96, (R) 102
Orotava, Valle de la 30
orujo 17, 199, 205
Osborne y Cia 154, 167, 204, 205-7
Osca 21
Oteros, Los 45, 50, 51
Otoñal 143
Ouro 94
Oyón 144, (R) 152

Pacharán 206, 208
Pacorrito 105
Pago de Carraovejas 51
Pagos Viejos 134
País Vasco 114-22
pajarete 167
Palacio, Bod. 144
Palacio de Bornos 47, 189
Palacio de los Guzmanes 56
Palacio de Monsalud 89
Palacio de la Vega 119
Palacios Remondo, Bod. 144
Palencia (R) 58
Palma de Mallorca 30
palo cortado 15, 104, 109, 155, 167
Palomino and Vergara 154, 165, 168
Pampano 45
Pamplona 119-20, (H, R) 122
Pando 173
Parker, Robert 49, 78, 129
Parxet 71, 72, 194
pasada 15
pasado 15
Pastrana 165
Pastrana, Carlos 69
Pata Negra 38
Paternina, Federico 130, 134, 144
Pavón 159
paxarete 167
Payuelos 50
Pazo 96, 98
Pazo de Barrantes, Bod. 96
Pazo de Señoráns 96
Pedro Domecq 154, 156, 166, 168, 202, 203, 206
Peñafiel 51, (R) 58
Peñalba López, Bod. 51, 54

Penedès (DO) 11, 13, 14, 59-60, 62, 72-3, 187, 194-5
Peninsular Palo Cortado 166
Perelada, Castillo de 195
Perelada Rosado 64
Pérez Barquero 109
Pérez Caramés 51
Pérez Marín, Hijos de Rainera 165, 168
Pérez Megía, Hijos de A 168-9
Pérez Pascuas, Bod. Hnos 51-2, 53, 56
Pernod 206
Pesquera 52
pétillance 8, 91, 116, 117, 188
Peynaud, Professor 39, 56
Piedmonte, Bod. 120
Pilar Aranda 166
Pilycrim 106
Pingadelo 100
Piñol, Vinos 73, 79
Piqueras, Bod. 35, 40
Pirineos, Bod. 23
Pla de Bages (DO) 13, 62, 70, 73
Plà y Llevant de Mallorca (DO) 13, 26, 30
plastering 169
Platja d'Aro (R) 83
Poblet, Monastery of 63, 73
Pompeyo 109
ponche 172, 200, 205, 206
Pontevedra 96-7, (H) 101, (R) 102
Pontons 74
Porrón (Porró) 74
Posada, Xosé 92
Poveda, Salvador 182
Prada, José Luís 52
Prada a Tope 47, 52
Prado Enea 142
Presidente 199, 206
Prieto Picudo 45
Prima Lux 72
Prima Nox 72
Prima Vesper 72
Príncipe 158
Príncipe de Viana, Bod. 120
Priorato (Priorat) (DO) 13, 59, 62, 74
Privalegeo del Condado 86
Protos, Bod. 52
Puebla (de la) Reina (R) 90
Puenta la Reina 120, (R) 122
Puente-Genil 110
Puerto 159, 166
Puerto de Santa María 154, 169, 198, (H) 175, (R) 176
Puig y Roca, Cellers 74
Pura Sangre 179
pupitre 191, 195
PX see Pedro Ximénez

Queimada 206
Quiles, Primitivo 182
quinine 206

Rabassa morta 60, 75
Raimat 75, 195
Ramón Bilbao 144
rancio (rancí) 59, 66, 74, 75

Raventós i Blanc, Josep María 75, 196
Ravina, Marcos Guimerá 29
raya 15, 110, 169
Real de Asua 134
Real Divisa, Bod. 144-5
Real Irache 118
Real Tesoro 169
refreshment 169
reglamento 13-14
Remelluri, Granja de Nuestra Señora de 145
Remírez, Fernándo 145
Remírez de Ganuza, Bod. 145
Renacimiento 203, 206
René Barbier 67, 74, 76
Requena (R) 186
reserva 16
Reserva Mont-Ferrand 196
Reus 76
Rías Baixas (DO) 13, 14, 92, 97
Ribas, Herederos de 30
Ribas, Hereus de 30
Ribeira Sacra (DO) 13, 92, 97
Ribeiro (DO) 13, 92, 96, 97
Ribeiro, Bod. Co-op del 96, 97
Ribera Alta 115, 120
Ribera Alta del Cea 50, 52
Ribera Baja 115, 120
Ribera de Burgos 52
Ribera del Duero (DO) 11, 13, 44, 45, 52-3
Ribera d'Ebre 76, 78
Ribera del Guadiana (DO) 13, 84, 88
Ricard 207
Río Viejo 155, 168
Rioja Alavesa 123, 145
Rioja Alta 123, 145-6
Rioja Alta, Bod. La 146
Rioja Baja 115, 123, 146-7
Rioja (DOCa) 8, 9, 11-12, 13, 14, 123-52, 187, 196
ageing 128-9
keeping 128
vintages 127
Rioja Santiago, Bod. 147
Rioja Vega 141, 147
Riojanas, Bod. 141, 147, 149
Rives 205, 207
Roch, Julia e Hijos 182
Roda, Bod. 147-8
Rodríguez, Telmo 116
rodrigón 98
Rodríguez, Don Jaime 145
Rodríguez, Telmo 46, 145
Rodríguez y Berger 40
Rojo y Negro 181
Romano 181
Roqueta, Ramón 73
rosado 16, 177, 188
Rosal, O 92, 97, 98
Rosas (Roses) (R) 83
Rota 170
Rotllán i Torra 64, 74, 76
Roura 76, 196
Rovellats, Cavas 196
Rovira, Pedro 76
Royal Ambrosante 171

Royal Carlton 189
Royal Corregidor 171
Rua 100
Rúa-Petín 100
Rueda (DO) 13, 44, 45, 53
ruedo 110
Ruedos de Montilla, Los 110
Ruíz y Cía, J 206
Ruíz Mateos, José María 154, 163, 170
Ruíz Mateos, Zoilo 170
Ruíz Torres, Bod. 88
Rumasa 148, 154, 170
Ryman, Hugh 68, 77

Sabatacha 182
sack 27, 170
S'Agaro (R) 83
Salas, Bod. 88
Salceda, Viña 148
Salnesur, Bod. 94
Salvatge 194
Salvatierra de los Barros 89
Salvatierra, Condado de 98, 99
San Asensio 146
San Domingo 164
San Isidro, Bod. Co-op del Campo 23
San Isidro, Co-op 182
San Isidro Gran Noval 182
San Martín de Valdeiglesias 40, 42
San Miguel de las Viñas, Cofradía de 76-7
San Patricio 163, 171
San Roman 50
San Sadurní de Noya (Sant Sadurní d'Anoia) 77, 187, 188, 196-7, (H) 83
San Trocado 93
San Valero, Bod. 23
San Vicente de la Sonsierra 148, (R) 152
Sánchez Romate Hnos 171, 201
Sánchez Rustarazo, Bod. 40
Sandeman-Coprimar 171,201
Sangre de Toro 77, 79
Sanguesa 120
Sanlúcar de Barrameda 154, 155, 166, 171, 198, (H) 175, (R) 176
Sanluqueña 160
Sant Cugat del Vallés, Monastery of 77
Sant Feliú de Guixols (R) 83
Santa Daría, Co-op Vinícola de 148
Santa Eulalia, Bod. 52
Santa María 162
Santa María de los Remedios, Co-op 98
Santamaria, Cellers 77
Santander 44
Santara 77
Santiago de Compostela 98, (H, R) 102
Santiago Ruíz 98
Santo Domingo de la Calzada 148, (H, R) 152
Sanz, Antonio 47
Sanz, Ricardo 47

Sanz, Vinos 53
Sarría, Bod. de 120, 121
SAT Masies d'Avinyo 73
Savin 132
Scala Dei, Cellers de 74, 77-8
Scala Dei, Monastery of 74, 78
scale 171-2
Schenk, Bod. 178, 182, 183
Scholtz Hnos 106, 110
Seca, La 53
seco 16
Secular 199
Segura Viudas 197
semiseco 16
Senador 199
Señor Atares 22
Señor de Cascante 119
Señor Lustau 204
Señorío de Agos 140
Señorío Amézola 133
Señorío, Bod. SAT 99
Señorío del Condestable, Bod. 183
Señorío Cuzcurrita 133
Señorío de Guadianeja 42
Señorío de los Llanos 38
Señorío de Nava, Bod. 53-4
Señorío de Robles 183
Señorío de Valdes Artesanal 55
Señorita 157
Serra, Jaume 78, 197
Serra, Simón 72
Serrada 53, 54
sherry 8, 11, 103, 153-76, 198
Sibarita 168
Sierra Cantabria, Bod. 149
Sierra de Gredos (H) 58
Sierra Negrete 183
Siglo 128
Silviño 98
sin crianza 16, 135
Sisseck, Peter 48
Sitges 78, (H, R) 83
SMS 150
Soberano 203, 207
sobre tabla 171
Socalco 99
soils 10
Sol y Luna 179
sol y sombra 207
Solagüen 137
Solar de Hinojosa 40
Solar de Samaniego 129
Solear 158
solera 11, 16, 45, 53, 59, 75, 86, 103-4, 110, 155, 166, 171-2, 198
Solera 1847 164
Solera Brandy de Jerez 198
Solera Gran Reserva 198
Solera Reserva 198
Solimar 69
Solís, Bod. Félix 35, 40, 41
Somontano (DO) 11, 13, 21, 23
Soto, José de 172, 206
SOVICOSA 88-9
sparkling wines 187-97
spirits 198-208

Sumoll 61
Sunflower 197
sunning 172

Tacoronte-Acentejo (DO) 13, 27, 31
Tafalla (R) 122
Tapada, Bod. 94
Tarragona 78, (H, R) 83
Tarragona (DO) 13, 59, 60, 62, 70, 78-9, 187
Tarragona Unión 80
Tea, Condado de 92, 97, 99
Tenerife 27, (H) 32, (R) 33
Tercia, La 110
Terra Alta (DO) 13, 62, 70, 79
Terras Gauda 92
Terras Gauda, Bod. 99
Terry, Fernando A de 154, 165, 172, 201, 207
TG 110
Tierra de Barros 84, 88, 89
Tierra de Campos 50
Tierra de Estella 115, 121
Tierra de Medina 53, 54
Tierra del Vino 54
Timon 70
tinajas 40-1, 88, 104, 110, 160
tinto 8, 16
Tinto Aragonés 45
Tinto Cazador 64
Tinto Fino 45, 126
Tinto del País 45, 126
Tio Benito 159
Tio Diego 172
Tío Guillermo 163
Tio Mateo 168, 169
Tio Pepe 155, 164, 172
Tirant 76
Toledo 41 (H, R) 43
Topacio 189
Toro (DO) 13, 44, 45, 54
Toro Albala 111
Torondos 48
Torre Muga 142
Torre de Oña 130, 149
Torremilanos 54
Torres, Miguel 14, 63, 68, 70, 71, 73, 74, 75, 77, 79-80, 188, 203, 204, 207
Torres de Quart 184
Tovar, Pablo Barrigón 48
Trajinero 107-8
tres cortado 167
Tres Lustros 192
Tres Palmas 154
Tres Pasas 109
Tres Rios 94
Triple Seco 204
Trobat, Bod. 80
Tudela (R) 122
tutor 99
Tuy (H) 102
Txakoliñ Gorri 116
Txakoliñ Zuri 116
Txakolí Txomin Etxaniz 117

Ull de Llebre 12, 35, 61, 126
Unión Agraria Co-op 80
Unión de Cellers del Noya 188

Unión Vitivinícola see Marqués de Cáceres, Unión Vitivinícola
Utiel, Co-op Agrícola de 183
Utiel-Requena (DO) 11, 13, 177-8, 183

Val do Salnés 92, 97, 99
Valbuena 54, 56
Valdejalón 23
Valdeorras (DO) 13, 92, 96, 99-100
Valdepeñas 41, (H) 43
Valdepeñas (DO) 11, 13, 35, 41
Valderas 50
Valdespino, AR 154, 172-3, 206
Valdevimbre 45, 50, 55
Valdizarbe 115, 121
Valduero, Bod. 55
Valencia 183, (H, R) 186
Valencia (DO) 11, 13, 177-86, 187
Valentino 184
Valeri Vila, Bod. 68
Vall de Sant Jaume 184
Valladolid 55, (H, R) 58
Vallformosa, Masía 80, 197
Valls, Co-op de 66
Valpiedra, Finca 149
Valsangiacomo, Cherubino 184
Valserrano 150
Valsotillo 50
Varvall 70
Vega Infante 183
Vega de la Reina, Vinos 55
Vega Sicilia, Bod. 45-6, 53, 54, 55-6
Velasco Charcón, Bod. 109
Veliterra 45
vendimia 16
Vendimia Cream 166
Vendimia Tarde 117
venecia 173
Venerable 168
Ventura, Jané 80, 197
Verbenera 110
Verdejo 45
Verdello 92
Verdial 37
Verdil 177
Verín 100, (H) 102
vermouth 8, 199, 201, 203, 205, 207
Veterano 205, 207
vi novell 72
Via Aurelia 68
Victoria 158
Viejísimo 111
Vigo, (R) 102
Vilafranca del Penedès 80-1, 197, (H, R) 83
Vilamar 183
Vilariño-Cambados, Bod. de 100
Villafranquina 47
Villagarcía de Arosa (R) 102
Villarrobledo 42
viña 16

Viña Abad Gran Vino Godello 95
Viña Alberdi 146
Viña Albina 147, 149
Viña Amalia 109
Viña Arana 146
Viña Ardanza 146, 149
Viña Bosconia 149
Viña Calderón 184
Viña Calderona 49
Viña Carrerón 109
Viña Cobranza 46
Viña Costeira 98
Viña Eguia 135
Viña Extremeña 89
Viña Herminia 138
Viña Marcos 117
Viña Mater 76
Viña Mein 100
Viña Mocen 46
Viña Montalvó 133
Viña Monty 141
Viña Odiel 89
Viña del Olivo 134
Viña Paceta 131
Viña Pedrosa 56
Viña el Pisón 134
Viña Pomal 131, 149
Viña Real 134, 149
Viña San Marcos 23
Viña Sol 79
Viña Tondonia 149
Viña Turzaballa 144
Viña Vermeta 182
Viña Vial 144
Viñadrián 136
vinagre de yema 168
Viñas de Gain 134
Viñas del Vero 24
Viñatigo 29
viñedo 16
Viñedos de la Marquesa 150
Vinícola de Castilla 37, 42
Vinícola Navarra 121
Vinícola del Priorat 74, 81
Vinival, Bod. 184
vino 16
vino de aguja 17, 100, 188
vino de color 173
vino commarcal (VC) 12, 17
vino corriente 17
vino de doble pasta 184
vino embotellado 17
vino gaseoso 17
vino generoso 17
vino de Jerez 17
vino joven 17, 115, 178
vino de lágrima 17
vino de mesa 12, 17
vino de pasto 17
vino rancio 17
vino de la tierra (VdlT) 12, 17
vino verde 17, 100
vinos de alta expresión 12
Vinos del Bierzo, Sociedad 47, 56
Vinos Blancos de Castilla 56
vinos jóvenes 135
Vinos de León-VILE, Bod. 54, 56

Vinos de Madrid (DO) 13, 34, 35, 38, 42
vinos quinados 201, 208
Vinos y Viñedos del Salón 24
vintage (sparkling wines) 188
Virgen 108
Virgen de las Viñas, Bod. Co-op 100
Visán 42
Vitivinícola Local SCA, Co-op 111
Vitorianas, Bod. 135
Vizconde de Ayala 147
vodka 199, 205, 208

Walnut Brown 173
Waltraud 79
whisky 202, 208
Williams & Humbert 154, 156, 173
Wisdom & Warter 173
Wisdom's Choice Cream 173

Xanandro 93
Xenius 190

Ycoden-Daute-Isora (DO) 13, 31
Yecla (DO) 13, 177, 184-5
Yelmo 80
Ygay 150
Yllera 50, 56
Yuntero 40

Zagarrón 40
Zamora (H) 58
Zapatos de Pisar 173-4
Zaragoza 24, 187, (H, R) 25
Zoco 206, 208
Zona del Albero 111